1980

The WISDOM *of the* SANDS

ANTOINE DE SAINT-EXUPÉRY

The Wisdom of the Sands

Translated
by Stuart Gilbert
from the French
CITADELLE

With a new Introduction
by
Wallace Fowlie

The University of Chicago Press
Chicago

This Phoenix edition
is published
by arrangement with
Harcourt Brace and Jovanovich, Inc.

The University of Chicago Press, Chicago 60637
Copyright 1950 by Harcourt, Brace and Company, Inc.
© 1979 by The University of Chicago
All rights reserved. Published 1950
Phoenix edition 1979
Printed in the United States of America
85 84 83 82 81 80 79   54321

Library of Congress Cataloging in Publication Data
Saint-Exupéry, Antoine de, 1900–1944.
    The wisdom of the sands.

    Reprint of the ed. published by Harcourt, Brace, New York.
    I. Title.

PQ2637.A274C52   1979   843'.9'12   79-15938
ISBN 0-226-73372-6

INTRODUCTION

At this moment, approximately thirty-six years after his death and thirty-one years after the posthumous publication of *Citadelle* (*The Wisdom of the Sands*), Antoine de Saint-Exupéry does not stand out as one of the truly great literary figures of his generation. He was regarded, however, as one of its heroes, and he was surely among its most widely appreciated writers. Two of his early books, *Vol de nuit* (*Night Flight*), 1931, and *Terre des hommes* (*Wind, Sand and Stars*), 1939, based on his experiences as an aviator, became best-sellers and were translated into several languages. His final aviation book, *Pilote de guerre* (*Flight to Arras*), 1942, dealing with his early war experience, was also enormously popular. *Le petit prince*, published in 1943 and translated into English the same year, became one of the best-known books of the forties and fifties. The reputation and popularity of this aviator-writer steadily increased during the fifteen years that preceded his death in 1944. During the years following the Liberation, from 1945 to 1950, he was one of the contemporary writers most deeply revered by French youth and was often placed with André Malraux and Albert Camus as an affirmer of man's heroic actions, as a believer in the power of man's will to oppose the hostile forces of the world.

After the resounding success of his aviation books and *Le petit prince*, *Citadelle*, which appeared in 1948, disappointed many of his most fervent readers. It puzzled them by its unexpected differences, in both content and style, from his other books. But a few critics tentatively suggested that it might turn out to be the most significant of all his writings. This prediction seems to be gaining credibility. Despite its length* and its strongly lyric form, *Citadelle* is today the most widely read, the most frequently analyzed, and the most highly regarded of his works. What were the stages of preparation leading to this, his ultimate work, which was so different from anything else he had written?

Perhaps all of his books grew, in one way or another, out of his experiences as a flier, experiences which began in the late twenties, when Saint-Exupéry pioneered as a commercial pliot. He had been an indifferent student through most of his early years, but he studied intensively the intricacies of the airplane engine and learned all that could be learned, both theoretically and practically, about aviation. He flew extensively over Europe, Africa, and South America, and established mail flights south of Buenos Aires and across Patagonia. He survived a forced landing on the Lybian desert and a crash in Guatemala. During the war, he made reconnaissance flights over occupied France, from the last of which, in July 1944, he failed to return.

To a majority of his readers, it had gradually become clear that for Saint-Exupéry, flying was an experience in solitude that encouraged meditation on the meaning of man's existence. The solitude of his flights allowed him—trained him, he often said—to return to the very source of man's life, and to the meaning of action, providing him with a perspective on man and civilization. Danger, of which there was no small measure, also played its role. For Saint-Exupéry, as for Camus and Malraux, danger and action had a mystique of their own that goes very far in explaining the character of his writings, and their popularity.

Like most intellectual Frenchmen, moreover, Saint-Exupéry was obsessed with history, with the effort to understand the present in the light of the past, and the tragedies of the past in terms of his hopes for the future. And related to this historical sense was his

* His early death prevented Saint-Exupéry from editing and possibly condensing his manuscript. Indeed, as Stuart Gilbert suggests in his Introduction, he may never have expected to do so. The French edition has 219 sections. Gilbert's admirable translation has reduced these to 122, and some of these sections have been translated only in part.

realization that he belonged to the community of mankind, a realization which had come to him in moments of solitude and great danger, and from which he drew inspiration for that quality, that power, we call heroism—and his was a simple, joyous form of heroism. At such moments of crisis, he seemed to rise above the normal human condition. It was an age-old story of adventure, of man alone, cut off from all other men, who learns in that very condition the mystical bonds that join him with all men.

In no sense an ascetic, Saint-Exupéry esteemed and welcomed all of the pleasures, sensual as well as spiritual, that life offered. He respected life in its completeness and considered it sacred. Literary and moral values replaced his early Catholicism, which ceased to have any importance for him. Courtesy appeared natural in him, and it seemed to have come down to him from the Age of Chivalry.

What gave him, from early in his manhood, a legendary quality was his modest heroism, the imperious demands he made on his friendships, the secrecy of his personal life, his youthful physical gracefulness, and the lofty moral code by which he lived. To his associates in aviation and in war, Saint-Exupéry was obviously more than a friend. He drew from them, by the power and appeal of his personality, an unusually strong bond of comradeship. Discreetly reserved in all his relationships, he could also, at the right moments, be witty, warm, and jovial. The testimonials of his friends speak approvingly of the extremes of his temperament: the sudden withdrawals, when he preferred or needed solitude, and his ebullient returns to their circle, when his warmth of heart and keenness of intelligence delighted them.

Vol de nuit and his earlier, less sucessful *Courrier sud* (*Southern Mail*), published in 1929, were brief reportorial books based on flight missions, cast vaguely in the form of stories. *Terre des hommes* and *Pilote de guerre* were further autobiographical accounts of flight missions, direct testimonials to the experience of a flier, but more reflective. In *Terre des hommes* the themes of action and meditation are closely mingled. From his position in the sky, the pilot came to perceive the meaning of the earth. In *Pilote de guerre* the experience and meditations of the flier are extended into the ordeal of war, defeat, and national tragedy. His meditations on the meaning and future of France while he served as a pilot in a defeated army are still relevant for many Frenchmen. During the Vichy regime, Saint-Exupéry spent two years in New York, unwilling at that time to join the forces of the Free French under de Gaulle. His attitude changed before the end of the war, and he returned to make those reconnaissance flights over occupied territory which ended in his death. Long before Jean-Paul Sartre used the word *engagé* to characterize a certain kind of writer, Antoine de Saint-Exupéry illustrated the meaning in his life and in his books.

If the aviation books were autobiographical accounts of action, meditation, and danger in the air, *Le petit prince* and *Citadelle* were imaginative, fictional presentations of moral and philosophical insights acquired on his flights. All of his biographers stress the fact that Saint-Exupéry had a happy childhood. He himself liked to say that he came from his childhood as one comes from one's native land. This happy childhood found its literary expression in *Le petit prince,* where his mature reflections turned this autobiographical material into a moralistic fairy tale for adults. After this charming tale of youthful happiness, the innocence of *le petit prince* grew into the knowledge and experience of *le grand caïd,* the great chieftain, builder of *la citadelle.*

The first pages of *Citadelle* were written in 1936. When questioned about the new writing, during the next eight years, Saint-Exupéry often referred to it as "my posthumous work." At one time he thought of calling the book *Le caïd.* He himself did not choose the title *Citadelle,* but the word is used frequently in the text, and the idea becomes the central image, representing the goal of the two principal speakers: the father and the son. Until this book appeared, in 1948, Saint-Exupéry had been looked upon primarily as a poet of action, as an adventurer whose exploits furnished the substance of his books. Brief adventures, narratives with dialogues, often appear in this long book, but they serve a purpose beyond the narrative: they are a means of initiating reflections and underscoring moralistic conclusions. Adventure in this final book has become inner and psychological, although one is aware, throughout, of the physical reality of a man's existence in the Sahara, and the desert seems a proper setting for the meditations. The most apparent literary form is the parable, the biblical parable, which occurs so often that it seems to be necessary for the expression of the writer's thought.

A young chieftain, *un jeune caïd,* the protagonist, is being gradually instructed by his father, who was the founder of the empire and who is in full control of its inhabitants. The younger caïd is taught to discern which moral and behavioral factors elevate, and which degrade the people. He learns to recognize those aspects of civilization that strengthen the empire, and those that may cause its decline. The form of a monologue prevails, somewhat monotonously, but it is preeminently a book of meditations cast in a decidedly lyric language. All of the themes will be familiar to readers of the first books of Saint-Exupéry. *Citadelle* was obviously destined to be the book of his life, the *summa* of his thought. By comparison, the earlier books are mere exercises leading to the composition of the last book and to the expanded and deepened thought of the writer.

It is certain that Saint-Exupéry himself attached great importance to this work, and the most recent commentators seem to agree with him. In his love for the desert, in the use to which he puts the desert, he recalls the writings of Père Foucauld, of Ernest Psichari, and even of Rimbaud. Like Malraux in his journey to the Far East, Saint-Exupéry belongs to a period in French literature when the young writer felt an imperious need to leave Paris, to escape from his familiar culture in order to refresh himself in one that was totally diffrent. Gide's *Nourritures terrestres (Fruits of the Earth)* was a guidebook for Saint-Exupéry, as it was for Camus in approximately the same years. The images and rhythms of Gide's early book are visible and audible in *Citadelle,* as well as in *Noces* of Camus.

These celebrated escapes from France (Psichari, Gide, Saint-Exupéry) were means by which France became more clearly understood and more deeply loved. Saint-Exupéry first learned as a pilot far from France to accept difficult duties in which, he believed, he saw the image of his destiny. He learned the harsh lesson of solitude and achieved a renewed sense of fraternity and of the strong attachment man has for his land. All of these lessons are exalted in *Vol de nuit, Pilote de guerre,* and *Terre des hommes.* And they are revived and revitalized in the many parables of *Citadelle.* In its fragmentary narrative, we see an old monarch leading his son to the top of a mountain which overlooks a sleeping city, where sentinels are on watch at every gate. We can see temples, buildings, the different sections of the city. It is a human citadel at the heart of an empire that stretches out to the desert sands, where barbarian tribes are camped. The symbolism is biblical, the poetry pastoral.

The metaphor of "the knot" (*l'homme un noeud de relations*) joining man to man appears on the last page as the summation of all the lessons. "For Thou, O Lord, art the common measure of us twain. Thou art the knot supreme, binding all things together." On the opening pages, the word *citadel* appears and is associated with the verb *to build.* "For I perceived that man's estate is as a citadel" (p. 13). "Citadel, I will build you in men's hearts" (p. 14).

The imposition of duty on a man, and his acceptance of duties to be performed, are defined as the only means by which a citadel may be constructed. This central moral lesson is expressed in a metaphor: "But the trees that I have seen shoot up the straightest were not those that grew in freedom" (p. 226).

With great insistence, even to the point of redundance, Saint-Exupéry patiently explains that all human adventure leads to knowledge and is, in the last analysis, an effort to elucidate the oldest problems facing man.

Undoubtedly, a large part of *Citadelle* was written in New York, at a time when Saint-Exupéry's principal themes had become permanently fixed in his mind. His last port of call (*la dernière escale*) as a writer was the African desert so suitable for the casting of his thought in its final form. The image of civilization for the young caïd is his father's palace. There he believes he will create, out of the many injustices of today, the justice that will be tomorrow's.

WALLACE FOWLIE

TRANSLATOR'S INTRODUCTION

CITADELLE, to whose English version the title of *The Wisdom of the Sands* has been given, is probably the most remarkable book that has come out of France since the catastrophe of 1940. The testament of a very unusual man, who combined great courage and powers of endurance with a prodigiously active mind and a high sense of moral responsibility, it evokes a vision of the world as it well might be, if men awoke to their almost infinite possibilities for well-being. Though Saint-Exupéry's philosophy of life differs *toto coelo* from that of Nietzsche, it is perhaps to *Also sprach Zarathustra* that *Citadelle* may best be likened; it has the same poetic texture, the same wealth of imagery, the same psychic tension, and the same exotic setting. But besides these qualities we are conscious of another, whose presence is delightfully felt in all Saint-Exupéry's work from *Night Flight,* which won him worldwide fame in 1932, to *The Little Prince,* which has charmed so many readers, young and old, since its appearance in 1943, and is indeed an emanation as it were of his many-sided personality. It is a tenderness, a sense of the pathetic vulnerability—never the vanity—of human life, and a compassion vast as the Buddha's.

This is admirably brought out in the *Life of Saint-Exupéry* by Pierre Chevrier which has recently been published in France, and which also gives, for the first time, I believe, the facts, so far as they are ascertainable, of that tragic last flight of his on July 31, 1944. In the summer of 1939, when the publication of *Wind, Sand and Stars* consecrated his fame, he was in New York. But, perturbed by the turn of events, he kept in telephonic contact with Paris, so long as the lines were open, and in August he returned to France. His early war experiences are described in *Flight to Arras*. After the fall of France he decided that he could serve his country best by returning to New York, where, after many difficulties, he arrived at the end of 1940 and settled into an apartment on Central Park South. Five thousand copies of his *Pilote de Guerre* (which had a big success in America under the title of *Flight to Arras*) were sold within a single week in France—before the German censorship intervened to suppress it. Thereafter the book was printed clandestinely at Lyons. Meanwhile Saint-Exupéry was moving heaven and earth to be able to resume active service at the earliest moment and in 1943, at last, he was allowed to sail in an American convoy going to North Africa. Many difficulties still lay ahead, due to his age—he was forty-three, over-age for a fighter pilot—and the poor state of his health. But with that indomitable persistence which was one of his characteristics he pleaded his cause with the military authorities and finally obtained permission from General Eaker to undertake five reconnaissance flights from the 2/33 Squadron Headquarters at Alghero in Sardinia. Somehow he managed to exceed the sanctioned five and his last flight was his ninth. He took off at 8:30 on July 31, 1944; the weather reports were good, the engines running smoothly, and the plane soared lightly into the shimmering morning air, northwards towards France. At one-thirty Saint-Exupéry had not returned and his friends were growing more and more anxious, as by now only an hour's fuel remained in his tanks. And at two-thirty he still had not returned. . . . That evening a young German pilot attached to Luftflottenkommando 2, entering up the day's report in his logbook, wrote: "Tribun (i.e. Avignon) has reported one enemy reconnaissance plane brought down in flames over the sea." Everything points to this plane's being Saint-Exupéry's *Lightning*. By a curious irony of fate this German airman who, after four crashes, had been assigned to an observation post on Lake Garda, was a cultured young man and amongst the most treasured books of his library,

now buried under the ruins of his home town, were those of—
Antoine de Saint-Exupéry.

"I do not mind being killed in war," Saint-Exupéry had written
to a friend. "What will remain of all I loved? I am thinking as
much of customs, certain intonations that can never be replaced, a
certain spiritual light. Of luncheons at a Provençal farm under the
olive-trees; but of Handel, too. As for the material things, I don't
care a damn if they survive or not. What I value is a certain arrangement of these things. Civilization is an invisible boon; it concerns not the things we see but the unseen bonds linking these
together in one special way and not otherwise. . . . Anyhow, if I
come out of it alive, there will be only one problem I shall set myself: What can one, what *must* one, say to men?"

The Wisdom of the Sands is Saint-Exupéry's answer to that question. It was a problem that had been haunting him throughout his
career. Writing nearly twenty years ago, Christopher Morley said
of *Night Flight*: "In its implicit suggestions this magnificent story
is not only an Ode to Duty but a profound essay on Discipline."
And André Gide in his preface to the French edition (1931) of
Night Flight wrote: "The quality which I think delights me most
of all in this stirring narrative is its nobility. . . . I am especially
grateful to Saint-Exupéry for bringing out a paradoxical truth
which seems to me of great psychological import: that man's happiness lies not in freedom but in his acceptance of a duty." All
Saint-Exupéry's writing was pervaded by an awareness of this truth
and it is one of the leading motifs of this his last work, which is
in fact a summing-up of the philosophy of life he built up through
some twenty-five years of pondering on the human situation.
Though intensely interested in aviation and one of its boldest
pioneers in the early adventurous phase, its "heroic age" as M. Gide
has called it, he saw in it far more than a means of access to the
thrills of speed and altitude; it had for him an almost mystical
significance. When I first met him—he was thirty at the time, and
Night Flight had just brought him fame—I was conscious, even
amidst the light-hearted chatter of a cocktail party, that mere physi-

cal adventure meant far less to him (though it meant much) than adventures of the mind. I happened to be reading Traherne's *Centuries* at the time and I remember thinking that this airman-poet shared the vision of that great mystic for whom "Eternity was manifest in the Light of the Day, and something infinite behind everything appeared, which talked with my expectation and moved my desire." And this impression deepened at each of our subsequent meetings. He had a sense of responsibility, a selfless devotion to his fellow men, a burning desire to see, and to make others see, the pattern behind the confusion of our age, which inspired immediate affection and respect. Yet he was always very human, almost boyish in his gay enthusiasms and, moreover, kept abreast of the advance of science, mathematics in particular, and could hold his own in argument with his friend Fernand Holveck, the eminent physicist and biologist, and with other leaders in the field of science. He had also a talent for invention, and between the years 1936 and 1940 took out no less than ten patents for various gadgets—concerned, as might be expected, with aviation.

The Wisdom of the Sands represents Saint-Exupéry's personal philosophy, his "Book of Wisdom" which lived and grew as he lived and grew; indeed he often in conversation referred to the book as his *œuvre posthume,* because he knew it would have no end so long as he was alive. He would work on it late into the night, sometimes speaking into a dictaphone the result of his labors. A considerable part of the book was written during his sojourn in New York, but, wherever he was, back in his beloved France and later in North Africa, the manuscript was always with him. He never tried to alter the text; whenever he wished to recast an idea in a new form, he put it down as it came to him under its new aspect. It was with the understanding of this background that the present edition was prepared; for it seemed clear that the occasional elimination of repetitive passages which in no sense affected the structure or essential meaning of the work could properly be made. This condensation, relatively slight, was made in France by recognized authorities on Saint-Exupéry's work, and we believe that they are such as he himself would have made, had he lived to see the book to press.

A few words regarding the form in which the book is cast and its directive ideas may be helpful to the reader before he embarks on the perusal of one of the most original, sincere, and thought-provoking books of modern times. The form of *The Wisdom of the Sands* is as far removed from the often dry-as-dust expositions of our professional philosophers as from the amiable guide-books to happiness of which we have recently seen so many. It abounds in vivid pictures of desert life, forays and sandstorms, mirage-born madness, beleaguered oases and cities, caravans going their perilous ways to safety or disaster. The narrator, ruler of a great empire in the desert, is no mere lay figure, an abstraction or a mouthpiece of the author, but a poignantly human personality, engaging not only our respect but, like the Little Prince, an intimate affection. For while fully conscious of his power, he is also conscious of his all-too-human imperfection and no stranger to that "dark night of the soul" which befalls all who ponder deeply on the riddle of existence. We see him first in his early days, when he is learning from his father the duties and responsibilities of the ruler of a vast, always imperilled empire. When he, in turn, takes up the reins of power, he both amplifies and deepens this legacy of wisdom. The keynote of his rule is love: he gives himself to his people, makes their problems and anxieties his own, sharing their predicaments and hopes with the selflessness of the true lover. Aware that a change is coming over the little world he governs, that essential values are being lost, the "infinite behind everything" being obscured by the diversity of things, he seeks to fix his subjects' gaze on that "divine knot binding things together" which alone bestows meaning on the chaos of appearances. He gives himself to his people and the more he gives the more he is enriched; he bids them, too, be givers, active helpers—not "sedentaries" placidly enjoying a hoard they have amassed—and thus enrich their lives with the best Life has to offer, which is neither the blind obedience of the anthill, in which individualities are submerged, nor the acquisitive, competitive activity of the self-seeker, but a love like his, embracing all alike, even the criminal, whom nevertheless it is his duty to punish, maybe with death. "When, in His good time, God receives this generation from me, it will be as He entrusted it to me—mellower, perhaps, and wiser, more skilled in fashioning silver cruses; but unchanged. I have wrapped my people in my love." For Saint-Exupéry was deeply conscious of the value of permanence, tradition handed down from generation to generation, a Rock of Ages amid the quicksands of modern life.

Related to this ideal of permanence is the amplification of a view already expressed in *Night Flight:* man's obligation "to endure, to create, to barter this vile body," this "barter" being the only means whereby he can give meaning and direction to his life. "Perfection is not a goal we reach; it is a bartering of one's all, in God." We are told of the hieratic goldwork "for whose perfection old craftsmen bartered a whole life's work," embroidered altarcloths "over which old women burnt their sight out," bartering themselves for that which is more precious than themselves, for "things of beauty incorruptible." Thus, roaming his city at the nightfall, the Prince pauses to gaze at an old craftsman, maimed and "groaning like a millwheel when he moved, for he was full of years and the light of words had grown dim for him—nevertheless ever was he becoming more luminous, apter for the task for which he had made the barter of himself. . . . Thus, escaping by a miracle from his old, gnarled flesh, he was growing ever happier, more and more invulnerable, more and more imperishable. And, dying, knew it not, his hands being full of stars." Saint-Exupéry believed that man's only way of release from the sad impermanence of his estate —his "escape from the wheel," as a Buddhist would describe it— is through self-dedication and a focussing of the mind not on things-in-themselves but on that which gives them meaning, "the figure in the carpet."

Other leading themes are the temple and the cedar-tree; the temple whose massive walls, like those of the great cathedrals, exclude the tumult, the fever, and the fret of the world outside, and favor prayer and meditation; the cedar-tree "which thrives on mud, but transforms it into a crown of leafage, fed by sunlight. Thus mud is transmuted into virtue. Would you save your empire, instil fervor. It will absorb men's activities and thrive on them, and the same longings, the same activities, the same efforts will serve to build your city instead of destroying it." Time and again he rebukes those who, wishing to learn the secret of the temple, take it to pieces and "seek to find the silence in the stones." Such "atomization" (I borrow the word from Mr. Geoffrey Gorer who, in a witty analysis of a famous Report, speaks of its "atomization of sex") was abhorrent to Saint-Exupéry. "Thus, if a man pulled his house to pieces, with the design of understanding it, all he would have before him would be heaps of bricks and stones and tiles; nor would he be able to discover therein the silence, the shadows, and the privacy they bestowed." It was the creative vision of the architect that had "the power of transforming stone into silence," and the ruler's function is to open his people's eyes to that creative vision.

Thus the ruler's responsibility is heavy; if his people fall on evil ways he is accountable, and it is not only his right but his duty firmly to direct their activities and to see to it that, like the stones of the temple, each is assigned his fitting place. A sharp distinction is drawn between equality (which obviously does not obtain in nature or in the relations between men) and fraternity, which is the relationship between members of a "well stablished" community like that of Plato's Republic. "I would have you know that the conditions of the fraternity you seek derive not from equality; for equality is consummated within God alone, whereas brotherhood is a recompense. . . . It stems from your acceptance of a hierarchy and from the temple that you build each for each." Those words "discipline," "hierarchy," and "constraint" which so often recur in *The Wisdom of the Sands* have there a special application; they are conditions of the fellowship of men in which each must do his duty by all, and all do theirs by each, at the behest of love. And perhaps in any case we would do well to ask ourselves

xvii

if the prevalent distaste for words like these is not but another symptom of our failure to come to terms with life and our quest of a futile freedom, that of ships which have slipped their moorings in a storm. Moreover, though the benign rule of Saint-Exupéry's Prince is authoritative, it is not authoritarian; if he insists on discipline for others, he has begun by disciplining himself.

It may be that the near-biblical tone and language of Saint-Exupéry's message to the world of today, whose divided aims, animosities, and incoherences must dismay all who have not fallen back on a barren fatalism, will take aback some readers, accustomed to the demotic stridencies of the literary marketplace. Yet it is but the immemorial language of a voice crying in the wilderness, the voice of a man of action, no mere Utopian dreamer or *littérateur,* a poet who faced death not once but often, and a great lover of his kind whose constant aim was to rebuild man in the likeness of that "Happy Warrior"

> *Who with a toward or untoward lot,*
> *Prosperous or adverse, to his wish or not,*
> *Plays in the many games of life that one*
> *Where what he most doth value may be won;*
> *Who, not content that former worth stand fast,*
> *Looks forward, persevering to the last,*
> *From well to better, daily self-surpassed.*

STUART GILBERT

6 July 1950
Paris, France

The WISDOM *of the* SANDS

From well to better,
daily self-surpassed

ALL TOO OFTEN have I seen pity led astray. But we who govern men have learnt to plumb their hearts, and we bestow compassion only on what is worthy of our concern. No pity waste I on the shrilly voiced afflictions that fret women's hearts. As I withhold it from the dying and from the dead. And I know wherefore.

A time there was, in my young days, when I pitied beggars and their sores. I hired physicians and procured balsams for them. Caravans from a far-off island brought me those rare unguents laced with gold that mend the torn skin above the flesh. Thus did I until the day when I discovered that beggars cling to their stench as to something rare and precious. For I had caught them scratching away their scabs and smearing their bodies with dung, like the husbandman who spreads manure over his garden plot, so as to wean from it the crimson flower. Vying with each other, they flaunted their corruption, and bragged of the alms they wrung from the tender-hearted. He who had wheedled most likened himself to a high priest bringing forth from the shrine his goodliest idol for all to gape at and heap with offerings. When they deigned to consult my physician, it was in the hope that the hugeness and virulence of their cankers would astound him. And how nimbly they shuffled their stumps to have room made for them in the market places! Thus they took the kindness done them for a homage, proffering their limbs to unctions that flattered their self-esteem.

But no sooner were they healed than they found themselves of no account, like barren soil that feeds nothing; and they made haste to revive the ulcers that formerly had battened on their flesh. Then, clad once more in a motley of scabs and sores, they strutted it, begging-bowl in hand, and squatted beside the caravan road where, crying up their noisome gods, they levied tribute of the wayfarers.

Also was once a time when I pictured the man whom I had sacrificed in battle in the desert as doomed to agonies of loneliness. Not yet had I learned that there is no solitude for the dying, neither had I come upon their condescension. But then I saw the egoist or miser—that selfsame man who had made so much ado if he were cheated of a penny—bid the members of his household gather round him at his last hour, and share out his chattels with scornful equity, like one scattering gewgaws to a pack of children. Likewise I saw the wounded coward—a man who would have screamed for help in the heart of some insignificant peril—once death's cold hand had touched him, wave help away, if he thought this help would bring his comrades into danger. We praise such selflessness. But there, too, I perceived only a covert form of scorn. And that man also is familiar to me, who shares his water-gourd when already he is shrivelling in the sun; or his last crust when famine stalks the city. This is because, having lost the craving for these things, he can fling away, with lordly lavishness, his bone or crust for anyone to gnaw.

I have seen women weeping for pity of their warrior dead. But it was we who had befooled them. Have you not seen them coming back, the survivors, blustering and bragging, making much of their great deeds and, in token of the risks they braved, trumpeting the others' death—a death they declared most hideous, for might it not have befallen them also? Why, even I myself when young thought fit to wear about my brows the red garland of sword-cuts dealt to others, and came back brandishing my dead comrades and the bitterness of their last end! But only he whom death has chosen, who is busy spewing blood or pressing back his entrails—he alone knows the truth of it: that death has no terrors. For now his body seems to him but an instrument for which he has no further use, of which he may as well be rid. A dismantled body, betraying all the flaws that Time has wrought. Thus, if that body thirsts, the dying man knows this is but a momentary craving, whereof the sooner he is rid the better. And how trivial they now appear, all the good things that once served to beautify and nourish and make glad that form of flesh, which is now become something alien to him, a mere chattel, like the ass tethered to its stake!

Then begins the last agony, which is no more than the ebb and flow of a mind, now filled, now emptied of the tides of memory. They come and go, bringing back, as they bore away, their store of half-forgotten scenes, the wrack of earlier days and empty shells of once-heard voices. Rising, they lave again the seaweed of the heart, and forthwith all the old loves quiver back to life. But meanwhile the equinox is mustering its last ebb, and presently the heart is drained; the tide and all its flotsam sink back into God.

True, I have seen men flee in panic when death loomed near. But, make no mistake, never have I seen a dying man take fright.

Why, then, should I pity the dying? Why waste time mourning their end? Too well have I understood the *perfection* of the dead. Nothing in my life weighed lighter on me than my meeting with that little captive girl who was given me, when I was sixteen, to be my plaything. When brought before me, she was already dying, hiding her cough with her scarf and gasping for breath like a gazelle at bay; yet seemingly unaware of her extremity, for she loved to smile. But her smile was like wind on a river, or a dream's afterglow, or a sign's faint hieroglyph; and day by day it grew more tenuous, rarer, harder to retain—till it ended as a thin straight line, the wraith of a sign that had fled for ever.

Then there was my father's death. Like an effigy hewn in granite, thus he lay, his life accomplished. The assassin's hair, they say, turned white when his dagger, instead of emptying the mortal shell, invested it with such regal majesty. Trapped by the silence he himself had made, the murderer lay hid all night in the royal bedchamber, confronting not a victim but the huge effigy on a sarcophagus. And at daybreak he was discovered, stricken to his knees by the mere immobility of the dead king.

Thus my father, whom a murderer had sped headlong into

5

eternity, when he fell on silence, made others hold their breath for three full days. To such effect that tongues were loosed, bowed shoulders straightened, only after we had laid him in the tomb. But such was the preponderance of this man, who had not so much ruled as weighed down on his people and stamped them with his massive imprint, that when we lowered him into the grave we seemed not to be burying our dead, but laying a foundation stone. That which hung on our creaking ropes seemed like the first slab of a temple. Thus we did not inter him, but sealed him in the earth, now that he had become what he was evermore to be, our bedrock.

He it was who taught me about death and forced me when I was yet young to face it squarely; for never did he lower his eyes. 'Twas said that in my father's veins flowed eagle's blood.

It was in the course of the baneful year which men named the Banquet of the Sun—for throughout that year the Sun magnified the desert. He blazed down on the sands amongst the bone heaps and dry thorns, the glossy skins of the dead lizards and the camel-grass all parched to bristles. He from whom herbs and flowers draw their sustenance had consumed his offspring, and lorded it over the far-flung devastation like a child amongst the toys that he has broken.

He drew up even the waters under the earth, and drank the limpid pittance of the wells. He despoiled the gold sheen of the sand, which grew so white and void that we called this land The Mirror. For a mirror, too, holds nothing, and the forms that fill it have neither weight nor stay; and sometimes, too, like a salt lake, a mirror sears the eyes.

If, straying from their path, the cameleers are lured into this trap which never yet has yielded up its prey, at first they know it not for what it is, for there is nothing to mark it out; and like shadows in sunlight they trail their spectral presences along the waste. Limed in viscid glare, they think they are advancing; drowned already in Eternity, they think to breathe. On and on they thrust the caravan, where no effort can avail against the creeping torpor. Pressing towards a well that has its being only in their dream, they welcome the cool advent of the dusk, though henceforth it is but a vain reprieve. Perhaps they lament, poor simpletons, the slowness of the nights, though soon unnumbered nights shall glide over them like the twinklings of an eye. And, hurling guttural reproaches at each other for fancied wrongs, they know not that already justice has been done.

Think you that a caravan makes haste? Let twenty centuries roll by, and then come back and see!

Foundered in Time and changed to sand, phantoms drunk up by the mirror, thus were they when I saw them for myself, after my father, wishing I should learn of death, had taken me behind him on the crupper and ridden forth.

"There," he said, "was once a well."

At the bottom of one of those long shafts, driven so deep they can reflect but a single star, the very slime had caked and the trapped star died out. Thus the lack of a single star can overwhelm, as surely as an ambush, a caravan upon its way.

Around the well head, as around a broken navel cord, men and beasts had massed together hugger-mugger, vainly hoping to draw from the earth's womb the water of their blood. But even the trustiest workmen lowered to the floor of this strait abyss had delved the hard, caked crust to no effect. Like the moth which, pinned while yet alive and fluttering to its death, scatters around it the silk and gold and pollen of its wings, thus the caravan, staked to the soil by a dry well, was already beginning to bleach in a medley of split yokes and axles, ripped saddlebags, diamonds strewn like pebbles, gold bars half sunken in sand.

While I gazed at these things my father said: "You know how looks the wedding feast when the bride and bridegroom and the guests have gone and day breaks on the havoc they have left. Broken jars, tables overset, charred embers—vestiges of a carousal that has petrified. Yet," my father said, "nothing can you learn of love by studying these tokens."

Also my father said: "The man who cannot read, for all he weighs and scans the Book of the Prophet, and though he pore upon the web of letters and the bright gold of the illuminations, never will that unlettered man find there the one thing needful—which is not the grace of forms but the wisdom of God. Thus, too, the virtue of the candle lies not in the wax that leaves its trace, but in its light."

But when my father saw that I was trembling at this first encounter, upon an empty highland like the high tables of the sacrifices of old, with the remnants of God's repast, he also said: "Not in dead dust will you discover that which matters. Linger no more upon this carrion. Here you may see nothing but a rubble of carts stuck fast for evermore, because there is none to man them."

"Then who," I cried to him, "will teach me?"

And my father answered: "You may discover that which is essential in the caravan when it is wearing its heart out in the wilderness. Forget the vain sounds of words, and watch. If a precipice halts its progress, it skirts the precipice; if a sheer rock towers up ahead, it rounds it; if the sand becomes too soft, it searches elsewhere a patch of firmer sand—but always it comes back to the same direction. When the crust of a salt marsh gives way under its weight, you see it struggling to extricate the beasts of burden from the slough and busily casting about for solid ground; but presently it forms up again, headed once more on its old course. If a beast stumbles and falls, they gather up the broken boxes and load them on another, tugging at the creaking cords to make them fast; then they set out again on the same onward way. Sometimes he dies, who acted as the guide. They gather round him. They bury him in the sand. They dispute amongst themselves. Then another man is appointed leader, and they set their course again on the same star. Thus, perforce, the caravan moves ever in the direction that rules its destiny, like a boulder rolling along an unapparent slope."

✦

The Wisdom of the Sands

It so happened that the judges of the town sentenced a you woman, who had committed some misdeed, to be stripped to 1 frail sheath of skin, and had her bound to a stake far out in the desert, by way of punishment.

My father said to me: "Now I shall teach you what it is men seek after." And again he took me pillion behind him.

While we rode, a whole day passed over her and the sun drank up her warm blood, her spittle, the sweat of her armpits. Drank also in her eyes the water of light. Night was falling, bringing its brief solace, when we came, my father and I, to the edge of the forbidden highland. Glimmering white and naked against the background of rocks, frailer than a young plant nourished with moisture but now cut off from the waterlodes hidden in the dank silence of the earth, she twisted her arms like tendrils writhen by a fiery blast, and called upon God's mercy.

"Listen," my father said. "She is discovering that which is essential."

But I was a child, and craven.

"Perhaps she is suffering," I answered him, "and perhaps she's frightened, too."

"No," my father said, "she has passed beyond suffering and fear. Those are diseases of the cattle pen, meet for the groundling herd. She is discovering the truth."

And I heard her lamenting her plight. Trapped in the vastness of this alien night, she was crying out for the evening lamplight of the home, for the room which would have taken her to its familiar bosom, and the latched door behind which she would have felt secure. Laid bare to the huge formless, faceless universe, she was calling for the child one kisses before lying down to sleep and who sums up the world. Engulfed on this high lonely place by a flood of the unknown, she sang of the husband's footfalls ringing on the threshold at the shut of day—those often heard, reassuring footfalls. Lost in an abyss of darkness and with nothing left to cling to, she besought that those safeguards might be restored to her without which life cannot be: that bundle of wool to card, that

9

one and only bowl, that one child to sing to sleep and not another. Forlorn, she cried for the safe eternity of a house, haloed with the whole village by the evening prayer.

My father took me back upon his horse when the woman's head drooped on her shoulder. And we were in the wind again.

My father said: "Tonight you will hear them muttering in the tents, you will hear them prattling of 'cruelty.' But heed not these stirrings of revolt—for I shall ram them down their throats. My work is to found men."

Yet inwardly I knew my father's kindness.

"I would have them love," he said, "the living water of the well-springs, and the smooth green garment of young barley woven upon the rents that summer makes. I would have them extol the seasons, returning in their good time. I would have them thrive, like ripening fruit, on slowness and on silence. I would have them mourn their bereavements and honor their dead for a long while; for slowly the inheritance descends from generation to generation, and I would not have them lose their honey on the way. I would have them be like the branch of the olive tree. That one which bides its time. Then they will feel within them, like the swirling gust which tests the tree, the impulse of God's breath. Thus He shall be their guide and lead them home from dawn to dusk, from summer to winter, from seedtime to harvest, from youth to age, and then from old age to the children of their children.

"For, as with the tree, of man too you know nothing if you spread him out across his allotted span and disperse him in his differences. The tree is more than first a seed, then a stem, then a living trunk, and then dead timber. The tree is a slow, enduring force straining to win the sky. So is it with you, my little man. God compasses your birth and growing up; He fills you, turn by turn, with longings and regrets, joys and griefs, angers and forgivings, and then He draws you back unto Himself. Yet none of these transiences is *you;* neither the schoolboy nor the husband, neither the child nor the old man. You are one who fulfills himself. And if you prove yourself a stable branch, well knit to the olive tree, you will taste eternity in all your works and days. And everything around you will become eternal. Eternal, the fountain singing its tireless song, that quenched your forefathers' thirst in other years; eternal, the light of the eyes of your beloved when she smiles on you; eternal, the coolness of the nights. Thus Time will be no more an hourglass squandering sand, but a harvester binding close his sheaf."

✵ 2

THUS, STANDING on the highest tower of the citadel, I perceived that we need not lament suffering, or death in God's bosom, or even our bereavements. For he who has gone, so we but cherish his memory, abides with us, more potent, nay, more present, than the living man. Nevertheless, knowing their anguish, I pitied men.

And I resolved to heal them.

For him alone have I compassion who wakes in the great ancestral night, thinking himself sheltered under God's canopy of stars, and suddenly feels himself a wayfarer—whither bound he knows not.

I forbid questionings, for I know that never any answer slakes our thirst. And that he who questions is seeking, primarily, the abyss.

I visit with punishment that restlessness of mind which prompts thieves to crime, since I have learned to read their hearts and know that, even though I rescued them from poverty, I would not save them. For they deceive themselves in thinking that they covet their neighbors' gold. The gold shines for them like a star and that love of theirs, which knows not what it is, yearns for a star that never may they capture. Thus they stray from gleam to gleam, pilfering

11

goods that serve them not a whit, like the madman who, thinking to trap the moon therein, draws up in a bucket the dark water of a well. They go their hollow ways, feeding the brief flame of orgies with the worthless ashes they have filched. Then they hark back to their night watches, pale with suspense like men on the brink of some momentous venture, keeping quite still for fear of giving an alarm, and dreaming that at last they will lay hands on something that may, if all goes well, fulfill their hearts' desire.

If I set such an one free, he will keep to his infatuation, and next day my men-at-arms, plunging through the undergrowth, will catch him yet again in another's garden, tingling with expectancy and fancying that, this night of nights, fortune will befriend him.

None the less I bestow my love on these men, for well I know their zeal is greater than that of the self-righteous merchant, smirking in his shop.

But I am a builder of cities. It is my purpose to lay well and truly, here and now, the foundations of my citadel. For here I have halted the progress of the caravan, which was but as a seed borne in the wind's lap. The wind wafts like perfume the seeds of the cedar tree, but I withstand the wind, burying the seeds in the earth, so that cedar trees may rise in their beauty for the glory of God.

Love must know its object. I succour him alone who loves that which is, and whose heart's desire can be satisfied.

That, too, is why I enforce the bond of wedlock and have her stoned, who is taken in adultery. And yet I understand her craving, and how compelling is the summons she obeys. For I can read her mind when she is leaning on the terrace wall; and comes the dusk, enabling miracles; when she is pent in on all sides by the ocean rim of the horizon and made over, as to an instant torturer, to love's bitter yearning. I feel her quivering like a fish trapped in a drying rockpool, waiting for her cavalier's blue cloak as for the solace of the waves' return. Across the shadows she launches her appeal, and whoever steps forth from them will bring appeasement. But in vain will she pass from cloak to cloak, for no man can sate her longings. Thus the foreshore craves the flooding tide to allay its drought; wave follows wave unceasingly and dies away in a thin line of foam. Where would be the gain were I to sanction her taking another husband? Whoever loves above all the approach of love will never know the joy of attaining it.

Her alone I succour who is able to *become* and to build up her life around the inner courtyard, as the cedar builds itself upon the seed; and who finds her life's fruition within the limits that befit it. Her I protect who does not love the spring in its diversity, but one particular flower in which all springtime is incarnate: a woman who is not in love with love, but with that one and only form which, for her, love has made its own.

That is why either I draw together, or blot out, the wife who, when night is falling, drifts asunder. I erect barriers around her: the tray of gleaming bronze, the stove, the kettle; so that day by day each of these common things may come to wear for her the look of a familiar friend, with a smile belonging to this place alone. And thus it will be as if, little by little, God's presence were being revealed to her. Then the child will cry for her to feed it, and the carding wool tempt her fingers; the embers will call on her to be fanned. Thus from henceforth she will be inured, schooled to the task assigned. For I am he who builds the urn around the perfume that it may be preserved. I am the use-and-wont that ripens the fruit. I am he who constrains the woman to take shape and being, so that in the fullness of time I may confide to God on her behalf, not a mere wistful sigh borne on the evening breeze, but an ardor, love and sorrows that are her own.

Thus for a long time I pondered on what is meant by "peace." It comes only from garnered harvests, from children, a house at long last set in order. It issues from that eternity into which return all things that are fulfilled. It is the stillness of full granaries, of sleeping flocks, of folded linen, of the perfected thing; of that which, well and truly done, becomes a gift to God.

For I perceived that man's estate is as a citadel: he may throw down the walls to gain what he calls freedom, but then nothing of him remains save a dismantled fortress, open to the stars. And then begins the anguish of not-being. Far better for him were it to achieve his truth in the homely smell of blazing vine shoots, or of the sheep he has to shear. Truth strikes deep, like a well. A gaze that wanders loses sight of God. And that wise man who, keeping his thoughts in hand, knows little more than the weight of his flock's wool has a clearer vision of God than that unfaithful wife laid bare to the witcheries of the night.

Citadel, I will build you in men's hearts.

There is a time for choosing out the seed corn; but there is likewise a time for rejoicing, once the choice is made, over the sprouting crop. There is a time for creation, but there is also a time for the creature. There is a time for the flaming bolts that rend the black dykes of the firmament, but there is a time for the cisterns in which the storm flood will be garnered. A time there is for conquest, but a day comes when empires are made stable. And I, God's servant, thirst after eternity.

I abhor that which changes. I will away with him who rises in the night and strews his prophecies upon the winds, like the tree smitten by a lightning flash when it splits and blazes up and fires the forest. When God moves, I tremble; for I would have Him, the Immutable, reseated in Eternity! There is a time for beginnings, but there is a time, a thrice-blessed time, for use-and-wont.

To pacify and fructify and polish, this is our task. I am one who heals the sun-scarred earth and hides from men the ravages of the volcano. I am the greensward mantling the chasm; the storeroom where the fruit grows golden; a ferryman to whom God has entrusted a generation and who bears them safe from shore to shore. When, in His good time, God receives this generation from me, it will be as He entrusted them to me—mellower, perhaps, and wiser, more skilled in fashioning silver ewers, but unchanged. I have enfolded my people in my love.

That is why I give my protection to him who in the seventh generation still carries on the task, striving to bring it to perfection, of shaping the ship's hull or cambering the shield. Him, too, I protect who, having received from his poet forbears a poem handed down by word of mouth, by dint of reciting it and changing the words unwittingly, infuses into it something of himself and sets his mark upon it. I love the woman suckling her child, as I love the ever-returning seasons. For, above all else, I am he who *dwells*. Citadel, my citadel and my dwelling place, I will shield you against the machinations of the sands. I will ring you about with clarions sounding defiance of the savage hordes without.

✄ 3

FOR I HAVE LIT on a great truth: to wit, that all men *dwell,* and life's meaning changes for them with the meaning of the home. And that roads, barley-fields and hillsides look different to a man according as they belong, or do not belong, to a domain. For once we feel that these divers things are bound together in a whole, then and only then, do they make an imprint on our hearts. Likewise, he who dwells and he who dwells not in the Kingdom of God do not inhabit the same universe. They are befooled in their own conceit, the unbelievers, who mock at us as dreamers, fondly thinking that the riches they seek are tangible. When they covet another's flocks or herds, it is but to gratify their pride; and the joys of pride are of the spirit and intangible.

Likewise with those who think to comprehend my kingdom by splitting it into parts: so many sheep and goats, so many barley-fields, dwellings and mountains—and then what more? Because there is nothing more for them to own, they feel poor and naked to the wind. But it became clear to me that those who reasoned thus were like a man who cuts up a dead body and says: "Lo, here you see what life is—but a conjunction of bones and sinews, blood and entrails." Whereas life is the glow those eyes once had, which are now but vacant dust. Far other is my kingdom than a sum total of sheep, goats, dwelling places and mountains; it is that which, ruling, binds them into oneness—the homeland of my love. And happy they who know this; for they dwell in my house.

And our immemorial rites are in Time what the dwelling is in Space. For it is well that the years should not seem to wear us away and disperse us like a handful of sand; rather they should fulfill us. It is meet that Time should be a building-up. Thus I go from one feast day to another, from anniversary to anniversary, from harvesttide to harvesttide; as, when a child, I made my way from the Hall of Council to the rest room within my father's palace, where every footstep had a meaning.

I have imposed my law, which is as the layout or the ground plan of my dwelling. Once there came to me a fool and said: "Do but free us from your constraints, and then we shall wax great." But I knew what my people stood to lose thereby: firstly, a visage they had come to know; and then, in ceasing to love it, their understanding of themselves. So I resolved to enrich them with their love, despite their unwillingness. For they were now proposing to me to lay low the walls of my father's palace, wherein every footstep had a meaning, so that they might roam at greater ease within it.

Vast was my father's palace, with one wing set apart for the women and a secret inner garden where a fountain sang. (And I ordain that every house shall have just such a heart within it, where a man may draw near to something and whereto he may retreat from something. A focal place of goings out and of comings in. Else, a man is nowhere. And there is no freedom in not-being.) Also there were barns and cattle sheds. At times it so happened that the barns were empty, or the cattle sheds unused. And my father forbade that either barn or shed should serve the other's purpose; for, said he, the function of the barn is to serve as a barn, and when you cease to know your way about a house, you are no longer dwelling in it. Thereto he added: "Little matters it if the one use or the other be the more productive or expedient. Man is not livestock for fattening, and love, for him, counts more than the use to which this place or that is put. You cannot love a house which has no visage, and where footsteps have no meaning."

Also there was a Hall of Audience, reserved for great embassies alone. It was thrown open to the light only on those days when horsemen could be seen approaching in a golden cloud of dust and on the horizon great banners billowed in the wind. That hall was left unused when lesser chieftains came. Then there was the hall where justice was administered; and another where the dead were laid. And there was an empty room, whose use none knew— and which perchance truly served no purpose but to teach men that there are things secret, that never may they reach the core of knowledge.

As they hastened down the corridors, bearing their burdens, the slaves thrust aside heavy curtains that lapped their shoulders. They climbed steps, opened doors, and went down other flights of stairs; and always, according as they were farther from or nearer to the central fountain, they raised or lowered their voices, growing still as death and moving on tiptoe when they were in the precincts of the women's chambers, to have entered which unwittingly would have cost them their lives. And the women, too, were sedate or arrogant or furtive according to their place in the household.

I can hear the voice of the fool, saying: See how much space is wasted here, what wealth left unexploited, what conveniences lost through inadvertence! Far better were it to lay low those useless walls and level out those short flights of steps, which merely hinder progress. Then men will be free.

But I make answer: Then men will become like cattle in the marketplace and to beguile the tedium of their days they will invent new, foolish pastimes, which likewise will be hedged about with rules, but they will be rules devoid of grandeur. For the palace may give birth to poems, but what poem could be made about such pastimes as their games of dice? Perchance for many years yet they might live in the shadow of these walls, and the

17

poems written in their shadow might still awaken yearnings in them for that which is no more; but, in the end, the very shadow would die out and they would understand the message of those walls no longer. And then—in what would they rejoice?

Thus is it with the man lost in a drab week of indistinctive days, of a year that has no festivals, no form or visage. Thus is it with the man without an hierarchy, who envies his neighbor if his neighbor excels him and fain would pull him down to his own level. But when all are levelled out into the flatness of a stagnant lake, what joy will they have of it?

My task is to set up rallying-points of power. I build dams in the mountains to hold in the water, and thus I set myself up—unjustly, if you will—against natural inclinations. Where men are becoming clotted together in a morass of uniformity I re-establish hierarchies. I bend bows. With the bricks of today's "injustice" I build tomorrow's justice. I renew directives where men have settled tamely down, each in his pothole, calling stagnation happiness. I scorn the shallow puddles of their justice, and release him whom a noble injustice has founded in his manhood. And thus my empire is ennobled.

For well I know their arguments. True, they could but admire the man my father founded, and dare not belittle a success so perfect. But then, on behalf forsooth of him whom those constraints had founded, they removed those constraints! Nevertheless, while these lingered on in men's hearts, they still took effect. Then, gradually, were forgotten. And by then the man whom they had sought to "save" was dead.

That is why I hate irony, which is not a man's weapon, but the dolt's. For the dolt says to us: "These practices of yours do not obtain elsewhere. So why not change some of them?" As who should say: "What obliges you always to house your harvest in the barn and the cattle in the shed?" But it is he who is the dupe of words, for he knows not that something which words cannot comprehend. He knows not that men dwell in a house.

And then his victims, now the house has lost its meaning for them, fall to dismantling it. Thus men destroy their best possession, the meaning of things: on feast days they pride themselves on standing out against old custom, and betraying their traditions, and toasting their enemy. True, they may feel some qualms as they go about their deeds of sacrilege. So long as there is sacrilege. So long as there still is something against which they revolt. Thus for a while they continue trading on the fact that their foe still breathes, and the ghostly presence of the laws still hampers them enough for them to feel like outlaws. But presently the very ghost dissolves into thin air, and then the rapture of revolt is gone, even the zest of victory forgotten. And now they yawn. On the ruins of the palace they have laid out a public square; but once the pleasure of trampling its stones with upstart arrogance has lost its zest, they begin to wonder what they are doing here, on this noisy fairground. And now, lo and behold, they fall to picturing, dimly as yet, a great house with a thousand doors, with curtains that billow on your shoulders and slumbrous anterooms. Perchance they dream even of a secret room, whose secrecy pervades the whole vast dwelling. Thus, though they know it not, they are pining for my father's palace where every footstep had a meaning.

That is why, now I fully understand these matters, I bring the weight of my authority to bear against this gradual attrition and pay no heed to those who prate of "natural inclinations." For too well I know that natural inclinations swell the lakes with the water of the glaciers, and level down the mountains, and fret the river's course, where it issues to the sea, into a thousand conflicting eddies. And I know, too, that natural inclinations lead to the splitting up of power and the levelling of men. But I govern, and I choose—knowing well that the cedar tree likewise triumphs over time's attrition, which else would humble it to the dust; and, year by year, fighting that force which drags it downwards, builds up the splendor of its leafy temple. I am life, and I control; I set up glaciers against the interest of the lakes. Little care I if the frogs croak, "Injustice!" I rearm man so that he may *be*.

That is why I care nothing for the babbling fool who chides the palm tree for not being a cedar and the cedar for not being a palm, and with his bungling booklore points the way to chaos. True, I know that the babbler seems justified of his foolish science; for, were life ruled out, cedar and palm would merge together and crumble into dust. But life withstands disorder and natural inclinations, and it is from the dust that it draws forth the cedar tree.

The purport and the purpose of my decrees is the man to whom they will give rise. As for the laws and customs and language of my empire, I seek not their meaning within themselves; for well I know it is by piling stone on stone that silence is built up. And that it is by dint of burdens borne and drudgery that love is quickened. Too well I know that the man who has anatomized a body and weighed the bones and entrails is none the wiser, for bones and entrails serve no purpose in themselves—no more than ink or paper. What counts is the wisdom the book bestows, which is of an essence different from that of these material things.

Likewise I will have no truck with controversies, for mere logic serves no purpose here. O language of my race, I will save you from decay!

I remember that miscreant who visited my father and said: "You bid your household pray with rosaries of thirteen beads. Why thirteen? May not salvation be had as well with a different number?"

Then he advanced subtle reasons why men had better pray with twelve-bead rosaries, and I, who was then a child, was taken by his cunning arguments. Anxiously I gazed at my father, doubting if his answer would outshine that specious brilliance.

"Tell me," the man continued, "wherein the rosary of thirteen beads weighs heavier. . . ."

"The rosary of thirteen beads," my father answered, "has the weight of all the heads I have already cut off in its defense."

God enlightened the miscreant, and he repented.

MAN'S DWELLING PLACE, who could found you on reasoning, or build your walls with logic? You exist, and you exist not. You are, and are not. True, you are made out of diverse materials, but for your discovery an inventive mind was needed. Thus if a man pulled his house to pieces, with the design of understanding it, all he would have before him would be heaps of bricks and stones and tiles. He would not be able to discover therein the silence, the shadows and the privacy they bestowed. Nor would he see what service this mass of bricks, stones and tiles could render him, now that they lacked the heart and soul of the architect, the inventive mind which dominated them. For in mere stone the heart and soul of man have no place.

But since reasoning can deal with only such material things as bricks and stones and tiles, and there is no reasoning about the heart and soul that dominate them and thus transform them into silence—inasmuch as the heart and soul have no concern with the rules of logic or the science of numbers—this is where I step in and impose my will. I, the architect; I, who have a heart and soul; I, who wield the power of transforming stone into silence. I step in and mold that clay, which is the raw material, into the likeness of the creative vision that comes to me from God; and not through any faculty of reason. Thus, taken solely by the savor it will have, I build my civilization; as poets build their poems, bending phrases to their will and changing words, without being called upon to justify the phrasing of the changes, but taken solely by the savor these will have, vouched for by their hearts.

For I am the ruler. I enact the laws, I prescribe the feast days, I ordain the sacrifices, and build up with their flocks and herds, their dwelling places and their mountains, a life well-ordered like my father's palace, where every footstep had a meaning.

Left to themselves, indeed, what could they have made of that heap of stones, however much they shifted it here and there? What but another stone-heap yet more confused? But I set order, governing and choosing. Mine alone are the reins of power. And thanks to this they can pray in the silence and the shadow my stones bestow—my stones erected in the likeness of the vision in my heart.

Mine is the lordship, mine the power; and the responsibility is mine alone. Nevertheless, I call on them to help me, having well understood that the ruler is not he who saves others, but he who calls on them to save him. For it is through me and the vision within me that is achieved the unity which I and I alone have summoned forth from my flocks and herds, my dwelling places and my mountains; and which, mark well, they love, as they would love a young goddess stretching forth her snowy arms in the sunlight, whom at first they knew not for what she is. Thus they love the house I have set up according to my vision; and, through the house, its architect. One who loves a statue loves not the clay, not the plaster or the bronze, but the achievement of the sculptor's mind. And I bind my people to their home, so that they may come to know it, little by little, for what it is. Only after nourishing it with their lifeblood and gracing it with their sacrifices, can they attain this knowledge; for it must take toll of their living flesh and blood ere it can body forth their full significance. But thereafter they cannot fail to know it for what it is, this divine structure with a human visage. Then they come to love it, and ardent will be their nightfalls. Fathers, when their sons first open their eyes and ears, will make haste to point them to it, lest it should be engulfed in the diversity of things.

Inasmuch as I took heed to make my dwelling vast enough to give a meaning even to the stars, thus when my people venture forth upon their thresholds at the shut of day and raise their eyes, they give thanks to God for so surely guiding the ships celestial of His firmament. And because I have made it so lasting as to encompass many lives within its span, they will go from festival to festival as they go from hill to hill, knowing where they go, and discovering, beyond life's infinite diversity, the face of God.

Therefore, my citadel, have I built you like a stout ship. I have bolted you together, ballasted you, and launched you forth into Time—Time which for you is as a favoring wind. The Ship of Men, lacking which they would not make eternity's haven.

None the less, well I know the perils threatening my ship. Ever is it buffeted by dark seas, by a host of other visions of what might have been; for always is it possible to lay the temple low and build another with its stones. But that other temple would be neither more nor less true, neither more nor less just. Thus none would be aware of the ruin that had befallen the essential quality of silence, which was not written upon the stones.

Wherefore I would have them fasten stoutly the breastbeams of the ship, so that they may voyage in safety from generation to generation. For how could I build the temple beautiful if ever and again I were to start it anew?

✖ 5

THIS IS WHY I would have them buttress firmly the breastbeams of the ship. Man's handiwork, resisting nature's blind, uncharted forces raging all around. He who forgets the might of the sea may be lulled into a rash confidence; for he deems it inviolate, this dwelling place that has been given him. Once he has taken stock of it, he who makes the ship his dwelling is no longer conscious of the sea. Or, seeing it, he comes to see it only as a setting for the ship. Such is the power of mind! The sea appears to him as something made to carry ships on its bosom.

But he is mistaken. The sculptor shows us the face he has wrought from the block of granite; yet another sculptor might have shown

23

us another face wrought from the same stone. And you yourself have seen the constellations. That one, you say, is a swan. But then another might tell you, "No, that is a reclining woman." His word would come too late; a swan it is and a swan it will always be for us, once that invented swan has gripped our fancy.

But fancying this or that inviolate, one thinks no longer of safeguarding it—and well I know how dangerous can be the clever fool. And the mountebank, who shapes beguiling faces by his sleight of hand. That is why I have such an one haled away to execution, and quartered. Those who watch him at his pranks lose all sense of their domain. But, mark this well, I act not thus out of deference to my jurists who prove the man was wrong. For he is *not* wrong. But neither is he right; nor will I permit him to set himself up as cleverer or juster than my jurists. Also, he errs in thinking he is right; for he, too, sets up as absolutes those newfangled signs of his, clustered and glittering on high, born of his hands but lacking substance, the hallowing of Time, the sanction of religion. His structure has not yet fulfilled itself; but mine has. That is why I pass sentence on the mountebank, and save my people from corruption.

For he who, ceasing to take heed, forgets that he is dwelling in a ship, is from the outset doomed to disintegration. One day he will see the billows rising in their might, and they will sweep him away—him and his pranks and follies.

This similitude of my empire to a ship came to my mind when it so happened that some of my people and myself were faring overseas on a pilgrimage. It happened in this wise.

The pilgrims were pent together within a great seagoing ship, where often in silence I walked amongst them. Squatting around trays of food, suckling babes or caught in the meshes of the prayers they droned above their rosaries, they had become denizens of the ship; for it was now their dwelling place.

Then one night the elements awoke. And when, in the silence of my love, I visited my people, I saw that nothing had changed. They were still busy carving silver rings, carding wool, or conversing in undertones; tirelessly weaving that web of fellowship, the bond that links men each to each so surely that if one of them dies, his death robs all of somewhat. And in the silence of my love, though I recked little of the subjects of their discourse, I listened to their chatter about kettles and ailments, and this or that; for I knew that the meaning of things lies not in the things themselves but in our attitude towards them. Thus a certain man whom I saw gravely smiling was making a gift of himself; and, if another wore a sullen air, this was by reason of his estrangement from God or from fear of Him. Thus I observed them, in the silence of my love.

But meanwhile the pounding of that monstrous thing beyond their ken, the sea, was telling on them, permeating them with its slow, tremendous rhythms. At each climax of a long upward slope everything seemed hanging in the void, out of space and time. The ship shuddered as though its frame were being wrenched apart. And so long as this break in reality persisted, they stopped praying, stopped talking, suckling babes or graving silver. But then came a single loud crack, like a short clap of thunder, and the ship lurched downwards, as if it were caving in, straining at all its transoms; and that headlong plunge set the men vomiting. Thus miserably they crouched, huddled together in that creaking stable, under the sickeningly swaying oil lamps.

Lest they should lose heart, I had a message sent them: "Let such of you as are workers in silver shape for me a silver ewer. Let those who cook the meals go about it with a will. Let those who are hale tend the sick. Let those who are praying plunge deeper into prayer."

To one whom I saw leaning against a crossbeam and listening, haggard-eyed, across the well-calked ribs of the ship, to the forbidden voices of the sea, I said: "You, my man, go down into the hold. Count up the dead sheep and tell me how many they be. In their panic they sometimes stifle each other."

He answered: "God is kneading his sea, and we are doomed. I can hear the breastbeams creaking. Ill is it that they thus disclose

25

their travail, for they are the very frame and fabric of the ship. Thus it is with the foundations of the earth to which we entrust our houses and the long rows of olive trees, and the frail lives of our fleecy sheep, browsing on God's pastures in the cool of the evening. It is good to tend our olive groves and flocks, and to cherish the love that dwells within the house. But evil is it when the solid frame begins to fail us; when that which has been made is once more in the making. Only behold today how that which should be silent is giving tongue. Thus woe betides men when the mountains set to growling. I have heard their voices, and never shall I forget the sound. . . ."

"What," I asked him, "was that sound you heard?"

"Sire, I once lived in a hamlet on a smiling hillside; a hamlet firmly rooted in the earth, under a sky that was its own, a hospitable sky. It was a village built to last, and lasting. The lustre of long use gleamed on the lips of our wells, on our doorsteps, on the curved brims of our fountains. Then unbewares one night something stirred in the bedrock of our village; it seemed that the ground underfoot was waking to life again, reshaping itself. What had been made was once more in the making. We trembled, not so much fearing for ourselves as for all those things we had labored to perfect; things for which we had been bartering ourselves lifelong. As for me, I was a carver of metal, and I feared for the great silver ewer on which I had toiled two years; for whose perfection I had bartered two years of sleepless nights. Another feared for the deep-piled carpets he had rejoiced to weave. Every day he unfurled them in the sun; he was proud of having bartered somewhat of his gnarled flesh for that rich flood of color, deep and diverse as the waves of the sea. Another feared for the olive trees he had planted. But, Sire, I make bold to say, not one of us feared death; we all feared for our foolish little things. We were discovering that life has a meaning only if one barters it day by day for something other than itself. Thus the death of the gardener does no harm to the tree; but if you threaten the tree the gardener dies twice. There was an old story-teller amongst us, who knew the fairest tales of the desert and had embellished them. And, being sonless, was alone in knowing them. When the earth began to slip he trembled for those poor ballads that never again would be sung by any man. For now the earth had wakened to life, it went on remolding itself and a great yellow tide came creeping down the hillside. And what of himself, I ask you, can a man barter to embellish a yellow flood that, slowly swirling, swallows all? What may he build on a formless moving mass?

"Under its pressure the houses gradually swung around, and in that all but unseen torsion the beams suddenly burst asunder like kegs of black powder. Or the walls began to shake and shake, until suddenly they fell apart. Such of us as survived found our lives had lost their meaning—all but the story-teller who had also lost his wits, and was singing, singing. . . .

"Whither are you taking us? This ship will founder and the sea engulf the fruit of our lives' toil. I can feel Time flowing by, outside. Flowing to no purpose. Surely Time should not thus make its flowing felt; but, rather, harden, mature and mellow. And little by little weld our work together. But henceforth what will it weld together that is of our making and shall endure?"

6

I WENT DOWN amongst my people, musing on the barter that can no longer be, when nothing remains stable from generation to generation; and on Time's river flowing to no purpose, like the sand in an hourglass. And I thought: Surely this dwelling is not vast enough and the work wherefor it was bartered not yet durable enough. I bethought me of the Pharaohs who had men build for them gigantic burial places, square-based and tapering skywards, like promontories jutting into the vast of Time that slowly wears them down to dust. I thought, too, of the wastes of virgin sand along the caravan roads, above which, here and there, looms up an old temple, half sunken and as it were unmasted by the invisible blue storms of the desert; still cumbrously afloat, but doomed. No, I thought, it is not lasting enough, this temple with its load of golden ornaments and treasures for whose making human lives have worn themselves away; with its honey stored up over many and many a generation, its filigrees of gold and hieratic goldwork for whose perfection old craftsmen bartered whole lives' work; and those embroidered cloths over which old women, working lifelong, burnt their sight out, and then, gnarled and wheezing, tottered down to death, leaving behind them a queenly train wrought in the semblance of a field of flowers. "What exquisite needlework!" they exclaim, who look on it today. "How strangely beautiful!" And it came to me that when these old women plied their needles they were like changelings and knew not how wonderful they were. . . .

Likewise I bethought me that it were well to build a great coffer to contain what these craftspeople had bequeathed, and the vehicle to carry it. For above all things I respect that which outlasts men, enshrining the ideals for which they have bartered their lives. Therefore am I building the great tabernacle to which they may entrust that for which they lived and died.

And again I pictured those slow ships in the desert, ever faring onwards. This I have learned, which is essential: that it behoves us to begin by building the ship and equipping the caravan, and erecting the temple which outlasts men. For, once this is done, you shall see them gladly bartering themselves for that which is more precious than themselves. Painters, gravers, silversmiths will arise. But place no hope in man if he works for his own lifetime and not for his eternity. Then it would be vain for me to teach him architecture and its laws. If they build houses but to live in, why should they barter their lives for these houses? For then each man's house is made to serve his own life and nothing else, and he calls his house "useful" and esteems it not for itself but for its utility alone. It serves him, and he busies himself therein, amassing wealth. But such an one dies barren, for he leaves nought of himself; no broidered cloth or hieratic goldwork sheltered in a ship of stone. Called on to barter himself, he preferred being provided for. And when such men depart, nothing remains.

Thus it was that, walking amongst my people in the loom of the nightfall, when all things fall asunder, and seeing them seated on the thresholds of their humble booths, in their work-worn garments, and resting from their bee-like toil, I took less thought for them than for the honeycomb on which daylong they had worked conjointly. And, pausing before one who was blind and furthermore had lost a limb, I pondered. So old, so near the grave was he, groaning like a rusty mill-wheel when he moved, and halting in his speech, for he was full of years and the light of words had grown dim for him—yet ever he was becoming more luminous, brighter, apter for the task for which he had made the barter of himself. With trembling hands he continued perfecting his fretwork, which had become for him as an elixir, ever subtler and more potent. Thus, escaping by a miracle from his gnarled old flesh, he was growing ever happier, more and more invulnerable. More and more imperishable. And, dying, knew it not, his hands being full of stars.

Thus toiled they all their lives, building up a treasure not for daily use and bartering themselves for things of beauty incorruptible; allotting only a small part of their toil to daily needs, and all the rest to their carvings, to the unusable virtue of chased gold or silver, the perfection of form, the grace of noble curves— all of which served no purpose save to absorb that part of themselves they bartered, and which outlasts mortality. . . .

Thus in the evening I walk, taking slow steps, amongst my people, wrapping them in the silence of my love. Disquieted by that alone which burns with unavailing light; the poet full of love for poems, who writes not his own; the woman in love with love yet, lacking skill to choose, unable to *become*. And I knew that I could heal them of the anguish that possessed them, did I bestow on them that gift which entails sacrifice and choice and forgetting of the outside world. For the flower you single out is a rejection of all other flowers; nevertheless, only on these terms is it beautiful. So it is with the object of the barter; and the fool who thinks fit to blame that old woman for her embroidery— on the pretext that she might have wrought something else—out of his own mouth he is convicted of preferring nothingness to creation.

Going my darkling ways, inwardly I can discern the prayer rising above the odors of the nightfall, wherein all things are ripening and taking form in silence, slowly, secretly, almost unawares. Embroidery and flower—each must first be steeped in Time for it to ripen.

In my long night walks it was revealed to me that the quality of my empire's civilization rests not on its material benefits but on men's obligations and the zeal they bring to their tasks. It derives not from owning but from giving. Civilized is that craftsman I have spoken of, who remakes himself in the thing he works on, and, for his recompense, becomes eternal, no longer dreading death. He, too, is civilized who fights and gives up his life for the empire. But those others who content themselves with luxury bought from the merchants are none the better for it—even though they feast their eyes only on perfection—if, to begin with, they themselves have created nothing. Well I know those tribes degenerate who no longer write their poems but only read them; who no longer till their fields, but have recourse to slaves. It is against such as these that the sands of the South are ever raising up more virile tribes, toughened by creative want, who go forth to sack the sterile treasures those others have amassed. No love have I for the sluggards, the sedentaries of the heart; for those who barter nothing of themselves *become* nothing. Life will not have served to ripen them. For them Time flows like a handful of sand and wears them down. What will I have to make over to God on their account?

Thus I understood the grief of men when the reservoir is shattered ere it is full. As for the passing of an old man, who is changed to dust after he has bartered himself wholly his life long —it is a glorious fulfillment, and what we bury is but the instrument, henceforth unserviceable. But also have I seen the children of my tribes who, when death is nigh, say not a word, their breathing labored, their eyes half-closed, the failing glow hidden under their long eyelashes. For it sometimes happens that God cuts down the flowers along with the ripe wheat; and when He binds up his sheaves, heavy with golden grain, He finds therein this useless luxury.

" 'Tis Ibrahim's child who is dying," people said, as I went by, and quietly, unnoticed, I entered Ibrahim's house. I spoke to no man, for I knew that when one cloaks oneself within love's silence there comes an understanding, striking behind the specious veil of words. None paid heed to me, so busy were they listening to his dying.

They spoke in whispers and shuffled their slippers when they moved, as though there were someone very timid in the room, whom the least noise would scare away. No one dared to move, or to open or shut the doors; it was as though a small, frail flame, fed by the thinnest oil, were feebly flickering, and they feared to quench it. When I saw the child I knew, by reason of his hurried breathing and the small clenched fists, that he was in haste to go, borne on the back of a galloping fever; and because of his stubbornly closed eyes, that shunned the light. And I watched those around him seeking to tame him as one tries to tame some small wild creature. Almost tremblingly they proffered him a bowl of milk, thinking perchance its sweet savor would take his fancy, give him pause, and he would drink of it. They spoke endearingly to him, as one speaks to a gazelle that is feeding out of one's hand. But he paid no heed, nor smiled at all; for it was not milk he needed. Then gently, very gently, as if they were murmuring responses to turtledoves, they began to croon a song, his favorite— that song about the nine little stars that went swimming in a pool. But too far away was he, it seemed; he neither heard, nor vouchsafed a backward glance, such was his haste to be gone. For in his dying the old loyalties were renounced. Then they prayed him at least to bestow that last look, the token of recognition that a traveller gives, without slackening of pace, to the friend he is leaving. Turning him in the cot, they wiped his clammy cheeks and forced him to drink—in the hope, may be, of rousing him from the drowsiness of death.

I left them to their task of laying snares to lure him back to life —snares that, alas, this child of nine could all too easily outwit. They held out toys, in the vain hope that these would catch his fancy; but ruthlessly the small hand brushed them away, as the hurrying traveller thrusts aside branches that impede his progress.

At the threshold I looked back, and standing there I saw all this but as a gleam, a moment, one of many aspects of the city—no more than that. Called by mistake, a child had risen and answered the summons. I saw him turn his face towards the wall. Already that child's presence was frailer than a bird's, and I left them to their weaving of a web of silence for the taming of the dying boy.

Walking down the narrow street, I heard voices behind closed doors chiding the serving maids. All within was being made trim and tidy; they were packing up for the journey through the night. Little cared I whether the reprimands were merited or not; all I marked was the fervor behind them. Then, farther on, I found a small girl leaning against the drinking-fountain, crying, her eyes buried in the crook of her elbow. Lightly I laid my hand on her hair and turned up her face that I might see it, but asked her not the reason of her grief, understanding well that it was unknown to her. For grief is ever begotten of Time that, flowing, has not shaped its fruit. Grief there is for the mere flux of empty days, or for a lost bracelet (a mourning for Time that has gone astray), or a brother's death (whereby Time has ceased to render service). When that little girl is older, her grief will be for the absence of the lover who, though she knows it not, serves as a secret path towards the real—the kettle singing on the hob, the well-shut house, the babe nuzzling her breast. And suddenly she will feel Time flowing through her, useless as the sand flowing through an hourglass.

Going a little farther, I saw a woman step forth on to her threshold, and when she looked at me her eyes were bright with joy—over, perhaps, the child that had just fallen asleep, or the fragrance of the evening soup, or a mere homecoming. And now at last having Time to and for herself.

I saw, too, my one-legged cobbler busy threading gold into his leathern slippers and, weak as was his voice, I guessed that he was singing.

"What is it, cobbler, that makes you so happy?"

But I heeded not the answer; for I knew that he would answer me amiss and prattle of money he had earned, or his meal, or the bed awaiting him—knowing not that his happiness came of his transfiguring himself into golden slippers. . . .

❧ 7

For I had lit on this other truth: to wit, that vain is the illusion of the sedentaries who think they can ever dwell in peace; for at every moment men's dwellings are in peril. Thus the temple you built upon the mountain, being exposed to the north wind, has gradually been eaten away like the stempost of an old ship. And your temple in the plain, beleaguered by the sands, will gradually be overrun by them, until nothing remains where it once was but a great sea of sand. Thus is it with all that men build, and likewise with my palace indivisible, wrought of flocks of sheep and goats, of dwellings and of mountains, which is the fulfillment of my love; but should the king die, in whom its visage is made manifest, it will once again break up into separate dwellings and mountains, flocks of sheep and goats. And then, foundered in the diversity of

33

things, it will be but a mass of raw materials—a quarrying place, perchance, for other builders. They will come, the men of the desert, and reshape these things into a new visage. They will come with this other vision in their hearts and reset, to body forth their message, the letters that served me for my book.

Thus did I myself in an earlier time; and never shall I weary of extolling them, those sumptuous nights of my forays! After aligning on the virgin sand the dark triangle of my camp, I climbed a hill, there to await the morning and, measuring with my eyes that black patch, hardly larger than a village marketplace, wherein I had massed my men-at-arms, my war gear and my horses, for a while I mused on their fragility. What, indeed, could be more vulnerable than that handful of half-naked men shivering under their blue cloaks, plagued by the night frost whereby the very stars seemed turned to icicles, and threatened by thirst—for it behoved us to go warily with the waterskins until we made the ninth day's well; threatened, too, by sandstorms uprising with the blind fury of a revolt; and, lastly, threatened by those wounds that set a man's flesh moldering like an over-ripe fruit. And then the man is fit but to be cast aside. What, I mused, could be more piti-ful than those little humps of blue cloth, but faintly stiffened by the steel of muffled weapons and strewn forlorn on the vastness of a desert that disclaimed them?

And yet—why need I be concerned for their "fragility"? Was I not knotting them together into a wholeness that would save them from dispersal and destruction? By the mere form of the triangle imposed on the encampment, I had wrested it from the clutches of the sands, and I had clenched my men like a fist. Thus may you see a cedar tree growing amongst boulders and guarding its wide branchage from destruction; for neither is there any sleep for the cedar tree, but day and night it wages war through every fibre, nourishing itself in a hostile world with the very forces that plot its ruin. At every moment the cedar stablishes itself, and at every moment I, too, was stablishing my dwelling place so that it might endure. So had I welded together that company of men, whom a mere gust might have dispersed, by setting up the dark triangle clamped to the soil, impregnable as a tower and lasting as a stempost. And lest my camp should sleep and founder in unwariness, I girt it about with sentries who culled all the drifting echoes of the desert. Thus, as the cedar draws into itself the stony soil and changes it into cedarwood, likewise my camp was nourished by those threatening it from without. How salutary is that exchange of tidings! And how blessed are the feet of messengers whom none hears approach and who suddenly loom up beside a camp fire and, squatting down, tell of the progress of a horde advancing southwards, or of the tribes combing the north for the camels that enemies have reaved from them, or of the turmoil in another tribe by reason of a murder, or (and above all) of the schemings of our foes who, silent beneath their cloaks, ponder darkly on the night ahead! You have heard them, these messengers who come with tidings of that uneasy silence. Blessed, too, are they who appear beside our camp fires so suddenly and with news so grave that in an instant all the fires are quenched with sand, the men fall flat, gun in hand, and a blue mist of powder smoke rings the camp!

For hardly has night fallen than it quickens with signs and wonders.

Thus evening after evening I gazed down at my camp becalmed like a ship in the vastness, but durable; for I knew that dawn would find it unscathed, jubilant as the cocks that crow for the sheer joy of another day. And then, while the animals were being harnessed, you could hear bursts of talk and laughter shrilling like bugle calls in the growing light. Drunk with the dawn's nectar, the men drew deep breaths of the new air, savoring the harsh tang of the desert breeze.

Presently I led them to the oasis we were to capture. One who understood men not would have thought to find the religion of that oasis within the oasis itself. But the dwellers in an oasis know nothing of their dwelling, and it is, rather, in some far-off desert

35

camp, beleaguered by the sand, that its inwardness may be discovered.

I said to my men: "There you will find fragrant grass and singing streams and women with long, gaudy veils who will run from you in panic, like a herd of gazelles, fleet indeed yet easy to be caught, made as they are for capture."

I said: "They think they hate you and will fight tooth and nail to fend you off. But you need only master them, clenching your fists in the blue-glinting tresses of their hair. But gently need you ply your strength to hold them. True, they will keep their eyes shut so as not to see you, yet your silence will oppress them like an eagle's shadow. Anon will they open their eyes upon you, and you will fill them with tears. . . . You will have been their vision of the vastness of the world: how could they forget you?"

And lastly I said to them, to whet their ardor for that earthly paradise: "There you shall see palm groves and many-hued birds. The oasis will yield to you because you have in your hearts the true religion of the oasis, whereas those you are driving out are no longer worthy of it. Why, even the women washing their linen in the stream purling over the smooth white pebbles think they are but sharing in a dull, trite duty when they observe a festival. But you, gnarled by the sand, scorched by the desert sun and salted with the fiery spume of salterns, you will wed them and as, your fists planted on your hips, you watch them washing their linen in the blue water, you will savor the fruits of victory.

"Here in the sand today you endure as the cedar tree endures, by reason of the enemies that beset and toughen you; and, after the oasis is yours, you shall still endure, provided the oasis does not become for you a refuge wherein you immure yourselves, oblivious of the world outside—but, rather, a lasting victory over the desert.

"You will have vanquished those others because they immured themselves in their contentment with the provisions they had laid up. In the sands that ringed them round and harried them they saw but an adornment, as it were a garland for the oasis. And they jeered at the spoiljoys who ruffled their peace, telling them that the sentries posted on the outskirts of this place of many waters should be punished if they slept at their posts.

"Thus they stagnated in that false happiness which comes of great possessions; whereas true happiness comes from the joy of deeds well done, the zest of creating things new. Those who have ceased to barter anything of themselves and draw their nourishment, be it the choicest and most delicate, from others—aye, even those men of taste who listen to strangers' poems but make not their own poems!—all such do but prey on the oasis without adding to its life, and batten on the songs that others provide for them. Thus voluntarily they have tethered themselves to the rack in their stables and, like cattle, are become ripe for servitude.

"When the oasis is taken," I bade them, "think not that anything vital has been changed. It will be but another kind of desert bivouac. For always is my empire threatened on all sides. Its stuff is but an assemblage of ordinary things, of flocks and herds, of dwellings and of mountains, and should the knot binding them give way, nothing will remain but fragments, scattered and dispersed for all who will to plunder."

❧ 8

I saw that they had fallen into error in the matter of respect. As for me, I have always borne in mind the rights of God, beyond the man himself; and, though I overrate not the importance of the beggar, I see him as one of God's ambassadors.

But never can I regard the rights of the beggar, his sores and scabs, as being worthy of respect for their own sake, or sacrosanct like idols.

What fouler place have I ever seen than that part of the town which, sprawling on a hillside, flowed seawards like a sewer? The corridors giving on its narrow streets exhaled noisome odors, and the squalid denizens of its glutinous recesses emerged from their lairs but to bandy insults in muffled voices, bringing to mind the flaccid bubbles that burst ever and again above a swamp.

There, too, I saw a leper guffawing till the tears came to his eyes, and then wiping them with a dirty rag: so gross and abject was he that he was making merry at himself!

My father resolved to have this plague-spot burnt out. But that spawn of the mire, clinging to its fetid hovels, waxed wroth and prated of its rights. The right to molder in its lazar-house!

"Natural enough!" my father said. "For these men justice means the perpetuation of that which is."

Shrilly they voiced their right to rottenness: founded on decay, they were all in favor of decay.

"Only let cockroaches multiply," my father said, "and you will presently hear them prating about the sacred rights of cockroaches. Which are self-evident. Then minstrels will arise to hymn them, and they will din into your ears the tragic plight of cockroaches, threatened with extinction. . . . For, to be just, we have to choose. Just towards the archangel, or just towards men? Just towards the skin disease, or just to healthy flesh? But why should I listen to him who pleads the cause of his disease?

"Rather, I shall make shift to save him, for this I owe to God. In that man, too, God dwells. But I shall not deal with the man according to his desire, for his desire is but the mouthpiece of the disease gnawing his flesh.

"After I have cleansed and washed and taught him, then his desire will be changed; he will disown the man he was. So why should I play ally to the man whom he himself will soon abhor? Why should I, as the creeping leper would have had me, hinder him from being reborn in comelier form?

"Why should I take sides with that which *is,* against that which *will be?* With that which vegetates, against that which promises better things?

38

The Wisdom of the Sands

"Justice, to my mind," my father said, "is to respect the trustee in virtue of the trust—no less than I respect myself. For he reflects the same light, however dim in him it be. Justice means regarding him as a vehicle, or a pathway. My charity is to help him to bring himself to birth.

"Still, when I see that human sewer oozing seawards, I can but be disheartened by its vileness. God is so sadly smirched therein. I await from one of them a sign revealing the man within, but never am I given even a hint of him."

"Yet," I said to my father, "sometimes I have seen one of them sharing his crust, or helping another still rottener than himself to unload his sack, or showing tenderness to a sick child."

"They put all in common," my father answered, "and of this hotchpotch make their charity—what they call charity! They share. And they would fain extol as a noble fellowship this pact of theirs, which jackals, too, observe when gathered round a heap of carrion. And bid us admire their munificence! But the value of a gift depends on who it is receives it, and here it is bestowed on the basest—like the proffering of strong drink to a drunkard. Thus the gift becomes a bane. As for me, I bring the gift of health; therefore do I extirpate that proud flesh—and it abhors me. . . .

"Thus their charity merely incites them to favor rottenness. But what if I, quite otherwise, favor health?"

Also my father said to me: "Do not give thanks to him who saves your life, nor overdo your gratitude. If he who has saved you looks to you for gratitude this is because his mind is base—for what does he think? That he has done *you* a service? Nay, it is God whom he has served by preserving you, if so be that you have any value. And if you speak overmuch of your gratitude, this proves that you are lacking in both modesty and pride. For the essential thing that he has saved is not your petty, precarious life, but the work in which you share and which needs your aid. And since the same task is allotted to him also, you have no need to thank him. He is recompensed by his own work in hand; in saving you he has helped on that work.

"Also you lack proper pride when you pander to his vulgarest emotions, flattering his pettiness by your servility. Were he noble-minded, he would wave away your gratitude.

"Nothing I see," my father said, "worthy of my concern but the fertile collaboration of one man through another. I make use of you as I make use of a stone; but who thanks a stone for having served to buttress the temple?

"These men, however, work not for anything beyond themselves, and that sewer plunging seawards feeds no hymns, nor does it breed marble statues, nor harbor conquests. All that interests these men is to drive the shrewdest bargain, enabling them to draw on the provisions that have been stored up. But make no mistake! Provisions are needful, but they are more dangerous than famine.

"They have split up man's works and days into two periods, which are meaningless: that of conquering, and that of enjoying the fruits of victory. Have you seen a tree growing up and, once it is fully grown, preening itself on its achievement? The tree grows because it must. And this I say to you: 'They are already dead who become sedentaries when the victory is won.'

"Charity, as my empire understands it, is co-operation.

"I bid my surgeon spare not himself when he is called in haste across the desert to succor a wounded man; to repair the damaged instrument. No matter if the man be but a humble stonebreaker· he needs all his strength to break the stones. No matter, likewise, if the surgeon be most eminent. For herein is no question of paying tribute to mediocrity, but of repairing the damaged vehicle. And both have the same driver. Thus it is with those who minister to the woman with child. Above all for the sake of that new life which the woman in her pangs and vomitings is serving; nor need the woman render thanks, save on her son's behalf. Yet we find women today demanding help, as if this were their due, on the score of their vomitings and pangs. If the women alone were in question I would away with them, so ugly are their vomitings. The only thing in them that has importance is the new life that they are serving; nor are they entitled to render thanks on their own behalf, since those who nurse them and they themselves are but the servitors of birth. Such gratitude were meaningless."

Not otherwise was it when a certain general came bragging to my father. "You yourself," my father said, "are nothing in my eyes. You are great only by virtue of the empire which you serve, and, if I have men treat you with respect, that is but to teach them to respect, by way of you, the empire."

Yet I knew my father's kindliness. "Whoever," he once said, "has played a lofty part and been honored may not be laid low. He who has reigned may not be divested of his kingship, nor must you reduce to beggary him who has given alms to beggars. Acting thus, you would be shattering the very design and fabric of your ship. Therefore I have my punishments befit the standing of those whom I punish. I execute those whom I have thought fit to ennoble, if they have proved unworthy, but I do not degrade them to the estate of slaves.

"One day I came upon a princess working at the washing trough, and heard the other women mocking her. 'What of your power and your glory now, O washerwoman? Once at a word from you a man's head fell under the axe, but now the tables are turned, and we can jeer at you to our hearts' content. 'Tis but justice.' For justice, to their mind, was compensation.

"But the woman kept silent under their taunts—humiliated, perhaps, on her own account, but chiefly on account of something greater than herself. Rigid, her face pale as death, the princess bent above the washing board, and the other women elbowed her aside without compunction. Yet there was nothing about her to incite their mockery, for she was fair to see, discreet in her gestures, silent. Thus I perceived that it was not the woman herself that her companions were flouting, but her degradation. For when one whom you have envied falls into your clutches, you have no mercy. . . . I had her brought before me.

"'Nothing I know of you,' I said, 'but that once you ruled. From this day on you shall have the power of life and death over the women who work beside you at the washing troughs. I restore to you your queendom. Go!'

"But when she had regained her place above the rabble, she was too much the queen to remember their offences. Moreover, those very women, now that they could no longer gloat over her humiliation, took heed of her nobility, and venerated her. For her welcome back amongst them they held high festival, and bowed to the ground when she passed by, feeling themselves the nobler for that they once had touched her with their fingers.

"This," my father said, "is why I will not have princes subjected to the insults of the mob or the coarse hands of jailers. But I have their heads fall in a vast arena, ringed round with clarions of gold."

"When a man abases another," my father said, "this is because he himself is base. . . . Never shall a ruler of men be judged by his inferiors."

❧ 9

THUS SAID to me my father: "Constrain them to join in building a tower, and you shall make them like brothers. But if you would have them hate each other, throw food amongst them."

And he said also: "Let them bring first to me the fruits of their toil; let them pour into my barns the river of their harvest; let them build in me their garner. For I would have them serve my glory when they thresh the wheat, and all around them the golden husks glitter in the sunbeams. Thus, instead of being a drudgery for the getting of bread, their task becomes an anthem. Thus, too, they are less to be pitied when their backs are bowed under the heavy sacks they carry to the mill, or bring back white with flour. Like prayer, the burden on his shoulders magnifies the man. So you may see them proudly smiling when they hold aloft the sheaves, like many-branched candlesticks, the spiked ears darting flashes of gold. For a civilization is built on what is required of men, not on that which is provided for them. True it is that, after the long day's work, this wheat supplies their food. But this is not the side of things that means most for a man: what nourishes his heart is not what he gets from the wheat, but what he gives to the wheat.

"Again I say it! Despicable are those peoples of the earth who chant others' poems, and eat alien corn, and hire architects from other lands to build their cities. Such people I call 'sedentaries.' Never will you see them clad in those veils of shimmering gold which hover round the threshing-floor.

"It is meet that I should receive, even as I give; so that I may be able to continue giving. How happy is this giving and taking which helps my people on their way and enables yet more giving! And, though the taking makes the body thrive, it is the giving alone that nourishes the heart.

"I have watched dancers composing their dances. And true it was that, once the dance had been devised and danced, none harvested the fruit of his work or could hoard it up. Like a flame, a dance gleams and is gone. Nevertheless I call that people civilized which makes dances, though for dances there is no harvest home or storing place. Whereas uncouth I call that people which aligns things on shelves, well chosen though these things may be, and though it have the wit to relish their perfection.

"Man," my father said, "is, above all, he who creates. And theirs alone is brotherhood who work together. They alone are alive who find not their peace in the goods they have stored up."

But, one day, certain persons were minded to naysay this.

"What mean you by 'creation'? For if you have in mind some noteworthy discovery, few indeed are capable thereof. Thus you are speaking only for a few—but what of the others?"

My father answered them: "To create may be to miss a step

43

in the dance; or to deal a chisel stroke awry when you are carving stone. Little matters it what the gesture brings forth. To you in your blindness such an effort may seem fruitless, for you bring your eyes too close. Only stand back and observe from a distance the activity in this quarter of the city. You shall see there a vast ardor and a golden cloud of dust billowing above the work. No longer will you notice gestures that go astray. Intent on their task, all these men are building, whether they will or no, palaces, cisterns, hanging gardens. Their hands are spellbound and these things are born of their enchantment. And, mark my words, these noble works are shaped no less by those who botch their gestures than by those who make them deftly; for you cannot divide men up, and if you will have none but great sculptors, you will soon have none at all. Who would be rash enough to choose a calling offering so little chance of a livelihood? The great sculptor springs from the soil of poor sculptors: they are the steps whereon he climbs towards the heights. Likewise the best dances come of a simple zest for dancing; that fervor which insists that everyone, even if he have no skill in dancing, shall join in the dance. Else you have but a joyless, pedantic exercise, an idle show of skill.

"Condemn not their mistakes as does an historian judging a bygone age. Who would blame a cedar tree for being no longer a seed, a young shoot, or a pliant stem? Let be, and from mistake to mistake will rise the forest of cedars scattering upon the breeze the incense of its birds.

"Mark well my words! One man may hit the mark, another blunder; but heed not these distinctions. Only from the alliance of the one, working with and through the other, are great things born. The vain effort furthers the successful, and the successful reveals the goal they both are seeking. One man who discovers God, discovers Him for all. For my empire is as a temple; I have mustered my people and they are ever building it at my behest. Yet it is *their* temple. And the rising of the temple ever spurs them on towards their best. Thus you see them inventing golden scrolls to deck the pillars; and even he who fails in his attempt, he too invents them. It is of this glorious, all-pervading zeal that those golden scrolls are born."

Another day he said: "Build not an empire where everything is perfect. 'Good taste' is a virtue of the keepers of museums. If you scorn bad taste, you will have neither painting nor dancing, neither palaces nor gardens. You will have acted like an over-squeamish man who never goes out for fear of being soiled by contact with the earth. At the core of your perfection will be emptiness, and you shall have no joy of it. Nay, rather build an empire where all is zeal."

❧ 10

WEARY WERE MY MEN, weary as those who have borne a heavy burden many leagues. My captains came to me and said: "When shall we return to our own country? The women of the conquered oases have not the savor of our women."

And another said to me: "Sire, I dream of her who was shaped by *my* Time, *my* care, *my* chidings. Fain would I go back and plant my own fields. For there a truth dwells, whereof I am losing grip. A longing takes me to muse upon my life. Let me go back, then, and mature in the friendly silence of my village."

Thus I understood that they needed silence; for in silence alone does a man's truth bind itself together and strike root. And, above all, Time imports, as in the suckling of a child. For even mother love grows out of many months of suckling. Who, at a given moment, can see the child growing? No one. 'Tis only those who come from elsewhere whom you hear exclaiming, "How he has grown!" But neither mother nor father has noticed him growing. He has *become,* in Time; and at each moment was that which he had to be.

Likewise my men needed Time—if only to come to understand

a tree. To be able to sit day by day on the same threshold, in front of the same tree, the same branches. For thus alone, little by little, does a tree makes itself known.

There was a poet who one night beside our camp fires fell to telling of his tree—no more than that—and my warriors hung on his words. Many of them had never seen anything but briars, dwarf palms and camel grass.

"You know not," he told them, "what a tree is. Once, as chance would have it, I saw one that had taken root within a derelict house, windowless and bare, and thence had set forth on its quest of light. For, as a man needs to be bathed in air, or a carp in water, so a tree needs to be bathed in sunlight. Earthbound by its roots, but with its branches tangled in the stars, it is as a bridge between us and the height celestial. Born blind, that tree had none the less unleashed its mighty sinews in the darkness, lurching and lunging this side and that against the walls; and the tale of the long struggle was written in the twistings of the trunk. At length, forcing its way through a fissure in the roof, it soared sunwards, straight as a pillar. And now, gazing at it, I could retrace, like an historian, the devious progress of its triumph.

"In splendid contrast with the knots and gnarls telling of the long, painful effort to break from its womb of darkness, it rose majestic and serene, spreading forth its leafage like a banquet table for the sun's regalement, suckled by the very heavens, gloriously nourished by the gods!

"With every sunrise I saw it awakening, from its broad base to the topmost twig. Tenanted by birds, it came to life and sang at peep of day; then, once the sun was up, turned loose on the air those hoarded lives, like a kind old shepherd turning loose his sheep across the meadows. Thus did my tree of many mansions, of leafy towers and turrets—and then stayed empty until nightfall."

So he spoke, and we perceived that it is needful to gaze long at a tree before it can take root and manifest itself within us; and all were envious of that man who had stored in his heart this wealth of leafage and of birds.

"When," they asked me, "will the war end? For we, too, wish to learn such things. 'Tis time for us to *become* . . ."

Sometimes one of my men would snare a sand-fox cub, young enough for him to teach it to eat from his hand, or tame a gazelle (if perchance she did not disdain to live). Every day the little fox would grow more precious to him; he would delight in its silky fur and playful ways, and above all in that need for food which called on him for so much care and solicitude. And in the simplicity of his heart he would hug the illusion that he was imparting something of himself to the little creature; that it was nourished, shaped and molded by his love.

But ever a day came when the little fox cub made off into the wild, answering the call of love—which left a void in the man's heart. Indeed one such perished because, taken in an ambush, he defended himself but half-heartedly. When we learned of his death, a strange remark of his came back to me; something he said when his companions, seeing how saddened he was by the loss of his pet, proposed to him that he should catch another. "Too much patience," he said, "is needed—not for catching, but for loving it."

Thus they wearied of the little foxes and gazelles, once they realized the vanity of their barterings; for a fox that love had lured away did not enrich the desert with them.

Another of my men said to me: "I have sons who are growing up, and I shall not have taught them. Thus I am vesting nothing in them. And whither will I go when I am dead?"

Then I, clasping them in the silence of my love, looked sadly on my army, which was beginning to melt away into the sands, like those storm-fed rivers that, lacking a clayey bed to save them, die sterile, since they have never changed themselves into grass or trees or food for men along their banks.

My army had dreamed of changing itself into an oasis for the empire's sake, so that my palace might be the goodlier for its far-flung habitations; and, speaking of it, men might say, "How sweet is the fragrance that comes to us from those new-won palm groves of the South, those villages where men carve ivory!"

But we were fighting without grasping what we won, and all longed for our return. The picture of the empire was dying within them, like a face which one has lost the knack of conjuring up and which is submerged in the diversity of things.

"What matters it to us," they asked, "if we be somewhat the richer by this unknown oasis, and how will it augment us? Wherewith can it profit us, once we are back at home in the peace of our villages? Him alone will it endow who dwells in it, plucking the fruit of his own palm trees and washing his garments in the living water of its streams."

❦ II

TRUE, THEY ERRED, but what could I do to set them right? When faith burns itself out, 'tis God who dies and thenceforth proves unavailing. When men's fervor goes, the very empire is breaking up, for it is compact of their fervor. Not that it is founded on illusion. But when I name "domain" a certain grove of olive trees and the hut amongst them, and, behold, the man who gazes on them feels a thrill of love and takes them to his heart—if a day comes when he sees but rows of olive trees like any others and amongst them a humble hut, meaningless save as a shelter from the rain, who then will there be to save the domain from being sold and dissipated, since that sale would change nothing as to the convenience of the hut, the produce of the trees?

But now look on the master of a domain when he is walking there in the dewy dawn and taking nothing from it, using none of the privileges of his estate. You might think him stripped of his possessions at this moment, for they are not serving him at all and (if rain has fallen) his feet sink in the mire like a laboring man's, and like any tramp he thrusts aside the dew-drenched branches

48

with his staff. Nor, from the sunken road in which he walks, can he see more than a tithe of his domain; yet all the time he is aware of being its lord.

When you meet him on his way and he gazes at you, there can be no mistaking him. Calm, self-reliant, he is assured of his seigniory by everything around him, though at the moment he is not putting it to use. His hands are empty, but he lacks nothing. Securely is he buttressed by these barley fields and pasture lands and palm groves that are his. The fields are at rest, the barns still sleeping, no gleams of broken light flash from the threshing-floors. Yet he has all these things locked within his heart. Not a nobody is this man going his quiet way, but the lord of the domain walking in his land.

Blind is he who sees man only in his deeds and fancies that the deed alone, or tangible experience, or the use of this or that prerogative, reveals him. What counts for man is not that which he is putting to use at any given moment; for this lonely wayfarer is putting to no use the handful of wheat that he might rub in his hands, or the fruit that he could pick. He who follows me to war is filled with memories of his beloved whom he can neither see, nor touch, nor clasp in his arms; and who, at this hour of daybreak, when he is taking deep breaths of the vastness and feels the pull of memories, is hardly living to the world on her bed so far away, but as it were derelict or dead—asleep. Nevertheless that man is fraught with an awareness of her; with a love he is putting to no use and which bides its time like the wheat stored in the granary. He is haunted by scents of which he is bereft, by that sound of leaping water which is the heart of his house and which he cannot hear. And laden, too, with the weight of an empire which makes him different from other men.

Thus, also, is it with the friend you chance to meet, who is bearing his sick child in his heart, though he is far from her. The fever of whose hands he does not feel, and whose whimperings he hears not. Seemingly at this moment nothing is changed in his life thereby; yet you see him as it were bowed down by the load of that sick child.

And thus it is with the man who, though he is a scion of the empire, can neither see it in its wholeness, nor employ its resources, nor have any profit whatsoever of them. Yet in his heart he is upheld and magnified by the empire, like the lord of the domain or the father of the sick child, or him whom love enriches though his beloved is not only far away, but sleeping. It is the *significance* of things that alone counts for men.

True, I know that many there are like the blacksmith in my village who came to me and said: "Little care I for what concerns me not. Let me but have my tea and sugar, my well-fed ass and my good wife at hand, and let my children wax in stature and goodlihead—then my cup is full, I crave nothing more. Why then all this ado for nothing?"

Yet how should he be happy if he stays in his house, cut off from all, or buries himself with his household in a tent far away in the desert? Therefore I bid such a man amend his thoughts. "And suppose," I ask him, "you meet other friends under other tents, and these have something to tell you, news of the desert to impart . . . ?"

For, forget it not, I have observed you, my people. I have watched you sitting around the camp fire, roasting a sheep or goat, and heard snatches of your talk. Then, walking slowly, in the silence of my love, I drew near. True, you spoke of your children, of the goodlihead of one, the sickness of another—but languidly. Only then did your interest quicken when there came amongst you a traveller from afar, and he fell to telling you of the wonders of a distant land, of the king's white elephants, or the wedding of a princess half a thousand leagues away, whose very name was unfamiliar. Or of the machinations of our enemies. Or else he would speak of a strange comet he had seen, or tell tales of love or courage in the face of death, and how some tribesmen hated and some greatly cherished you. Thus, linked up with many far-off things, your minds ranged widely, and your tents, threatened but well guarded, took on their full meaning. You were enmeshed in a great network which magically changed you into something vaster than yourselves. For you have need of the vastness that such words alone impart.

I remember what befell those three thousand Berber refugees whom my father lodged in a camp north of the city; for he would not have them mix with our people. Being kind of heart, he furnished them with food and clothing, tea and sugar; but asked no work of them in return for his munificence. Thus they had not to take thought for their livelihood, and any man of them might have said: "Little care I for what concerns me not. Let me but have my tea and sugar, my well-fed ass and my good wife beside me, and let but my children wax in stature and goodlihead—then my cup of happiness is full, I crave nothing more."

Yet who could have deemed them happy? Sometimes, for my instruction, my father took me to their camp.

"See!" he said. "They are turning into cattle, and rotting away; not in their bodies but in their hearts."

For everything was losing its significance for them. You need not stake your fortune on a throw of the dice, but it is well that the dice should conjure up for you a dream of a vast domain and many herds, of gold bars and diamonds that never will be yours— though certainly they exist. But comes a day when the dice no longer conjure up dreams, and then no play is possible.

Thus these men we had kindly entreated soon had nothing more to say to each other; having used up their family tales (which were all alike) and described to each other over and over again their tents (though all their tents were much the same). They had done with hoping and fearing, and with inventing. And now they used words only for the simplest purposes. "Lend me your cooking stove," one would say, and another: "Where's my son?" What desire could have stirred this human herd, sprawling on the straw beside its manger? For food? They had it. For freedom? But within the limits of their little world they were quite free— sunk in that inordinate freedom which often saps the vitals of the rich. To vanquish their enemies? But they had enemies no more.

My father said to me: "You could come here with a whip, by yourself, and walk through the camp, slashing each man on the face, but all you would elicit from them would be the snarls of a pack of curs, that slink away, itching to bite but daring not. None will sacrifice himself, and so you are not bitten. Then you fold your arms and gaze on them. Despising them."

Also he said: "These men before you are mere husks; no longer is there any man within. True, they may stab you in the back, like cowards; but they will not face your gaze."

Yet like a slow disease dissension spread amongst them, a vague hostility that did not split them up into two factions but set each against his neighbor; for by consuming his own share of the common stock each deprived the others of a moiety. They eyed each other like dogs prowling around their trough and presently, on the strength of what they called "justice," took to murdering each other. To their mind, justice meant, above all, equality, and anyone who excelled in any way was crushed out ruthlessly.

"The mass," my father said, "hates the sight of one who proves himself a man; for it is formless, straining all ways at once, and tramples on the creative impulse. True, it is evil that a single man should crush the herd, but see not there the worst form of slavery, which is when the herd crushes out the man."

Thus, on the pretext of ill-defined rights, daggers ripped bellies in the darkness, and each night brought forth a crop of corpses. At daybreak they haled the bodies, like so much ordure, to the limit of the camp, where they were loaded on our scavengers' carts. And I remembered my father's words. "If you wish them to be brothers, have them build a tower. But if you would have them hate each other, throw them corn."

We found that little by little they were losing the use of words, now that words had ceased, for them, to serve any purpose. And my father had me walk amongst them and mark those vacant, brutish faces which gazed at us without a sign of recognition. The only sounds that came from them were grunts like those of hungry animals. Thus they drowsed their lives away, without desire, or love, or hate. Some even gave up washing and did not trouble to destroy their vermin. Which greatly prospered. So, presently, boils and blains began to break out on their bodies; the whole camp stank to high heaven, and my father feared the outbreak of a pestilence.

Doubtless he gave thought also to man's honor, for thus he said to me: "Now must I seek to rouse up the archangel crushed and buried beneath their dunghill. For though I respect them not, I respect God in all His creatures."

❦ 12

"HEREIN YOU MAY DISCERN," my father said, "a great mystery in man's estate; often he loses what is his most precious possession without knowing what he has lost. Thus it is with the sedentaries of the oases, clinging like limpets to the hoards they have amassed. And indeed their loss has left no trace on the solid things they set such store by. Thus, too, is it with the men of dwelling places and mountains when these no longer form part of a domain.

"They do not perceive that they are wilting, draining themselves of their substance and depriving all things of what gives them worth, when they lose touch with the meaning of the empire. True, things keep their outward aspect, but what is a diamond or a pearl if none desires it? And the child you rock to sleep has lost something of himself, if he is no longer dedicate to the empire. But at first you know this not, for his smile has in nowise changed.

"This is because things of daily use remain outwardly the same, after they have lost their inner virtue. But what is a diamond's daily use? And what the use of finery, if there are no festivals? And what is the child if there be no empire; if you dream not of making of him a conqueror, an architect, the lord of a domain? If he is abased to being a mere lump of flesh?

"They disregard the breast unseen that suckled them night and day; for the empire nourishes your heart as your beloved nourishes you with her love, changing for you the whole meaning of the world, though she be very far away, and sleeping, and like one dead. Though its fragrance cannot reach you, a soft breath flutters in that far land, making the world a miracle for you. Even so, walking in the dewy fields at daybreak, the lord of the domain bears all things, even the sleep of his husbandmen, in his heart.

"Likewise the mystery of him who bemoans his lot, if his beloved withdraws herself from him, or his own love dies, or he ceases to venerate the empire, is that he has no inkling of his own impoverishment. He merely tells himself, 'Less beautiful is she than the beloved of my dream, or less lovable. . . .' And, reassured, he goes his way as the wind lists. But for him the world has ceased to be a miracle. No longer is any dawn for him a dawn of homecoming, or of awaking in her arms. No longer is the night love's sanctuary and by the grace of her whose light breath fans his cheek, a shepherd's great blue cloak enveloping their love. The lustre has gone out of everything, all is turned to stone. Yet he who is blind to this havoc of his life grieves not for his bygone plenitude, but is contented with his new-won freedom, which is the freedom of having ceased to exist.

"Thus, too, is it with the man in whose heart the empire has died. 'My fervor was but blind infatuation,' he says—and indeed this is true for the man he has come to be; for nothing now exists outside him but a farrago of sheep and goats, mountains and dwellings. The empire was a creation of his heart.

"But wherein lies a woman's beauty, if there be none to be moved by it, or a diamond's prestige, if none longs to possess it, or an empire, if there be no more servants of the empire?

"That man who bears a vision in his heart and can interpret it, and, cleaving to it, like a child to his mother's breast, draws his very sustenance from it; if for him it be a corner stone, the one

54

thing that gives meaning, breadth and fullness to his life and brings magnificence within his grasp—such a man, if he be sundered from his wellspring, is as it were dismembered and he pines away like a tree whose roots are cut. Never will he find himself again. Nevertheless, though the passing of that vision has laid waste his life, he does not suffer; nay, he grows reconciled to his abasement, being unaware of it as such.

"Wherefore it is our bounden duty to quicken whatever is great in man, and to exalt his faith in his own greatness.

"For the nourishment of which he stands in greatest need is drawn not from things themselves but from the knot that holds things together. It comes not from the diamond but from a certain relation between the diamond and Man; not from a tract of sand but from a certain relation between it and the tribesmen; not from the words in the book but from a certain relation between the words in the book—love, the poem, the wisdom of God.

"And when I bid you join together and build in fellowship a mighty whole whereby every man will be the richer, each sharing in all and all in each; and if I enfold you in the kingdom of my love—how can you fail to be the greater for it, how can you naysay me? The beauty of a face lives but in the interplay of the features, each with each. Yet the sight of it may overwhelm you with joy. Thus, too, it is with a poem that wrings tears from your eyes. Stars, water-springs, regrets—with these and nothing more my poem is built up. Yet when I have remolded these as my inspiration listed, they are a pedestal for a divine presence looming above and not contained in any of them."

To that mass of rotting humankind my father sent a singer, and at shut of day he took his stand in the centre of the camp and sang. He sang of far-off things that ring their changes on each other, and of the wonderful princess whose palace lies two hundred days' march across a treeless, waterless expanse of sand. But the very lack of wells becomes a holy sacrifice, quickening love's ecstasy; and the water in the waterskins a prayer, for it leads the seeker to the beloved. "Ah, how I longed for the coolth of palm groves," he sang, "and for the soft fingers of the rain; but above all I yearned for her who would perchance welcome me with her smile at journey's end—till I could no longer distinguish between the fires of fever and my love."

Hearing, they grew athirst for thirst and brandished their fists at my father. "O cruel man, thou hast robbed us of that thirst divine and the ecstasy of sacrifice for love!"

He sang of the fears that darken counsel when a war breaks out, making the whole desert a viper's nest and swelling each dune with presages of life or death. And then they yearned for the peril of death, making the sandy waste a living, venomous thing. He sang of the terrible imminence of the foe when his onslaught is awaited on every hand and he ranges from horizon to horizon like a sun whose rising place none may foreknow. And then they thirsted for an enemy to gird them with his enveloping splendor, like the sea.

But when they thirsted after love, glimpsed in the likeness of a face, daggers flashed from their sheaths. And, stroking their swords, they wept for joy. Those rusty weapons, long forgotten and discarded, now seemed the earnest of their lost manhood; for they alone enable man to recreate the world. Then suddenly, glorious as a conflagration, rebellion blazed up amongst them.

And, to a man, they died like men!

❧ 13

THUS WE MADE essay of poets' songs upon our army, now beginning to fall asunder. But a strange thing befell: the songs took no effect, our soldiers laughed at them.

"What care we for all those old wives' tales?" they said. "Let the minstrels sing *our* truths: the fountains in our courtyards and the good smell rising from our cooking pots when we come home at nightfall."

And so I learned this other truth: to wit, that power once lost is not to be regained. And that the vision of the empire had lost its efficacy. For visions wither like the flowers of the field when their life force is spent, and then they are mere dead matter, leaf mold for another sowing. Therefore I withdrew to a lonely place to ponder on this riddle. Nothing is truer or less true, but only less or more efficacious. The mystic bond that held together their diversity had slipped from my hands, and the empire was disintegrating from within. For when a cedar tree is rent by the blast and the desert winds ravage it, this is not because the sands have waxed stronger but because the cedar has already given up the fight and opened its gates to the barbarians.

Thus when a poet sang they murmured: "He protests too much, too passionately." And truly the emotions he voiced rang false in our ears, like echoes of a bygone age. "Is he himself the dupe," they asked, "of this great love he professes for all those sheep and goats, dwelling places and mountains, which are but so many separate things? Is he taken in by this great love he professes for the reaches of rivers that no war threatens and which merit not that blood be shed for them?" And indeed there was no denying that even the singers had qualms of unease—as if they were telling clumsy fairy tales to children who had outgrown belief in them.

In their crass stupidity my generals complained to me of my minstrels. "They sing out of tune," they grumbled. But I knew what made their voices sound thus; they were praising a dead god.

Then, in their crass stupidity, my generals asked: "Why have our men lost heart for fighting?" (As who should ask: "Why have they lost heart for reaping wheat?") But I changed the question which, put thus, led nowhere. For what was at stake was not a task to be performed. And in the silence of my love I asked myself: "Why have they lost heart for *dying?*" And my wisdom sought an answer.

A man does not lay down his life for sheep or goats, for dwellings or for mountains. Such things will go on existing though nothing be sacrificed to them. A man lays down his life to preserve the unseen bond which binds them together, transforming them into a domain, an empire—that becomes to him like a familiar face. A man will barter himself for that unity, for even in the act of dying he is building it up. By reason of his love his death is worth the dying. And he who has slowly bartered his life for a work well done, which will endure after he is dead—for a temple far outlasting him—such an one is willing enough to die, if his eyes can distinguish the temple from the diversity of materials composing it, if he is captivated by its beauty, and desires to merge himself therein. Then he is absorbed into something greater than himself, giving his all for love.

But why should they have been willing to barter their lives for tawdry, self-interested ends? Self-interest bids men save their lives. Despite their zeal, my singers were offering them counterfeit coin as recompense for their sacrifices. They were unable to conjure up for them the visage that would have stirred their hearts. To die in love—that happy death was not vouchsafed my men; why then give up their lives?

Some few there were, steeled by their devotion to a duty blindly accepted and ensued, who gave up their lives; but they died sadly, their eyes grim and set, in stubborn silence.

Therefore I cast about for a new message, one that would fire their ardor; though well I knew no arguments or wisdom would avail, since my task was, rather, to mold a visage—like a sculptor imposing his creative will on inert stone. And I prayed God to enlighten me. . . .

Thus all night long, unsleeping, I watched over my sleeping men, amidst the ceaseless rustle of the sand as it coursed over the dunes, unravelling them and remaking them a little farther on. And all night long the moon shone down or vanished behind redly glowing sand-clouds whirled by the wind. I could hear the sentries hailing each other from the three terminal watchtowers of the vast triangle of the camp, and their voices were devoid of faith, and pitiful in their forlornness.

And I said to God: "Their words ring dead on the void, for our old order is outworn. My father's prisoners were miscreants, but compassed by a mighty empire. My father sent to them a singer, who spoke with the voice of the empire, and thus in a single night, by the power of his words, their hearts were changed. But that power emanated not from him but from the empire.

"But I have no such singer, no truth have I, nor shepherd's cloak. Needs must they fall to killing each other wantonly, fouling the darkness with knife-thrusts in the belly, futile as a leper's sores. What message shall I give my people, to weave them together again?"

Now and again false prophets arose and won over some of them. And, though few in numbers, those who believed in them took heart and were ready to die for their faith. But their faith meant nothing to the others. Thus all these diverse faiths set them at odds, and many small sects sprang up, each hating all the rest, since it claimed alone to know what was truth, and what was error. Now that which is not truth is error and that which is not error must be truth; this there is no denying. Yet well I know that error is not the *opposite* of truth, but a different arrangement, another temple built with the same stones—neither truer, nor falser, but unlike. And when I saw them ready to die for their phantom truths, my heart bled, and again I prayed to God.

"Canst thou not make known to me a truth that overrides their private truths, welcoming them all into its bosom? For, could I make out of these diverse growths that prey on each other a tree quickened by a single soul, then each branch would profit by the welfare of its neighbors, and the whole tree become a vast participation, waxing and proliferating sunwards. And would not my heart be big enough to contain them all?"

But then came the heyday of the hucksters, and well-doers were put to scorn. All was bought and sold, and virgins were traded like cattle. The stocks of wheat I had laid up for times of famine were pillaged. Men were murdered. But I was not simpleton enough to ascribe the breakdown of the empire to this breakdown of morals; too well I knew that the breakdown was due to the decline of the empire.

"O Lord," I prayed, "impart to me the vision for which they will barter themselves with all their hearts, and all, through each, will wax in power. Then virtue will shine forth, betokening the men they are."

❧ 14

IN THE SILENCE of my love I had many of them executed, but each death fanned the revolt smoldering underground. Men accept that which is made plain; but therein nothing was made plain, and they could not clearly understand the principle behind each new death sentence. And then it was that by grace of God, His wisdom, I learned how power should be exercised.

For power does not justify itself by severity, but wholly by the simplicity of the language it sponsors. True, severity is needed to impose that new language, for there is no proving it by logic; nor indeed is it truer or falser, but only different from its precursor. Yet how could discipline impose a language which of its very nature sets men at odds by giving them opportunities of quarreling over it? By imposing a language of that sort you merely impose dissension and fritter away discipline.

I can enforce my will when I *simplify,* when I constrain each man to become different, clearer visioned, more generous and more fervent—in a word, at one with himself in his aspirations. Once he has thus *become,* since, now that his eyes are opened, he abjures the undeveloped self that formerly was his, then he is astonished, nay, ravished, by his sudden splendor and is henceforth my ally, a soldier schooled by my severity. And this severity rests solely on the part he has to play; it is as it were a mighty portal through which the herd must pass, driven on perhaps by blows, so that it may slough its old self and be transfigured. Yet it is not true that such men are compelled; they are converted.

But severity or discipline fails of its end if, once he passes through that gate, the man who has been stripped of his old self, and released from the chrysalis, does not feel his wings unfolding, and if, instead of glorifying the pangs which brought this new self into being, he feels maimed and bereft, and struggles back to the farther bank of the river he has crossed.

And then surely the river will run red with blood, shed all in vain.

That I had been unable to convert those men whom I put to death proved that I had fallen into error. And I prayed to God.

"O Lord, my cloak is too short and I am a bad shepherd, who cannot shelter his flock. I satisfy the needs of some, and I leave others in their want. I know that all aspirations are alike to be commended: the yearning for freedom no less than the cult of discipline. The desire to get the children's bread, and the desire to sacrifice bread. The thirst for knowledge which weighs things in the balance and the craving for submission which accepts and stablishes. For hierarchies which deify; and for the sharing that provides for all alike. For time, which enables meditation; and for work which fills up time. For spiritual love which mortifies the flesh but ennobles man; and for pity, which heals his wounds. For the future that is yet to build; and for the past and its preservation. For war, which sows the seed; and for peace, which brings the harvest home.

"But I also know that these dissensions are mere quarrels about words and the more a man rises above himself, the greater the height from which he views them—until at last they dwindle into nothingness.

"O Lord, bestow on me a fragment of thy cloak whereunder I may shelter all alike and their burden of great longings. I am weary of putting men to death, lest they whom I cannot take under my cloak undo my work. For I know that these men imperil both the others and the boons, such as they are, of my precarious enlightenment; but equally I know that they are noble and they, too, have their truth within them.

"O Lord, I fain would safeguard the nobility of my warriors and the beauty of our temples, for which men barter their all, and which give meaning to their lives. But, walking tonight in the desert of my love, I came on a little girl in tears. Gently I drew her head back so as to see her eyes, and the grief I read in them abashed me. If, O Lord, I give no heed to this, I am excluding a part of life, and my task is incomplete. Not that I turn away from any of the lofty goals I set before me—but that little girl *must* be consoled. Thus alone will all go well with the world; for in her, too, the meaning of the world is manifest."

✳ 15

HARD IS THE WAGING of war when it no longer answers to a natural inclination or is not the expression of a desire. In their crass stupidity my generals studied the art of tactics, arguing interminably, and seeking perfection, before they could bring themselves to act. For they were but worthy, conscientious men; not God-possessed. Therefore they failed. And I had them gather together to hear my words.

"You will never win battles," I told them, "because you seek perfection. But perfection is a—museum-piece! You rule out mistakes. You never move until you are fully justified by precedent. But where have you ever seen the future proved by dialectics? Just as you seek to hinder throughout the land the coming forth of painters, sculptors, great inventors—even so you will hinder victory. For, mark well my words, a tower, a city, or an empire grows like a tree. They are manifestations of life, since they are made by man. True, he fancies that his reasoning controls the setting up of the stones. But that gradual ascent of stone on stone is primarily born of his desire. The city is immanent within him, a vision cherished in his heart, as the tree is immanent in the seed; and all his reasonings and calculations serve but to give form to his heart's desire, to make it visible. For you do not explain the tree by telling of the water it has drunk, the minerals it has absorbed, and the sunlight that strengthened it. Nor do you explain the town by saying, 'For such and such a reason that arch does not cave in. . . . Here are the architect's figures.' If the town is to come into being, you will always find calculators, who handle figures skilfully. But these are mere menials; if you advance them to the front rank, thinking that their handiwork can bring a town into being, no town will rise up from the sands. They know *how* towns are born, but not *why*. But take an unlettered conqueror and set him down with his people on even the rockiest, least promising patch of land, and then after a while come back. Lo, a goodly city crowned with thirty domes, gleaming in the light! And each dome stalwart as the spreading branches of a cedar tree! For the conqueror's desire will have fulfilled itself in his new city, and he will have found, to forward the work, all the calculators no less than all the roads and implements he needed.

"Thus it is," I told them, "you will lose the war. You have no desire or natural inclination urging you on, nor do you co-operate: rather, you destroy each other's work by contradictory orders. Consider the stone, and how its weight tells when it rolls down to the bottom of the ravine. The stone is a co-operation of all the particles of dust wherewith it has been molded, and all weigh in the same direction. Or consider the water in the reservoir. Ever it presses on the walls, biding its time; for surely a time will come when it has its chance. Night and day, indefatigably, the water thrusts against its confines, seemingly inert, but none the less alive. And no sooner does a tiny rift develop, than, seeping in, it launches its attack; and when it comes on an obstacle, turns it if this may be done, or else returns to its feigned slumber, biding its time until a new rift promises another path. Thus promptly when an opportunity arises it grasps it, and in the end, by countless devious ways, that no calculator could have reckoned out, that steady pressure drains the reservoir and all your store of water is lost in the sand.

"Your army is like a sea that does not chafe its dykes. You are like dough without leaven, or unsown soil; a crowd without a guiding desire. Instead of leading, you administer. You are but feckless lookers-on. But as for the dark forces pressing on the dykes of the empire, these need no administrators to enable them to whelm you in their flood. Later, of course, historians yet stupider than you will explain the reasons of our downfall, and attribute our enemy's success to his superior prudence, foresight and calculation. But I tell you that when a flood breaks through the dykes and engulfs a city of men, it owes nothing to foresight or prudence or calculation.

"But, like the sculptor whose chisel strokes draw forth the statue from the marble, I, too, will shape the future, and one by one will flash and fall the flakes that hide the visage of a god. Some indeed will say, 'The god was within the block of marble, and he but disclosed him by the deftness of his chisel strokes.' But I reply that he made no calculation but shaped the stone, and that smile on the god's face is not composed of chisel strokes and of sweat and flakes of light; it comes not of the stone but of the creator. Set man free, and he will create."

In their crass stupidity my generals took counsel together. "We must ascertain," they said, "why our men are thus at odds and hate each other." And they summoned the men before them.

The generals heard them patiently and sought to compose their differences and do justice, restoring to this man his due and taking from another what he had no right to keep. When the motive of their hatred was jealousy the generals sought to determine who was in the right and who was wrong. And soon they were at their wits' end, so tangled were the problems to be solved, and so often did the selfsame act have several facets: being noble in a certain light, sordid in another, at once mean and generous. These debates lasted far into the night and my generals went short of sleep, and their stupidity grew ever crasser, until one day they came to me and said: "There is but one solution to this imbroglio—another Flood, like Noah's!"

But I remembered my father's words: "When mildew attacks the wheat, think not its cause lies in the crop, but move the wheat into another granary. When men hate each other, listen not to the futile reasons they give for their hatred; for always there are motives other than these, whereof they have not thought. They have quite as many motives for loving each other. As many, too, for living in a state of indifference. But as for me—I who pay scant heed to words, knowing that what they convey is but a symbol hard to decipher (even as the stones composing a building reveal not the shadow or the silence it bestows, and as the particles of which a tree is made do not explain the tree)—why should I be interested in the ingredients of their hatred? They built it with the same stones that might have served to build up love."

Thus I watched, aloof, this hatred of theirs which they tricked out with specious arguments; nor did I hope to cure them by the practice of a justice that would have served no end, but, rather, reinforced their arguments, by confirming their grievances or prerogatives. Confirming, too, the rancor of those against whom I had decided, and the insolence of those whose cause I had espoused. Thus I would have dug the gulf still deeper. But I remembered my father's wisdom.

It came about that, after conquering some new territories, he found that order was slow in being established in them, and he therefore appointed generals to second the governors he had set up. But a time came when travellers returning from the new-won provinces brought ill tidings to my father.

"In such and such a province the general has insulted the governor, and they are no longer on speaking terms."

And a traveller from another province said: "Sire, the governor has taken a dislike to the general."

And a third: "Sire, your arbitration is sought in our new province for the settling of a grave dispute. The general and the governor have arraigned each other in the law court."

In the beginning my father had them explain the motives of these conflicts. And always the motives were quite cogent. Anyone enduring such affronts would have felt moved to avenge them. Likewise there were tales of shameless acts of treachery and venomous disputes, of kidnappings and outrage. And always, to all appearance, one party seemed in the right and the other in the wrong. But soon my father wearied of this interminable tittle-tattle.

"I have better things to do," he said, "than trying to decide these foolish quarrels. They are breaking out in every corner of my new territory; each time different, and yet alike. How strange it is that I should always choose generals and governors who cannot endure each other!

"When the cattle you have lodged in a shed start dying one by one, do not examine them, thinking thus to find the cause of the trouble. Examine, rather, the cattle shed—and burn it."

Therefore he called a messenger.

"I have ill defined their prerogatives. They know not which of the two has precedence at state banquets. They watch each other, glowering, and walk forward side by side to the banqueting table. Then one of them—the more brutal or quicker-witted of the two—sits down in the seat of honor. The other scowls at him, vowing to be less foolish next time and hasten to snatch the first place at table. And soon, naturally enough, they come to stealing each other's wives, reaving each other's cattle, hurling insults at each other. And for all their futility, these grievances rankle bitterly, for they believe in them. But, as for me, I will not hearken to their clamor.

"You would have them love each other? Then fling not down before them the grains of power for them to share and peck at.

Let one serve the other, and let that other serve the empire. Thus, because each seconds each and they build conjointly, they will live in amity."

Therefore he punished them ruthlessly for their unseemly bickerings. "The empire," he said, "will not permit these scandals. Clearly a general should obey the governor. Therefore I shall punish the governor for being unable to make himself obeyed. And the general for failing in his obedience. And I counsel you to hold your peace."

Whereat throughout the new territory these men made up their quarrels. The stolen camels were given back; the unfaithful wives restored to their husbands, or put away; and insults were atoned for. Moreover, he who obeyed found a new source of joy laid open to him, for the praises of him who gave the orders rang sweetly in his ears. And he who ordered rejoiced to demonstrate his power by magnifying his subordinate, and at the state banquets urged him forward that he might take his seat the first.

"It was not," my father said, "that they were stupid. But that the words of current speech convey nothing worthy of interest. Learn, my son, to listen, not to the sounds of words that weave the wind, nor to reasonings that throw dust in your eyes. Learn to look farther. Their hatred was not mere aberration. If each stone be not in its place there is no temple; but if each stone be in its due place, and serve the temple, then nothing matters but the silence born of the stones and the prayer taking form amongst them. And then—what need to speak of the stones themselves?"

Therefore I paid no heed to the perplexities of my generals who came to me and fain would have me seek in men's acts the causes of their quarrels, so that I should set order in these by dispensing my justice. But, in the silence of my love, I walked across the camp and watched my soldiers scowling at each other. Then I withdrew, and voiced my prayer to God.

"O Lord, thou seest how these men are at enmity because they are no longer building up the empire. It were mistaken to believe that they cease to build because of their dissensions. Enlighten

67

me as to the tower that I must have them build, enabling them to barter themselves for it and fulfill in it their aspirations. A task which will absorb the best in each and, calling forth the greatness in him, rejoice his heart. My cloak is too short and I am a bad shepherd, who cannot shelter his flock from the night winds. And because they are cold they hate each other. For hatred is but dissatisfaction, and in every hatred is a meaning secret and compulsive. Thus clustering weeds hate and devour each other, but it is not so with the solitary tree, whose every branch thrives on the welfare of the rest. Grant me, O Lord, a fragment of thy cloak whereunder I may gather in my soldiers, my tillers of the soil, my sages and the husbands and wives of my people, that all may be enfolded, even the little ones who cry at nightfall. . . ."

⚜ 16

THUS TOO WITH VIRTUE. In their crass stupidity my generals came and prated to me of virtue.

"See," they said, "how our men are taking to evil ways. That is why the empire is decaying. Laws must be stiffened, sterner punishments devised. All who offend must be beheaded."

But I thought in my heart: Perchance it may be needful to behead. Yet virtue is primarily a consequence, and the corruption of my men is due, above all, to the corruption of the empire which shapes and founds them. Were it alive and healthy it would stimulate the best in them.

And I recalled my father's words: "Virtue is perfection in man's being, and not the absence of vices. When I wish to found a city I gather together the thieves and the lowest of the low, and I uplift them by the grant of power, offering them joys far other than the squalid thrills of plundering, ravishing, money-snatching. Then you will see them fall to building manfully, their pride becoming towers, battlements and temples, and their cruelty grandeur and discipline. They are serving a city of their own begetting, for which they barter themselves wholeheartedly. They will die on the battlements in its defense. And now you will find in them the gold of virtue without dross.

"But if you be of those squeamish ones who resent the dark power of the earth, the ugliness of the soil with its rottenness and worms, surely you are asking man not to be himself, not to smell of manhood. You are blaming him for the very tokens of his strength. Then you set impotents to rule the empire, and they harry evil-doing—which is energy misdirected. It is life and potency that they are harrying, and in the end they become museum-keepers, curators of a dead empire.

"The cedar tree," my father said, "lives on mud, but transforms it into a crown of leafage, fed by sunlight. Thus mud is transmuted into virtue. Would you save your empire, instil fervor. Then it will absorb men's activities and thrive on them, and the selfsame longings, the same activities, the same efforts, will serve to build your city, instead of destroying it.

"But now mark well my words! Once completed, your city will die. For these men live not by what they receive but by what they give. Whenas provisions have been laid up, they will fight over them and become once more like wolves in their lairs. Or else, if your harshness masters them, they will become like cattle in the stall. For a city is never completed. I say, 'My task is ended,' only when my fervor fails. Thus those men die—because they are already dead. But perfection is not a goal we reach; it is a bartering of one's all in God. And never have I 'completed' my city."

Wherefore I questioned if it were enough that heads should fall. True, if any man is corrupt it is well to extirpate him, lest he taint the others. Not otherwise do we cast a moldy fruit out of the storehouse, or put a sick animal out of the cattle shed. But better is it to set up a new cattle shed or storehouse; for primarily it is these that are to blame.

69

And why punish a man whom perchance one can convert?

Therefore again I prayed to God: "O Lord, bestow on me a fragment of thy cloak whereunder I may shelter all these men and their burden of great longings. I am weary of putting men to death, lest they whom I cannot take under my cloak undo my work. For I know that these men imperil the others and the boons, dubious as they are, of my partial truth; but equally I know that they are noble and they, too, have their truth within them."

❧ 17

THUS EVER HAVE I scorned the lure of words that weave the wind, and abhorred sleights of speech. When in their crass stupidity my generals came to me and said, "The people are revolting, we counsel you to be adroit," I sent them about their business. Adroitness is but an idle word, and no devious course is open in creation. What you do, you stablish; and that is all. If when progressing towards a certain goal, you make-believe to move towards another, only he who is the tool of words will think you clever. For, when all is said and done, you stablish that on which your heart was set; that with which you concerned yourself and nothing else. Even if you made it your concern to fight against it. Thus, when I fight my foe, I stablish him, for I shape and harden him on my anvil. Likewise when, on the pretext that this is to ensure a wider freedom in the future, I stiffen my discipline, it is discipline that I stablish. Life admits no trickery. We do not deceive the tree; it grows as we train it to grow—and all else is words that weave the wind. If I profess to sacrifice my generation for the welfare of future generations, it is living men whom I sacrifice. And all else is words that weave the wind. When I make war in order to secure peace, I stablish war. Peace is not a state we finally achieve by dint of war. If, trusting to the peace that I have won in battle, I disarm, then all is lost. As for peace, I cannot ensue it unless I stablish it on sure foundations: to wit, that I receive and draw men towards me, so that each can find in my empire the fulfillment of his heart's desires. For though each man loves it in a different way, the vision is the same. What sets men at variance is but the treachery of language, for always they desire the same things. Never have I met a man who longed for disorder, squalor or catastrophe. From one end of the earth to the other the vision haunting them, which they would wish made good, is similar: only the ways in which men seek it differ. One thinks that freedom will enable man to fulfill himself; another, that strict discipline will lead him on from strength to strength—but both alike desire his greatness. This one thinks that charity will unite men; another scorns charity, as pandering to the ulcers flaunted by the beggar, and constrains his people to build a tower whereat they will work together for the good of all, each stablishing the other. And both alike work in the cause of love. Some think that prosperity solves every problem; for, once freed from the thrall of daily cares, a man finds time to cultivate his heart and mind and soul. But another believes that the quality of men's hearts and minds and souls is nowise affected by the food and comforts provided for them, that it depends on the gifts which are asked of them. To such a man's thinking there is beauty in those temples only which are born of God's behest and are made over to Him as men's ransom. Yet both alike desire to beautify the heart and mind and soul— and both are right. For who can better himself in an atmosphere of cruelty, of thralldom or soul-deadening toil? Yet likewise who can better himself in an atmosphere of licence, of esteem for what is rotten to the core and futile activity that is a mere pastime for idlers?

Thus you see men gladly unsheathing their swords on behalf of the same ideal, and then comes war—which is a quest, an ordeal, a groping towards an all-compelling gleam, like that of my poet's tree which, being born blind, thrust up and battered at its prison walls until it broke a window in the roof and then rose, straight at last and proud and glorious, sunwards.

As for peace, I impose it not by force. If I do but crush my enemy, I stablish him and his undying hate. The better part is to convert; and to convert is to welcome in. It is the offering to each man of a garment to his measure, in which he feels at ease. The same garment for all. For all incoherence is but the lack of genius.

Therefore once more I prayed to God: "Enlighten me, O Lord. Enable me to wax in wisdom so that I may bring reconcilement, without compelling these men or those to forgo some aspiration they have cherished fervently, but by revealing a new vision which to all will seem the same. Is it not thus with the ship? Those who, being devoid of understanding, haul the sheet to starboard contend with those who are hauling it to port, and in their blindness hate each other. But, if they understand, they work together in the service of the wind."

Peace is a tree whose growth is slow. Like the cedar we must absorb ever more and more of the stony soil, to stablish its unity.

Building peace is building the shed large enough for all the herd to sleep in it; building the palace vast enough for all men to gather within it without abandoning any of their belongings. There is no question of maiming them so that it may hold them all. Building peace is persuading God to lend his shepherd's cloak so that all may be enfolded under it, in the fullness of their desires. Thus it is with the mother who loves her sons; one of them mild and gentle, another bursting with the zest of life, and, perhaps, a third a cripple. All are equally dear to her, in their diversity, and all, in the diversity of their love, enhance her glory.

But slow in the rearing is the tree of peace. The light I have is not enough: nothing is clear as yet. I can but choose and reject. All too easy would it be, this making of peace, were they all alike already. . . .

Thus the adroitness of my generals led to nothing; for, in their crass stupidity, they came to me with endless arguments, reason-

ing about it and about. But I remembered a saying of my father:
" 'Tis the art of reasoning that leads men to make mistakes."

"If," they said, "our men are failing in their duty to the empire,
this shows that they are growing soft. We must arrange some
ambushes for them; then they will harden, and the empire be
preserved."

Thus speak the wiseacres who argue from cause to effect. But
life *is;* as the tree *is.* And the stem is not a means the seed has lit
on for developing into a branch. Seed, stem and branch are the
selfsame process of fulfillment.

Therefore I gainsaid them. "If our men are growing soft this
is because the empire, which nourished their vitality, has gone
dead within them. Thus it is with the cedar that has spent its gift of
life and is beginning to scatter itself upon the desert. To renew
their life they need to be converted."

But this my generals could not understand. In my indulgence
I let them play their games and send men forth to meet death
round a well that no one coveted, for it was dry; but near which
the enemy, as chance had it, were encamped.

True, there is beauty in a skirmish round a well, that dance
around a flower; for he who wins the well weds the earth and
sweet is the taste of victory on his lips. Then, with the wide sweep
of a flurry of startled crows, the enemy swings round, dislodged
by your advance, and re-forms behind you in a place where they
feel safe from your attack. But soon the sand that has drunk
them up is charged with gunpowder, and you must play the great
game of life and death, glorying in your manhood. And you dance
round a central point, withdraw, and then swerve in upon your
target.

But if this be a dry well, your play is changed. For that well is
futile, meaningless as the dice in a game in which you do not stake
your fortune. Having seen men kill each other when there was
cheating, my generals believed in the dice game and set them
playing around that well, which was no more than a blank die.
But no one kills another over dice that have no numbers on them.

Nor did my generals grasp what love is. They had seen the lover thrilling to the dawn that kindled his love anew when the first rays waked him. Likewise they had seen the warrior thrilling to the dawn, when its first rays waked him with a promise of victory, whereat his heart was uplifted and he laughed for joy. They thought it was the dawn that had worked this magic; not love. But, as for me, I say that without love nothing can be achieved. A die which betokens nothing worthy of desire cannot lift up your heart; nor can a dawn that only wakens you to your forlornness. Likewise, death for a useless well is but vanity and vexation of spirit.

True, the harder the task wherein you consume yourself for love's sake, the more it will exalt you. The more you give, the greater you become. But there must be someone to receive; and losing is not giving.

But, having seen men rejoice in giving, my generals had not had the sense to know that there was always someone who received; and that merely to strip a man of what he has cannot suffice to exalt him.

I came on a sorely wounded man, and bitter was his heart.

"Sire," he said, "I am dying. I have given my blood, and got nothing in exchange. But the enemy whom I laid low with a bullet in his belly, before another could avenge him—I watched him dying. And methought in death he was winning the crown of life, for he was possessed by faith. Thus, rewarding was his death. But not so mine; it is merely because I obeyed the orders coming to me from my corporal, not from some other whose gain would have recompensed my loss, that now I die; with honor, but despite."

As for the others, they had fled.

THAT EVENING I clomb a tall black crag overlooking the camp, and gazed down on its glimmering triangle flecked with black, with watchmen on the tops of the three corner towers, and, well stocked though it was with guns and powder, liable to be swept away at any moment and scattered on the desert like a dead tree—and I forgave my men.

For I had understood. The caterpillar dies when it has made its chrysalis; the plant, when it has run to seed. Thus all that is changing its condition travails and suffers. All within it wastes away till it is but a shell of death and vain regrets. These men of mine, having worn out the old empire whose youth none might renew, were waiting for that great change to come on them. No renewing is there for the caterpillar, nor for the plant once it has run to seed, nor for the stripling whose childhood has left him, though fain would he recapture its carefree joys and still delight in toys whose colors have faded, and relish his mother's fond embraces and the sweet flow of milk. But from those childish things the glamor has departed; there is no refuge in his mother's arms, the milk has lost its savor—and sadly he goes his way. Thus the old empire was outworn and these men, though they knew it not, were hankering after a new one. The boy who has grown up and no longer needs his mother's care will know no rest until he has found the woman of his choice. She alone will reassemble his scattered selfhood. But who can make their empire manifest to men? Who, by the sole might of his genius, can hew out of the diversity of things a new visage, and force them to lift their eyes towards it and know it for what it is? And, knowing it, to love it? This is no task for a word-spinner, but one for a sculptor and creator. Only a man who needs not to justify himself by words can shape the marble and grave it with the power of quickening love.

✣ *19*

THEREFORE I SUMMONED my architects and said: "It is on you that the city-to-be depends, not as to its spiritual import but as concerns the form it is to take, which will body forth its meaning. I am at one with you in holding that men must be suitably housed therein, so that they may enjoy the amenities of the city and not fritter away their strength in wasted efforts and needless inconvenience. But I have long learned to distinguish that which is important from that which is urgent. True, it is urgent that man should eat, for else he cannot live, and death abides no question. Yet love, the sense of life and the quest of God are more important. No thoughts waste I on a breed that merely fills its belly. The problem I set myself is not that of knowing whether or not the man will be prosperous, well housed and happy. Nay, I begin by asking myself *what* man will be prosperous, well housed and happy. For to my fat hucksters, squatting snug on their money bags, I prefer the lean nomad, for ever vagrant in the wake of the wind. The service of so vast a lord invests a man with beauty. Constrained to choose, were I to learn that God withholds His greatness from the former and grants it only to the latter, I would lead my people out into the desert. I would have each man shed his light, and I pay no heed to the fatness of the candle; I value it for its flame alone.

"But I have not observed that the prince is inferior to the stevedore, or the general to the sergeant, or the foreman to the workman he controls. Nor have I found those who build brazen ramparts inferior to such as build mud walls. Nor do I frown upon that stairway of achievement which enables a man to climb to high estate. But I have not confounded the means and the end; the temple steps with the temple. Needful it is that a flight of steps give access to the temple, else it would stay empty; but only the temple is important. It is well that a man should live and have at hand the means of waxing great. Yet these are but the steps leading up to the sanctuary, the soul that I shall build for him; and only this matters.

"Thus I blame not the priority you give to things of daily need; but I blame you for making them your end. Very necessary are the palace kitchens, but the palace alone counts; the kitchens are but to serve it. Nevertheless, when I call you together and say to you, 'Tell me, what part of your work is the important part?' you gaze at me tonguetied.

"Or else you say: 'We cater for men's needs. We give them houses to dwell in.' Very true. As one caters for the cattle housed in the cattle shed. Surely a man needs a closed place wherein he may strike root and, like the seed, *become*. But also he needs the great Milky Way above him and the vast sea spaces, though neither stars nor ocean serve his daily needs. Some I know who have slowly, painfully, climbed the mountain, tearing their hands and knees on the rocks, wearing themselves out in the long upward struggle, so that they might reach the summit before dawn and steep their gaze in the cool depths of the still blue plains, like thirsty men straining towards a lake whence they will drink. Once they were on the mountain-top they sat down and gazed their fill, drawing deep breaths of eager air, their hearts surging with joy. For here was a sovereign remedy for all life's disappointments.

"Some, too, I know who seek the sea in their slowly moving caravans, and the sea lures them on and on until at last they reach a headland and feast their eyes on all that vast expanse of depth and silence. They breathe deeply the harsh tang of brine. They are enraptured by a sight that serves none of their instant needs, for there is no laying hold of the sea. Nevertheless, their hearts are washed clean of the thrall of petty things. For perhaps, ere this, like men behind prison bars, they would gaze with wry distaste at the cooking pots arrayed upon the hearth and listen to the shrill complainings of their wives; and were sickened by all that too familiar drudgery and drabness, which, though they may

77

compose but an aspect of reality into which we read a deeper meaning and significance, are also apt to thicken and close in on us like a grave.

"Thus men can lay up stores of vastness in their hearts and fare homewards, the happier for these beatific visions. And then the house is changed for them, because they can recall that vast plain glimmering in the dawn light, or the splendor of the sea. For behind all seen things lies something vaster; everything is but a path, a portal, or a window opening on something other than itself.

"So do not tell me that your everyday walls suffice for men; for if they had never seen the stars and if it were in your power to build them a Milky Way hung overhead on mighty arches—even were a fortune swallowed up in building such a dome, would you dare to say that fortune was ill spent?

"Therefore I say to you: if you build a temple that is 'useless,' in that it does not serve for rest, or cooking, or gatherings of the notables, or the storage of water, but solely for the greatening of men's hearts and the tranquillizing of the senses, and for Time that ripens (for it is like a secret chamber of the heart whither a man can retire to steep his soul for some hours in the peace that comes of comprehension, when passions are lulled and justice rules without reprisal)—if, then, you build a temple where the sufferings of the body are transformed into hymns and offerings and where death's imminence seems like a tranquil haven, glimpsed through the murk of the storm, dare you say that your labor has been in vain?

"If for men whose hands are torn by tugging at frozen ropes when the tempest rages, men who have wrestled night and day to keep the ship afloat, until their bodies are become but raw flesh rasped by the bitter spindrift—if for these men you make it possible to shelter now and again in a harbor of still, shining waters, where the waves are at rest and there is no more strain or struggle and Time itself seems sleepbound, where there is an all-pervading silence hardly broken by the low sound of ripples as the ship glides to her moorings—dare you say your labor has been in vain? Sweet it is to men, this landlocked harbor, after the foam-fringed breakers, the white manes of the coursers of the sea.

"And this it lies within your power to bestow on men; you need but bend your genius to it. You can create the savor of the water of the harbor, of silence, and of immortal hopes, by the mere disposal of the stones you use.

"Then your temple will draw them to it like a magnet and in its silence they will search their souls—and find themselves! For else there would be nothing to allure them but the market stalls, no desire quickened in them but the lust of buying, whetted by the merchants. And never would they be reborn in their greatness, or know the vastness that is latent in them.

"But, you will tell me, those fat merchants are fully satisfied; they ask for nothing more. How easy it is to sate him whose heart is shallow!

"True, a foolish habit of speech brands your work as 'useless.' But men's behavior gives the lie direct to such arguments. In every country of the world you can see them eagerly seeking out those masterworks in stone that you have ceased building—granaries for the heart and soul. And when have you known a man feel moved to roam the world so as to visit warehouses? True, merchandise has its uses, but a man needs it only as a standby: great is his misjudgment of himself if he thinks he desires it in and for itself. Nay, men's journeyings have other aims. Have you not watched them on their travels and observed what they seek out? Sometimes, no doubt, a snowclad mountain or a smiling bay or a red volcano smothered in its vomit allures them, but above all they are drawn to those half-buried ships of stone, which alone take man somewhere.

"They visit and go round them, dreaming, though almost unawares, that they have embarked on them for the great voyage. But, in truth, they are not on the way to anything. No longer do these temples draw to themselves the mass of men and carry them afar and transmute them, like the chrysalis, into a nobler race.

79

These emigrants no longer have a ship, nor can they undergo a change and, in the long voyage, build up their poor, maimed souls into rich and splendid souls. Therefore you see all those visitors roaming round the sunken temple, peering and prying as they tread the flagstones worn to lustrous smoothness, listening to the echoes of their voices in the great domed silence, lost in the forest of the granite pillars and thinking simply that, like history students, they are gleaning knowledge. Yet surely from the throbbing of their hearts they might have guessed that what they seek from pillar to pillar, aisle to aisle and nave to nave, is the Captain; and that they are gathered there, awe-struck and full of a vast yearning, to invoke a Helper who comes not, and waiting for a change of heart that is denied them, because they are wrapped in themselves—because there are now but dead temples sunken in the sands, stranded ships whose store of shadows and silence is ill-guarded, which leak at every seam, with great strips of blue sky showing through the crumbling dome, and sand hissing in through the rifted walls. And hungry are they with a hunger that nothing can sate.

"Thus, I tell you, you will build because the deep forest is good for men; good, too, the Milky Way and the blue plain seen from the mountain-top. And yet—what are those vastnesses of sea and plain and Milky Way, compared with the pregnant darkness of the stones of the temple when the architect has found a way of filling them with silence? You, the architects, will be the greater for having looked beyond the daily needs of life and raised your eyes towards the one task truly worthy of your achievement. It will absorb the best of you, since, no longer serving your self-interest, it will force you to serve itself. And it will lift you up above yourselves. For how should great architects arise, if the work to be done lack greatness?

"You will become great only when the stones you claim to charge with power are not mere edifices for the convenience of men; when they serve not merely useful, measurable ends, but become pedestals, stairways, ships, that bring Man nearer God."

80

20

My GENERALS WEARIED ME with their arguments. They were always holding conferences and wrangling about the future: thus they sought to prove their competence. They had begun by learning history, and knew all the dates by heart: the dates of my victories and conquests, the dates of births and deaths. They were convinced that events can be deduced each from the one preceding it, and they saw history as a long chain of causes and effects, taking its rise in the first line of the first book of history and inevitably proceeding to that last chapter in which it was recorded, for the enlightenment of generations to come, that creation had reached its acme in the galaxy of generals of which they were the major stars. Thus, carried on by their own momentum, from consequence to consequence, they made bold to prognosticate the future. Then they came to me, laden with their cumbrous conclusions, saying: "Thus and thus should you act for the happiness of man, and to ensure peace and the welfare of the empire. We are learned men," they added, "we have studied history."

But I knew that only that which repeats itself can be grasped by study. The man who plants a cedar seed can foresee the rising of a cedar tree, just as he who flings a stone foresees its fall. The cedar begets itself and the stone's fall likewise is a repetition, albeit the stone our man throws or the seed he plants has never served thus before. But who can claim to foretell the destiny of the cedar, ever and ever transforming itself, from seed to tree and from tree to seed, from chrysalis to chrysalis? Therein is a genesis for which I have no precedent to go on, since each cedar tree is a new growth which perfects itself without repeating anything I wot of. And I know not whither it is going; even as I know not whither men are going.

True they make great play with logic, do my generals, when they

seek out and detect a cause for each effect that is pointed out
to them. Every effect, they tell me, has a cause and every cause has
an effect; so from cause to effect they go blundering on towards
a false conclusion. For to go back from effects to causes is one
thing, but to go forward from causes to effects is another.

I, too, have read the advance of my enemy written on the virgin
sands like an inscription scrawled in chalk. I knew that each step
is always preceded by another sponsoring it and thus the chain
proceeds, link by link, nor may any link be lacking. Unless perchance a high wind has arisen and, scouring the sand, expunged
the script, like writing on a schoolboy's slate, I can go back from
imprint to imprint up to the starting point; or, following after the
caravan, can surprise it in the gully where it has thought fit to
linger. But, in perusing this script, I find nothing that will enable
me to predict its route and to forestall it. That which guides its
destiny is other than the record of the sand; and what the foot-
prints give me is but an idle token, telling me nothing of the hates
and fears and loves that chiefly rule men's lives.

"But," firmly entrenched in their stupidity, my generals would
say, "this, too, goes to prove that everything's a matter of reasoning. Once we know the hates and fears and loves that rule their
lives, we can foretell men's acts. Thus always the future is immanent in the present."

I answered them that no doubt it is always possible to foretell
the progress of the caravan one step ahead. That new step will
certainly repeat the one preceding it, as to its direction and its
amplitude. This is a lore of that which repeats itself. But presently
the caravan will swerve from the track my logic has mapped out
for it, for its desire will change. . . .

And then, since they still failed to understand, I told them the
tale of the great stampede.

It took place in the region of the salt mines, where men were
ever struggling desperately to survive amongst a waste of minerals;
for nothing here countenanced life. The sun bore down on them
and burnt them. And far from yielding clear well water, the

bowels of the earth gave forth but a spume of salt that would have ruined the water, had not all the wells been dry. Trapped between a glaring sky and the sheen of rock salt, these men who had come from afar with their water skins well filled made haste about their task of hewing out those crystalline blocks whose forms betoken life and death. Then, linked to these as by an umbilical cord, they fared back to a happier clime and the life-giving waters of their homeland.

In this place the tyrant sun was cruel and white as famine; and here and there around the salt mines rocky shelves thrust through the sands, shouldering up a great crag, hard as a black diamond, at which the desert winds gnawed seemingly in vain. Any man who had studied the age-old tradition of this stretch of desert would have said it was certain to endure unchanged for many centuries. Slowly, imperceptibly, as if a too weak file were fretting it, that crag would go on being worn away: men would go on bringing water and victuals, and, now and again, a new gang would be sent to relieve the unfortunates forspent by toil.

Nevertheless there came a dawn when men turned their eyes towards the mountain—and, behold, something met their gaze that never yet had they seen!

The winds that had been gnawing haphazard at the cliff for centuries had shaped on it the likeness of a huge scowling face. And now, above the desert and the salterns underground and the tribesmen camped on a soil more hostile to man than the salt water of the sea, there lowered a furious black face hewn in the rock, opening its mouth to curse them under the bright immensity of the sky. When they saw it for what it was, the men took fright and fled. Their panic spread to the depths of the pits, the miners poured up from the workings, cast a quick glance at the cliff, and then, with horror in their hearts, rushed to the tents, packed up their goods in haste, cursing the women and children and slaves for their slowness, and, trundling before them their belongings, doomed henceforth, betook them along the northward trails. To a man they perished on the way for lack of water.

Thus were proved vain the forecasts of the logicians who had said that the cliff would continue to be worn away and men go on hewing salt for many and many a century. How could they have foreseen that which was to come to pass?

When I plunge back into the past, I split up the temple into stones—a simple task, whose course is easy to forecast. So it is, also, if I anatomize a dead body into bones and entrails, or the temple into rubble, or the domain into sheep and goats, mountains and men's dwellings. But if I look towards the future, then always I have to reckon with the birth of new beings that will be added to the stock, and regarding whom nothing can be predicted since they will be of another essence. Such entities I call simple and single, because they die and vanish if they are taken asunder. Thus silence is something superimposed upon the stones; yet it dies if they are taken apart. Thus, too, the visage is something superadded to the marble or to the elements of which the visage is composed: it perishes when they are broken up, or when the lineaments are isolated. Similarly, the domain is something superadded to its goats and sheep, its dwellings and its mountains.

I cannot predict, but skilled am I to found. The future is what we build; and if I weld together the diversities of my age in a single, unique visage, and have I the sculptor's godlike hands, my desire will come into being. But I would be wrong were I to say I had been able to forecast, when what I did was to create. Out of the chaos of appearances I shall have fashioned a visage and made it good, and it will rule over men. As does the domain, which sometimes claims even their lifeblood.

Thus was revealed to me this new truth: to wit, that giving much thought to the future is vain. Only one task is worthy of the doing and that is to express the Here and Now. And to express means building, out of the infinite diversity of the Here and Now, a visage dominating it. It means shaping silence out of stones.

Any other claim is but an ado of words that weave the wind.

21

THERE IS NONE of us but knows how reasoning can mislead, and some of the men before me were not convinced—even by the subtlest arguments, the most impressive proofs. "No doubt," one of them would say, "you are right. But all the same I think otherwise." Such men passed for stupid. Yet I knew they were not stupid; rather, the wisest of all. For they revered a truth that words could not convey.

Those others thought that words can cover everything; that with words men express the universe, happiness, stars and the sunset, love and silence, architecture, the domain. But I knew better; I had seen man face to face with the mountain it devolved on him to grasp, spadeful by spadeful.

I admit that, when they have planned the battlements, my draughtsmen have in their hands the truth of the battlements, which can then be built according to their figures. One of the truths of the battlements is the draughtsman's; but what draughtsman understands their real meaning? What in his plan shows that ramparts are a dyke; or brings out their likeness to the bark of the cedar tree, within which that living thing, the tree, builds itself up? What plan shows that these ramparts are to be a sheath for fervor, guarding a stronghold perdurable, within which generation after generation will barter its life to God? The draughtsman sees in them only bricks and mortar, measured lines and stresses. True enough, calculations, bricks and mortar go to their making; but the ramparts are also the bulwarks of a ship and a shelter for individual destinies. And I believe above all in the destiny of the individual, which is nowise to be scorned for being so limited. A solitary flower can be a window opening on the vision of spring, and a springtime that brought no flowers would mean nothing to me. . . .

Sometimes I was taken to a mountain-top that I might contemplate the city. "Now behold our city!" I was told. And I admired the disposal of the streets, the layout of the battlements. "There," said I, "is the hive where the bees sleep. At daybreak they sally forth across the plain to harvest their golden store. Thus do men sow and plough and reap. And long strings of little asses bring back the fruit of the day's toil to granary, market place and storeroom. At dawn the city scatters forth its people and then draws them back, laden with their provisions for the winter. Man is he who produces and consumes, and I can best befriend him by studying his problems and administering the anthill."

But others, wishing to show me the city, had me cross the river and admire it from the farther bank. Outlined against the sunset glow, rose the long lines of houses, some low, some tall, and round the summits of the minarets, slender as masts, floated light skeins of bluish mist. I thought of a fleet setting sail. And then I perceived this other truth about the town: that it was no mere geometric scheme, but, rather, a human challenge to the world, a sea venture sped by the great wind of man's endeavor. Gazing, I thought, "There beacons the pride of victory in the making. I will appoint captains to rule my cities, for it is in the compelling zest of high adventure and of victory, and in creative action, that man finds his supreme joys." This truth was neither truer nor less true; but different.

And, yet again, others, wishing me to admire their city, took me within the ramparts and led me first to the temple. No sooner had I entered than I was taken by the shadows and the silence and the coolness. Then I fell to musing, and now this musing seemed to me more important than food or conquest. For I had eaten to live, I had lived to conquer, but surely I had conquered so as to return to this good place and feel my heart the vaster for the hushed silence that encompassed me. "Herein," I said, "is the truth of man; he lives by his soul alone. I will appoint priests and poets to rule my city, and they will make men's hearts blossom forth like flowers." And this, too, was neither truer nor less true; but different.

Thus now, in the ripeness of my knowledge, when I use the word "city" it is not for purposes of argument, but simply to express all that "the city" conjures up in my heart and what I have learned of it by experience, by lonely wanderings in little streets and the breaking of bread together in its dwellings, by its glory seen in outline across the plain and its gracious symmetry viewed from the mountain-top. And much else which I have no words for, and cannot clearly recall. So how could I use that word for purposes of argument, since what is true of one sign is false of another?

❧ 22

BUT ABOVE ALL methought there was a dark compulsion in all that concerns man's heritage, handed down from generation to generation. This I felt when, in the silence of my love, I walked slowly in the town and saw a woman talking to her beloved and smiling to him with tender fear; and another woman waiting for her soldier to return, another scolding her servant, or a man—one of those who sow dissension—rising in his wrath and championing the weak; or another man placidly carving an ivory ornament, trying again and again to draw nearer to the ideal of perfection in his mind. Or when I gazed at my city on the verge of sleep, making that low murmurous sound (like the sound, long in dying, of a beaten gong), as though daylong the sun had fostered its activity, as it fosters that of the bees, but then comes nightfall, wearying their wings and sealing up the fragrance of the flowers, and they have nothing left to guide them home but wraithlike trails on the bosom of the wind. Or when I saw the lamps being put out one by one and the fires banked under the ashes, now that each man had brought home his belongings: one man, his corn under cover of his barn; another, his dog or his ass; another, his children playing in the doorway; an old man, his three-legged stool—and all thoughts and prayers and plans for the morrow, impulses to grasp or cast away, fears and hopes, problems to be solved, hates that would not kill before the next day's sun, ambitions that could lead nowhere until the dawn, and all the prayers that link men unto God—all these were laid by, in abeyance, dead to all seeming, yet but dormant, since this vast and varied patrimony, which for the moment served no purpose was not lost but kept in reserve. For once the first rays waked the swarm to new activity the heritage would be restored, and each man would return to his quest, to his joy or his toil, his hatred or ambition, my swarm of bees to its lilies and its thistles. . . . And then, pondering on these things, I asked myself: "What is the significance of all these stored up impressions?"

Thus it was clearer than ever to me that, had I to start with a mankind not yet fully conscious, had I to train men and instruct them and stock their minds with all these infinitely various emotions, the bridge of language could not have sufficed thereto.

Though words suffice for daily intercourse, our patrimony cannot be comprehended by the words used in our books. And were I to take children in hand and knead and shape them, giving each a trend that I had arbitrarily selected for him, I would have left out not a little of our patrimony. Thus with my army if it lack the keeping-touch between man and man which makes of it a dynasty unbroken. True, my men are trained by their corporals, and obey their captains' orders; yet the words that corporals and captains dispose of are but counters, utterly inadequate to convey from one to the other a sum total which cannot be assessed or stated in set phrases. A trust that no word, no book can transmit. For it concerns attitudes of mind and personal views, impulses and antipathies, the relations between thoughts and things. Would I expound these and make them plain, I should be constrained to tear them to pieces—and then nothing would be left. So it is with the domain, which calls for love: I should have said nothing about it did I talk of the sheep and goats, the mountains and dwellings it comprises; for its secret treasure is not transmissible by words, but by the bond of love lengthening down from generation to generation. A love that dies, if once you break a link between the generations. Thus, should you break the link between the older men and the younglings in your army, it will be like the frontage of a gutted house, that falls at the least shock. Likewise, should you break the link between the miller and his son, you will ruin all that is most precious in the mill: its fervor, its inner meaning, no less than all those innumerable manipulations and movements for which reason can account but little, yet which are needful. More wisdom is latent in things-as-they-are than in all the words men use. And then, forsooth, having snapped the links, you would ask them to rebuild that fallen world by the mere reading of some little "book of words" that is but a parade of pale reflections, void and insignificant as compared with the sum total of man's experience. Thus you would make of man a beast of the field, naked and uncouth; having forgotten that the ways of man are like the ways of a tree and grow and transmit themselves one to the other, as the life force of the tree flows through its knots and twistings and the proliferation of its branches.

Mighty is the organism to which I minister, and when I survey my city from the mountain-top that word "death" becomes meaningless to me. For while here and there leaves are falling, new buds are putting forth; and, throughout all, endures the solid trunk. These private misfortunes harm nothing vital: you see the temple rising steadily, the granary being filled, emptied and replenished, the poem gathering beauty, and the rim of the fountain growing ever more lustrous as the years smooth it down. But if you make a rift between the generations, it is as if you bade a man start life again in middle age, and, having stripped him of the knowledge, feelings, comprehension, fears and hopes that were his, you sought to replace, by the meagre precepts of a book, this sum of experience enfleshed. But then you would have checked the flow of sap rising within the trunk and robbed him of all the endowment of the past save that which can be codified. And since words simplify to teach, falsify in the imparting, and kill in the understanding, you would but dam the stream of life within men.

But, as for me, I say it is well to favor the rise of dynasties within the city. If my healers are drawn from a small group, but enjoy an heritage handed down in its entirety and not merely a batch of formulas, I shall come to have healers of a far higher calibre than if I were to choose them indiscriminately from my people and enrol the sons of soldiers and millers. And it is not that I discountenance vocations; nay, this solid trunk will be sturdy enough for me to graft thereon branches of another stock. Thus my dynasty of healers will take into itself the new aliments furnished by such as have a natural vocation.

Thus yet again I learned that logic is the death of life, and avails nothing in itself. For all those makers of formulas err when they speak of Man; they confuse the formula, which is the flat shadow of the cedar, with the tree itself. To convey its weight and mass, its colors and its freight of birds, far more is needed than a mere covey of words that weave the wind.

It became clear to me that to rule out contradictions is no less rash than futile. Thus I made answer to my generals when they came and talked to me of "order," but confused the order wherein power is immanent with the layout of museums. As for me, I say that the tree is the very embodiment of order. But its order is that of unity overriding diversity. Thus on one branch birds have made a nest; another branch has none. One branch bears fruit, another is barren. One points to the sky, another droops earthwards. But, haunted by their habit of parades, my generals hold that those things only are in order which have ceased to differ from each other. Did I let them have their way, they would "improve" those holy books which reveal an order bodying forth God's wisdom, by imposing order on the letters, as to which the merest child can see that they are mingled with a purpose. My generals would put all the A's together, all the B's and so forth; and thus they would have a well-marshalled book; a book to the taste of generals.

How, then, could they countenance that which may not be formulated or has not yet matured? Or conflicts with another truth? How should they know that in a language which describes but fails to grasp, two truths can be at variance; that I can speak without contradicting myself of "the forest" or "the domain" though my forest extends over several domains without, perhaps, covering the whole of any one of them; and, conversely, my domain includes several forests though, perhaps, none of them is wholly contained in it? And that these truths do not naysay each other. If my generals, however, hymn the domains, they see to it that the poet singing of the forest is beheaded.

For truths may clash without contradicting each other; indeed there is but one truth whereby I stand, and that is Life; and but one order, which is that of mastering the materials to hand. Little care I if these materials are of diverse kinds. My order is the co-operation of all through each, and this order enjoins on me a creative activity that never ceases. It compels me to build up a language which, ever fusing contradictories into one, is itself a living entity. To create order it is never needful to reject. True, were I to begin by rejecting Life, and did I align men like posts along a roadside, then I might well achieve an order perfect of its kind. Likewise, if I reduced my people to the condition of ants in an anthill. But what love could I have for human ants? Rather, I love that man whom his religion sets free and whose life is quickened by intimations of divinity within him: the kingdom of God, the empire, the domain, his home—so that day in, day out, he barters himself for something vaster than himself. Why, then, should I not let them dispute amongst themselves, knowing as I do that every gesture which succeeds is made up of all those which fail to hit the mark, and that to become greater man must create, and not repeat himself? (For to repeat himself would mean but the consuming of stores laid up in the past.) And, lastly, because I know that everything, even the shape of the hull, must live and grow and constantly transform itself; else it is mere dead matter, a museum piece, a product of routine. And I am careful not to confound continuity with routine, or stability with death. Neither the stability of the cedar tree nor that of the empire derives from any decrepitude. "This," my generals say, "is perfect; therefore it will change no more." But, as for me, I abhor sedentaries, and maintain that completed cities are dead cities.

❦ 23

EVIL IS IT when the heart vanquishes the soul. Evil, too, when emotion vanquishes the mind.

Yet I discovered that it was easier to weld men together in my empire by emotion than by the mind, arbiter of emotion. Which seemed to show that, though in itself emotion counts for little, processes of mind must make good through emotion.

Thus I learned also that we must not subject him who creates to the desires of the multitude. It is, rather, his creation that must become the multitude's desire. The multitude must accept the mind's gift and transmute it, once received, into emotion; for the mass of men is but a belly whose function is to transmute the nourishment it receives into grace and light.

The prince, my neighbor, shaped his world because he felt it in his heart, and of his people made a hymn to God. Nevertheless it befell that many of them feared the solitude of the mountain height where darkling you can see the long steep slopes flowing away beneath you like the prophet's train and, holding converse with the stars, you quail before their icy questioning. Then a great hush falls and through it comes that still small voice which speaks only in silence. And he who has scaled these heights comes back refreshed by the honeydew of the gods. But only he to whom the right of an escape from the crowd has been accorded can bring back that golden dew. And it will seem bitter on the tongue; for all new, pregnant words seem bitter, inasmuch as none has ever undergone a change of heart without suffering. Thus it is and must be when I raise you up out of your old selves, enabling you to slough your past and, like the snake, don a new skin. Then, like the spark that kindles a forest fire, your plain-song will swell to a vast hymn of praise. But he who shuts his ears to it, and likewise a people that forbids one of its number to break free from the herd and isolate himself on the mountain-top—surely they are murderers of the spirit. For the domain of the spirit, where it can spread its wings, is—silence.

❦ 24

WHENCE I WAS LED to reflect on those who consume more than they bestow. Thus it is with the lies of the rulers of a nation; for the efficacy and power of their words reside in men's belief in what they tell. True, much may be achieved by lies; yet when I lie I blunt my weapon in the using of it. And, though I may begin by besting my opponent, there comes a day when I must face him, weaponless.

A like case is that of the poet who makes his effects by playing traitor to the time-proved rules; for scandalizing, too, is a technique. But such a man is an ill-doer. He shatters for his personal ends a vase containing an age-old treasure, common to all. In order to express himself, he ruins the possibilities of expression for others; like one who, to light his path, should set fire to the forest, leaving nothing but ashes and charred embers for the rest of men. Moreover, when once grammatical mistakes have become the rule, I can no longer scandalize or startle. But also, by the same token, I am unable to express myself in the beauty of the oldtime style, for I have made havoc of its usages and ruled out the mutual understanding, the signs and symbols, the speaking glances that are a code built up from generation to generation and that enable me to transmit my thought down to its subtlest shades. I shall have expressed myself, perhaps—but at the cost of ruining my instrument, and others', too.

Likewise as regards irony which is the weapon not of a man but of a dolt. Once, to my shame, I myself made sport of one of my governors, a much-esteemed man; I even named him "a jackass in office"—to the amazement and amusement of those around me. But there came a day when I had linked "jackass" and "governor" so closely that I no longer roused laughter when I spoke my mind. Thus I ruined an hierarchy, a possibility of ascent, ambition that might have worked for good, and a vision of greatness. I had pillaged a granary and squandered the good grain. And the crime, the treachery of it, was that, if I could thus drag down my governor, this was because others had stablished him in greatness. Given the opportunity of expressing myself, I had used it for his downfall and played the traitor.

But he who disciplines his writing and shapes his instrument to the advantage of his art finds his weapon ever the keener for the using; and thus, the more he draws on his store, the more his store increases. Thus, also, he who, despite difficulties and cruel setbacks, rules his people by the truth of his words, and augments the trust accorded him the more he draws on it, will be followed more loyally than another in the forefront of the battle. So is it with him who instils the sense of human greatness into his people: he is tempering an instrument which will serve him in tomorrow's need.

THEREFORE I SUMMONED the teachers before me and I said to them: "It is not your task to kill the Man in the children of men, nor to change them into ants trained to the life of the anthill. Little matters it to me whether a man be more or less amply endowed; what matters is whether he is the more or the less a man. Nor do I begin by asking whether or not he will be happy; I wish first to know *what* man will be happy. And little care I for the prosperity of the sedentaries, waxing fat like stall-fed cattle.

"You shall not fill them with hollow formulas, but with visions that are the portals of creative action.

"Nor must you begin by imparting the dry bones of knowledge, but you shall impart to them a mode of thought enabling them to grasp the Here and Now.

"You shall not assess their abilities by any seeming gift for this or for that. He goes farthest and best succeeds who has worked the hardest against the grain.

"Lay not much stress on use and wont; but rather on the creation of the man the boy will be, so that he may plane his boards in loyalty and honor. Thus he will plane better.

"Teach respect, for irony is the habit of the dolt and forgetfulness of due esteem.

"Strive to break the bonds that tie man to his worldly goods; thus you will stablish the Man in the child of man by teaching him above all to barter himself for something greater than himself—for, otherwise, he is but warped.

"Teach prayer and meditation, for these add virtues to the soul. And the practice of love; for what can replace love? But self-love is the opposite of love.

"Above all, punish lies and delation—though these may serve the man himself and seemingly the city. But fidelity alone breeds the strong man; and a fidelity that holds good in one camp and not in the other is no fidelity. Once faithful, always faithful: he who can bring himself to betray his fellow laborer is unfaithful. As for me, I desire a city that is strong, and I will not base its strength on men's corruption.

"You shall teach the love of perfection, for every work whereunto a man sets his hand is a step upon the path leading Godwards, and only death can stay that progress.

"You shall not begin by teaching forgiveness and charity. These are liable to be misapprehended and become but condonation of injuries and ulcers. But you shall teach the young how wonderful it is for men to work in amity together, each seconding each and all. Then the surgeon will hasten across the desert to set a worker's knee, slight though be the injury. They are voyaging in the same ship and the captain is the same for both."

⚘ 26

THUS WAS I LED to study that great miracle, the sloughing and renewal of one's self; for there was a leper in the town.

"Come," my father said, "and you shall see the bottomless pit."

After leading me to the outskirts of the town, he had me halt on the margin of a ragged, scurvy field. Round the field was a fence and in the centre the low hut where lived the leper, cut off from men.

"Think you," my father said, "that you will hear him howling his despair to the skies? Nay, when he comes forth, you shall see him yawning, listlessly indifferent.

"Neither more nor less than he within whom love has died. Neither more nor less than one fordone by exile. For, mark me well, exile does not break the heart; it wears you down. You have to live on dreams alone, and you play with dice that bear no values. Little matters the exile's wealth; he has become but a king of shadows.

"Salvation lies," my father said, "in necessity. You cannot play with dice that bear no values. You cannot satisfy yourself with dreams, because dreams offer no resistance. Even thus it is with youth's callow flights of fancy, which bring but disillusion. That alone is useful which resists you. The misfortune of that leper is not that he is rotting, but that nothing resists him. He dreams his life away, a sedentary, amongst the provisions he has laid up."

Sometimes the townsfolk came to watch him, and gathered round the field like men who, having climbed a volcano, line the crater's edge and peer into the depths. They blench each time they hear strange rumblings underfoot, as though the monster were preparing to belch forth. Thus they crowded round the leper's field, like men watching some great mystery. But there was no mystery.

"Have no illusions," my father said. "Picture him not as desperate, wringing his hands through long sleepless nights, and raging against God or against himself or against his fellow men. There is nothing within him save a vast insouciance. What indeed should he have in common with other men? His eyes are running, his arms falling from him like dead branches, and all he knows of the town is a far-off rumble of carts. Life is for him a pageant empty of concern; it nourishes him no more. You cannot live on an empty show, but only on that which you transform. Nor can you live by that which is stored in you, as in a warehouse. That man would come to life again, could he whip up his cart-horse, transport stones and join in building the temple. But, as things are, all is given him."

In time there grew up a custom: touched by his affliction, the townspeople came daily and flung offerings over the stakes fencing him in. Thus he was clad, served and tricked out like an idol; fed on the best dishes and on feast days honored furthermore with music. Yet though he had need of all, none had need of him. He had all good things to hand, but none to proffer.

"So is it," my father said, "with the wooden idols that men load with gifts. Before them glow the lampions of the faithful, the savor of burnt offerings rises to their nostrils, diadems glitter on their heads. But, mark my words, though that crowd flinging golden bracelets and jewels to its idols greatens itself thereby, the idol remains a mere dead block of wood. It transforms nothing. Whereas the living tree clutches the earth and molds it into flowers."

Presently I saw the leper come forth from his lair and survey us with his lacklustre eyes—as indifferent to the clamor which greeted him as to the sound of sea waves. He was cut off from us, and inaccessible for evermore. When one of the crowd voiced his pity, the leper eyed him with a vague disdain. He had nothing in common with them, and was sickened by a game where nothing was at stake. For what value has compassion that does not take its object in its arms? As for him, though something of the animal remaining in him stirred him to anger at being made a sight to gape at, like a freak in a village fair, that anger had little force behind it. We were no longer of his world; we were like children peeping into a pool wherein a solitary carp is slowly swimming. And, as for us, what mattered his anger, an anger that could not strike, but only spend itself in a babble of words blown on the wind.

Thus I saw that his very affluence had stripped him of everything. And I recalled those lepers in the South who levied their toll of the oases on horseback, because they were forbidden by the leper laws to alight from their mounts. Each proffered his begging-bowl on the end of a stick. Their eyes were hard, unseeing; for happy faces were to them but a hunting ground like any other. Why indeed should they have resented a happiness as alien to their world as the frolics of small animals playing in a patch of sunlight? Slowly they rode past the booths, now and again letting down baskets slung on ropes, and waiting patiently till the merchants had filled them. In that patience of theirs there was something terrifying, for in their silent immobility they seemed not men but festering growths of the disease, vials of corruption. And for us they were but halting places on the way to death, malignant caravanserais. What were they awaiting? Nothing. For a man awaits nothing within himself; he awaits something from another than himself. And the more rudimentary your language is, the cruder are your links with others; the less you can know of tedium and awaiting. But what could these men, so utterly cut off from us, have awaited of us? Nothing whatever.

"Observe him," my father said. "He has even stopped yawning. He has bidden farewell to everything, even that tedium which is men's awaiting."

✹ 27

THUS, ABOVE ALL, I saw the misery of their estate. My people dwelt in darkness, and that darkness was like a ship in which God has pent his passengers without a captain. Then, wishing to begin by understanding in what happiness consists, I resolved to separate them into two groups.

I had the bells ring, and, "Come to this side," I said, "all ye whose lives are crowned with happiness." For happiness is something immediately perceptible, like the savor of a ripe fruit. Thus have I seen a woman bending forward, pressing her hands to her breasts, so great a flood of happiness was welling up within her. So came those happy ones and stood on my right hand.

Again I had the bells ring, and, "Come to this side," I said, "all ye who are unhappy. Stand on my left." And now that I had separated them, I sought to understand, and asked myself: What lies at the root of their distress?

I have no faith in arithmetic. Neither joy nor sorrow is a matter of multiplication. If but one of my people suffers, his suffering is as great as that of the whole people. Yet likewise it is wrong if this man does not sacrifice himself in the service of the people.

Thus it is with joy. When the queen's daughter weds, the whole nation dances. The tree has shaped its blossom. And I judge the tree by its finest flower.

✥ 28

VAST DID IT SEEM to me, my solitude. Yet it was the selfsame silence and quiet growth I preconized for my people. And this aloofness, this weariness of spirit on the mountain-top—I drank them to the bitter dregs. Below me I saw the city sparkling in the dusk, and heard that multitudinous invocation which rises from a city when all doors are shut, all are gathered in and drawn together in intimate communion. I watched the windows closing one by one and lamps put out; and I knew the love of those who dwelt there. And the weariness of spirit love can bring, unless it barter itself for something vaster than itself.

Some windows remained lighted, sick-room windows. And near the ramparts shone a light apart, where perhaps a man was wrestling with a task undone; for he could not sleep until his sheaf was perfected. Likewise a few lighted windows told of fond awaiting, hopeless hope. God had gathered in his harvest for the day, but some there were who would nevermore come home.

Thus, like sentries, some were keeping watch, confronting the night as men who watch a darkling sea. These men, I thought, are sponsoring life, confronted by the ocean of the unknown. Like outposts in a forward line. Thus it falls to a few of us to watch over the sleep of men, to whom the fateful stars owe their answer, and to stay wakeful at our posts, keeping tryst with God. While the sedentaries sleep, we, a chosen few, guardians of the city, feel the night wind billowing down like a cold mantle let down from the stars, and lashing our cheeks.

Captains, my comrades, hard is the night before us. Those others wrapped in slumber know not that life is made of changes, fibres straining and creaking within the cedar tree, painful transformations. We, the few, bear the load for them, and keep ward at the frontiers on behalf of those within whose breasts disease is smoldering and who slowly work their boats upstream towards the dawn; those who, like lookout men in a crow's-nest, search the gloom for an answer to their questions; those who still hope for a return of the beloved one.

And then it became clear to me how narrow is the frontier between fervor and anguish of mind. For these are the lot of the same men; and both are an awareness of space and vastness.

They alone keep vigil with me who are fervent and suffer in their hearts: meanwhile let the others take their rest—all who have created in the day and are not called on to hold the front line against the powers of darkness.

That night, however, the whole town was astir because of a man who was to expiate a crime at dawn. Some believed him innocent. So patrols went the rounds, hindering the townspeople from gathering together; for that night something drew men from their dwellings and towards each other. Then, "See," I told myself, "how great a fire is kindled by one man's plight! That prisoner in jail is hovering above the city like a flaming brand!"

Then a desire came to me to see him, and I betook myself to the prison. Foursquare and black it loomed against the stars. The men-at-arms unbarred to me the gates, which swung open, rumbling on their hinges. The walls seemed of a prodigious thickness, the windows were strongly barred. There, too, I met dark patrols prowling the corridors, and they turned hastily, blinking like startled nightbirds, as I went by. Everywhere was a smell of overcrowded, airless rooms, and when anyone dropped a key or trod heavily on the flagstones, he woke a volley of echoes, as in a crypt.

And I thought, "How dangerous this man must be that, weak though he is and of so frail a body that a nail would suffice to drain it of his lifeblood, they needs must heap a mountain on him!"

All those footsteps I heard were trampling on his belly; the walls, posterns and buttresses weighing him down. "This man," I told myself, "is surely the prison's soul, its focal point, its inmost truth and meaning. Yet, to look at, he is but a heap of rags and tatters sprawled alongside the bars! Asleep, perhaps, and struggling for breath. Yet, such as he is, the leaven of a town. And if he mumbles to himself or rolls over against another wall, a whole town quakes."

They opened the spy-hole and I gazed at him. For well I knew that here was something I must understand.

And I thought: Perhaps he has nothing to reproach himself with save a very human love. But he who builds a dwelling gives a form to it. And, in truth, any and every form may be desirable. Yet not all forms can coexist together. All might have been beautiful; but not all at once. . . . Perhaps his dreams are beautiful.

We, he and I, are on the mountain crest. Alone together. Tonight, at the world's summit, we meet and are at one. For on these heights there is nothing to sunder us. He, too, desires justice. Yet it is a different justice and this man must die. . . .

And I was heavy of heart.

Nevertheless, for wishes to blossom into deeds, for the life force of the tree to become a branch, the woman to become a mother, a choice must be made. It is from the injustice of all choice that life springs. Thus, being beautiful, a certain woman was loved by many and many a one. And, being what she was, she reduced them to despair. For always that which is, is unjust. And I understood that cruelty lies at the heart of all creation.

I shut the spy-hole and made my way back along the corridors, my heart full of esteem and of love. "Since his greatness is his pride, what good were it to leave to him his life, in bondage?" I passed patrols, warders, sweepers at work, heralding the daybreak—

and all, it seemed to me, were his prisoners. These grim walls guarded their prisoner, like those ruins whose sole significance comes from a treasure buried under them. Then again I turned and gazed at the prison and, with its turret like a garland proffered to the stars, it seemed fraught with fervor, a great ship in full sail, carrying its freight. "Who is the victor, when all is said and done?" I asked myself. In the distance, hunched in darkness, the prison had had the grimness of a powder magazine.

Then I thought of the townsfolk. "True, they will weep for him. Yet also is it good that they should weep."

I fell to musing on the songs and sounds and meditations of my people. "They will bury him." But, methought, there is no burial of the dead; what is buried is a seed. No power have I over life, and one day he will come into his own. I hang him on a rope; but I shall hear his death breaking into song. And its echoes will fill the ears of those who seek to reconcile that which is divided. But I, what shall *I* reconcile?

I weld men into one hierarchy; but never, at the same moment, into another. Wrong were it for me to confound beatitude with death. My course is set towards beatitude, but I must not exclude contradictions; rather, welcome them. One thing is good, another evil—I hate those compromises which are possets for the weak and sap their manhood. It is for me to greaten myself by the acceptance of mine enemy.

❧ 29

GAZING AT THE dancing-girl's face, I pondered. Sullen she seemed, and dogged, weary of the world. And then I fell to thinking of the empire; how in its great days its aspect was a visage. Today it is but the lid of an empty box. There is no emotion left in men's hearts, and injustice is a dead word. No man any longer suffers for his convictions. And of what worth are convictions that bring not suffering?

He desired to acquire. He has acquired. And has he now achieved happiness? But happiness lay in the effort of acquiring. Consider the plant that shapes a flower. Is it happy for having shaped its flower? Nay, rather, self-fulfilled; and now it has nothing to look forward to but death. First we have desire, a zest for work, and the craving for success. Then comes repose. But no man can live by that repose, which nourishes him not; for what is aimed at must not be confounded with that which nourishes. Thus a man may run the fastest, and win the race; but he cannot live on his won race. Nor another, lover of the sea, on the great storm he has bested. That storm was but a single arm-stroke in his swimming; it called for another and another stroke. And the pleasure of forming a flower, of riding out a storm, of building the temple is other than the pleasure of possessing a full-blown flower, a memory of riding out a storm, a standing temple. Vain is the hope of finding pleasure in that which one has hitherto disdained; as when the warrior hopes to find pleasure in the joys of the sedentaries. Yet, while seemingly the warrior fights to achieve that which nourishes the sedentary, he has no right to feel frustrated if, when peace comes, he is changed into a sedentary—for false is the lament of one who tells you that, like a will-o'-the-wisp, fruition eternally flees before desire. He is mistaken as to the object of desire. What you seek eternally, you say, hovers eternally just out of reach. But it is as if a tree were to lament: "I have shaped my flower and, lo, it is turning into a seed, and the seed will become a tree again, and the tree once again put forth a flower." Thus, now you have bested the storm, the storm is become repose, yet this repose is but the harbinger of another storm. This I tell you: that there is no divine grace to absolve you from the process of becoming. You fain would *be;* but you can *be* only in God's good time. He will gather you into his garner when your slow process of becoming ends and you are fully molded by your deeds; for, mark you, man is slow in coming to birth.

Thus are men stripped of all, because they thought to acquire and own, and halted on the way so as, forsooth, to batten on the stores they had laid up. For there is no laying up of stores. Well I know it, I who for so long let myself be bewitched by the lures of His creatures, knowing that the bodies of women now being molded into beauty in a foreign land, and anointed with rare, fragrant oils, lay within my grasp. These heady visions I called love, and it seemed to me that I would die of thirst if I failed to win her on whom my heart was set.

Great were the rejoicings to celebrate the betrothal; great and for my whole people hued and hallowed by the rites of love. Basketfuls of flowers were scattered on the streets, perfumes floated in the air and they burned diamonds that had cost men blood and tears and sweat, born of the toil of many, like the single drop of scent distilled from cartloads of flowers. And, half unwittingly, each sought to plunge himself into love's ecstasy.

But then I saw her on my terrace, a gentle creature with the wind blowing her veils about her. And I gazed on her, I the man, the conqueror, at last possessing the handsel of my war. And now, suddenly, confronted by her, knowing only that I must *become.* . . .

"My dove," I murmured, "my little turtledove, my lithe-limbed gazelle. . . ." For with these weak words I had conjured up I thought to grasp her, elusive as she was. Evanescent as snow in sunlight. It was withdrawn, the gift I was awaiting, and "Where are you?" I cried. For she had slipped away from me. "What is the barrier between us?" I was becoming a dungeon, a keep. And meanwhile the bonfires blazed merrily to celebrate love's triumph! But I, alone in my bleak wilderness, gazed down on her as she slept, naked in beauty. "I took the wrong direction," I lamented. "I pursued the wrong quarry. Swiftly she fled, but I hunted her down and seized her. Only . . . once seized, she ceased to be." And then I saw my error. What mattered was the pursuit, the hunting down. Yes, I had been as great a fool as the man who, because he loved the music of the wellspring, filled his pitcher at it and placed it in his cupboard.

But if I touch her not, I build her up before me like a temple: I build her in the light, and the fields and woods are comprehended in her silence. Thus I can love her beyond herself, beyond my self; and compose hymns of praise lauding her empire. Then her eyes shut, eyelids of the world, and in my arms I can hold her like a darkling town. She is but one step more on my upward climb to God. . . . She was made to be consumed, burnt up; not to be trapped and held.

And presently, lo, the whole palace in tears, the townsfolk heaping ashes on their heads, for I straightway called up a thousand men and marched them out through the great gates towards the desert—so sore was my discontent!

Thus did I understand the limits of my empire. Indeed these very limits made it known to me—for I love that only which resists. Him I love who proves his manhood by resistance, who is self-contained and silent, who keeps himself hard, whose lips are sealed under torture, who has resisted torture and love alike. Him who chooses and is unjust in his not-loving—and her, that woman on the terrace, who is like a staunch tower, impregnable.

For I hate complaisance. He who never says "no" is no true man, but worthy of the anthill, wherein God has ceased to have a place. A man without leaven. This, indeed, was the miracle revealed to me in my prison: that man was stronger than I, than you, than all my jailers and my drawbridges and ramparts. This it was that lay behind the problem that had fretted me; which was the same problem as that of love, when I held her, naked and yielding, in my arms. The greatness of man, and withal his littleness; for I perceive that he is great in his faith, not in the arrogance of his revolt.

30

THUS IT WAS SHOWN to me that a man was unworthy of interest not only if he was incapable of sacrifice, of withstanding temptation and facing death serenely, but likewise if, merged into the mass and swayed by it, he truckled to its laws. The wild boar, the solitary elephant and the man on his mountain-top have their appointed way of life, and the herd must permit his silence to each, nor drag him from it through hatred of all that is like a lonely cedar tree eminent on the heights.

When some busybody comes forward, claiming to expound man with his logic and neat definitions, I liken him to a child who has settled down with spade and bucket at the foot of Atlas and proposes to shovel up the mountain and install it elsewhere. Man is what he is, not that which can be expressed. True the aim of all awareness is to express that which is, but expression is a slow, elusive task, and it is a mistake to assume that anything incapable of being stated in words does not exist. Stating is, by the same token, comprehending. But small indeed is the part of man which I have learned, so far, to comprehend. Yet that which on a certain day I come to comprehend existed none the less the day before; and foolish indeed were I to deem that all in man for which I cannot find the words is unworthy of consideration. Neither do I express the mountain; I can but signify it. But to signify is not to grasp. I can signify to one who knows already; but if a man knew nothing of it, how could I bring to his mind the mountain with its stonefields, crevasses, lavender-clad slopes and its crags buttressing the stars? And for me the mountain is far other than a derelict fortress, or a helmless ship which can be loosed from its moorings and towed wherever anyone lists; it is a whole world in itself, with its own laws of gravity and an inner silence yet more majestic than the silence of the stars upon their courses.

Thus was I led to a pregnant paradox; of admiring at once the subservient man and him who is untamable and ever shows himself in his true colors. The problem I could understand, though words failed me to state it. For those men who are governed by an iron discipline and, at a mere sign from me, brave death; those very men whom my faith inspires with ardor, but who are so thoroughly inured to obedience that I can taunt them to their faces and scold them like children—those very men, when high adventure beckons and they clash in battle, have the temper of tried steel, godlike rage, and courage in the face of death.

Clearly these were but two aspects of the same person. He whom we admire as the essence of intractability (like her whom there is no subduing and who, clasped in my arms, is remote as a ship on the high seas), he whom I call a lion, inasmuch as he never palters or comes to terms or, through greed or weariness or suppleness, abandons the least part of himself; he whom I can crush between the millstones without squeezing from him one drop of the oil of his secret, for he is like the hard stone of the olive; that man whose heart is like a diamond and whom I will suffer neither the masses nor the tyrant to constrain—always in such a man have I discerned another side. He is disciplined, respectful, full of faith and self-abnegation; for he is the wise scion of a high-minded race and custodian of its virtues.

But as for those whom I once called "free," who decide solely for themselves and are ineluctably alone—such men are ships that answer not to the helm, but are at the mercy of every current. Their resistances are but futile whims.

Thus I, who loathe those cattle—men who are drained of their human substance and have no world within—I, who, neither as master nor as leader, would wish to unman my people and change them into blind, servile ants—I have learned that by my constraint I can, and should, quicken their lives abundantly. And likewise that a man's obedience, his helpfulness to others and reverence in my church, are not signs of a weakling or a half-man: rather, such an one can serve me on the frontiers of my empire, as a bulwark.

Thus as regards that man penned beneath the ramparts, on whom my sentries were keeping watch, and who would not abjure even were I to crucify him, but would laugh his scornful, defiant laugh even when my torturers were crushing his bones together—were I to deem him a mere callous brute I should judge him wrongly. His strength comes from another religion than mine; he has another aspect, and a gentler. Well can I picture him sitting in his home, his hands on his knees, and smiling amiably as he listens to his friends' talk. Thus, too, with her whom I hold captive in my tower; who paces to and fro within the cage of the horizons, cannot be held or ravished, and withholds the words besought of her. And who is simply of another country, another tribe; consumed by another fire, and faithful to her own religion. Save by way of conversion, I could not reach her heart.

Most of all I hate those who *are* not; curs who vaunt their freedom because they are free to turn their coats and to play the renegade (yet how should they know their treachery, since each claims to be a law unto himself?). Thus free are they to cheat and to abjure; but I soon make them change their minds, when hunger nips them, by pointing to their trough.

Thus was the night of nuptials and of the man sentenced to death. Therefrom I learnt this much of the meaning of existence: that it behoves men to be staunch as the stem-post of the ship. Let not your form alter, but like the cedar change into your own substance what you take in from without. I am the frame, the structure, the creative drive that brings you into being; and then it is for you, like the great tree which multiplies its own branches and not another's, shapes its own leaves or needles and not another's—it is for you to grow and steadfastly endure.

But them I call the rabble who hang on others' words and gestures, and, chameleon-wise, take their color from them, truckling to their benefactors, relishing applause, and making themselves the mirror of the multitude. Never do you find such men faithful wardens of their heritage, like a citadel; nor do they hand down their password from generation to generation; but rather let their children grow at random, without molding them. And everywhere they breed, like fungus, on the face of the earth.

31

WHEN MY COUNSELLORS came and spoke to me of "comfortable conditions" I bethought me of my army. For well I know the efforts men put forth to achieve a life of balanced ease, though, once balance is attained, life ceases.

Therefore loved I war, which paves the way to peace—peace with its warm, reposeful sands, and its virgin sands alive with vipers, and its sheltered, inviolate places. A picture rose before me of children I had seen playing with white pebbles and transfiguring them. "Here," they said, "is an army on the march; yonder a herd of cattle." But the passer-by saw only pebbles; for the riches of the child's hearts are unapparent. Thus is it with him, too, who draws his life-force from the dawn, plunging into its frosty sheen as into a pool of living water, then warms himself with the first level rays. Or, yet more simply, that man who when he is thirsty goes to the well, hauls at the chain, and lifts the brimming pail on to the rim of the well, his ears full of the sound of tinkling drops, a shrill, sweet water-music. And thus his thirst infuses a meaning into his going-forth, his arms and his eyes, for that thirsty man's walk towards his well is like a poem. But there are others who beckon a slave, and he lifts the water to their lips, and they know not the song of the wellspring. Their "comfortable conditions" are but a lack; and because they have no faith in suffering, joy withholds itself from them.

Thus have I seen it with him who listens to music and feels no need to penetrate it. Like a man carried in a litter, with music sounding in his ears, but unwilling to rise and walk towards it; or like one who disdains a fruit because the rind is bitter. But, mark me well, no fruit there is without a rind. No landscape is discovered from the mountain-top, if you have not struggled up the slopes; for the landscape is not a mere sight but something achieved and conquered. If you have yourself carried to the summit in a litter, you will see but a more or less uninspiring pattern, and how will you add savor to it from within yourself? But for him who, having scaled the heights, folds his arms contentedly, that landscape is imbued with memories of the arduous ascent, the pleasant ache of limbs resting after long effort, no less than with the blue haze of sundown; and also with the satisfaction that comes of what is well ordered, for his upward steps have somehow helped to impose a pattern on the rivers under his eyes, aligned the foothills, knit together the pebbles of the village roads. That landscape is begotten of him, and I liken his joy to the joy of the child who, setting his stones in order, has built his town and feasts his eyes on it, imbuing it with himself. But what child would delight in a mere heap of stones, a sight which has cost no effort?

I have seen men suffering from thirst—thirst which is a lust for water, crueller than a disease; for the body knows its remedy and craves for it as it craves for a woman, and sees in fancy others drinking. (Thus, too, one pictures the woman one desires bestowing her smiles on others.) Nothing has meaning until I mingle my mind and body with it; nor is there adventure unless I share in it. When my astrologers spend studious nights poring hour after hour upon the Milky Way, they see there as it were a great book spread open before them, its pages gloriously rustling as they turn—and they praise God that He has vouchsafed to flood the firmament with an elixir so compelling.

Wherefore I tell you: "You have no right to shirk an effort, save in the cause of another effort; for your life's work is ever to greaten yourself."

❦ 32

THAT YEAR died he who reigned beyond the eastern marches of my empire. Many a hard battle had I joined with him, and therewith I had come to understand that I leaned on him as on a wall. Still can I recall our meetings. A scarlet tent was pitched out in the desert, and each of us made his way into the tent, leaving his army afar—for it is not well for the men to mingle together. The crowd lives only in and for its belly. And shallow gilding flakes all too easily away. Thus warily they gazed at us, standing to their arms for prudence' sake, and not to be beguiled by any insidious softening of their mood. For wise was my father when he said: "Forgather not with your adversary on the ground level, but in the topmost tower of his heart and soul and mind. Else, by seeking to find common ground in your tawdrier emotions, you will come to shedding blood, needlessly."

Thus, taking to heart his counsel, I went forth to meet my man, stripped of superfluities and fenced by threefold walls of solitude. We sat down on the sand, facing each other. I know not which of us two was the more powerful; but in that sanctuary of solitude, power became measure; for though our gestures shook the world, we measured them.

Sometimes we fell to speaking of the grazing grounds. "I have twenty-five thousand head of cattle dying," he would say, and add: "The rains were good in your country, I am told." But I could not suffer them to import their alien customs, and doubts that breed corruption. Those shepherds from another world—how could I admit them into my empire?

"We," I said, "have twenty-five thousand young children who must learn the prayers of their own people and not another's; else will they grow awry."

So we had recourse to the arbitrament of war, and we were like tides flowing and ebbing, but neither gaining ground. And though each brought his full weight to bear, neither yielded; because we both were primed to the utmost, each hardening his enemy by defeat. "You have gained a victory; thereby am I grown the stronger."

Not that I misesteemed his greatness, or the hanging gardens of his capital, or the perfumes sold by his merchants, or the delicate craftsmanship of his goldsmiths, or his great dams for the storing of water. Only a small mind traffics in scorn; a mind whose truth accords no place to others'. But we who knew that different truths can coexist thought not that we were lowering ourselves by countenancing another's truth, unpalatable though it might seem. An apple tree does not, to my knowledge, scorn the cedar, or the palm tree, or the vine; but each toughens itself to the utmost and mingles not its roots. Thus it retains its form and selfhood, a capital inestimable, which it were unbecoming to debase.

"True bartering," he was wont to say, "means the box of spikenard, or the seedling; it is the gift of golden cedar-wood that imparts the fragrance of my house to yours. Or, it may be, my war cry when it reaches you from my mountains. Or, perchance, the coming of an ambassador, if he has long been trained and shaped and tested, and he both rejects you and takes you to his heart. He rejects you on his lower levels; but on the heights where human esteem rises above hatred, he finds common ground with you. The only esteem worth having is an enemy's; for that of friends is worthless unless it be something higher than their kind regards or the trivial emotions of the marketplace. Die for your friend if you will, but pity not yourself therefor."

Thus I would lie, were I to say I had a friend in him. Nevertheless, always we met with deep-felt joy—but here words would lead astray by reason of men's pettiness. My joy was not for him, but for God; he was a bridge leading towards God, and our meetings were keystones of the arches. And our silences were understanding.

May God forgive me for weeping when he died! Too well I knew it, my sorrow's flaw. Surely, I told myself, it is because I am not yet pure enough that I shed these tears. Whereas I pictured him, had I been first to die, simply walking forth into the vastness of the desert twilight and contemplating the great change that had come on our world as calmly as he watched the shadows gathering. Or as a drowning man when the world changes under the slumbrous mirror of the waters. "O Lord," would he have prayed to his God, "the day dawns and the night falls according to Thy will. But nothing has been lost of the sheaf that has been gathered up, of the epoch that has passed away. *I have been* . . ." Thus he would have gathered me into his peace ineffable. But I was not pure enough, nor as yet fain enough of things eternal. Like a woman, I still felt that vague melancholy which comes when the evening wind withers the flowers in my rose-garden. For in my roses it withers me, and I, too, die in them.

In the course of my life I had deposed statesmen, buried my captains, won women and lost them; and I had left about the world a host of vestiges of myself, as a snake leaves its sloughed-off skins. Nevertheless, as punctually as returns the sun ruling the tides of light and dark, or summer ruling the year's fruition, even so from colloquy to colloquy, from one treaty to another, did my men-at-arms pitch that empty tent far off in the desert. And every year we repaired to it, he and I. Thus arose a hallowed custom, and ever I saw that smile of his, crinkled like old vellum, and his serenity as death drew near. And that silence which is not of man, but God's.

But now I was alone, sole trustee of my past, with none left to bear witness to my works and days. Or to those activities which I had not deigned to unbare to my people, but which he, my neighbor in the East, had understood; all those heart searchings which never had I paraded before others but in his silence he had discerned. Those responsibilities which had all but overwhelmed me and of which none of my people had even an inkling (for it was well that they should think I gave my every whim free rein), but which he, my neighbor in the East, had weighed, never with fellow-feeling but with fine aloofness; for he judged these matters quite otherwise than I. And now behold he was sleeping in the glittering cerement of the sand, having drawn it over him as a shroud. Silence had enwrapped him, and on his lips was taking form that final smile, forlorn yet God-enkindled, of a man who is content with having bound up his sheaf, his eyes closed on their treasure.

In my discomfiture how much was due to self-esteem! Weak as I was, I ascribed high importance to the course of my destiny, though it had none at all; I rated the empire in terms of myself instead of sinking myself into the empire, and I saw my life like a long track steadily rising towards the peak I had attained.

That night, on the lonely table-land, I stood at a parting of the ways: after climbing to the heights I must now begin the long descent. For the first time I knew that I was old; all men seemed strangers, there were no familiar faces left. I felt detached from all, now that I was growing detached from myself. On that upward slope I had abandoned, one by one, my captains, my loves, my enemies, and perchance my only friend. Henceforth I was alone in a world peopled by men I knew no more.

Yet, dark as was the hour, I found strength to take up life again. "I have broken through my last husk," I told myself, "and now I shall step forth the purer. I had rated myself too high, and because I was growing soft this trial has been sent me. For I was puffing myself up with ignoble fancies; but now will I be able to enshrine him, my dead friend, for ever in his majesty, nor will I weep for him. Simply—*he will have been.* And the sand will seem to me the richer, since often in the vastness of this desert I have seen him smile. And for me all men's smiles will be enriched by that one man's smile; for I shall see in Man that secret image which no sculptor has been able to wrest forth from the stone enshrouding it. Across the unhewn block I shall discern Man's countenance the better for having looked one man straight in the eyes.

"True, I am treading now the downward slope; but have no fear, my people. I have restored the broken link. Ill was it that I should have depended on a man. The hand which healed me and sewed up my wound is no more, but the suture remains. As I descend my mountain I pass sheep and lambs. And fondle them. I am alone in the world under God's providence, but when I fondle lambs which open the wellsprings of the heart, I am caressing not so much these little creatures nuzzling my hand as all the weakness of mankind; and thus I return to you."

As for that other king, I have throned him in majesty; I have immortalized him in death. Every year a tent is pitched in the desert, while my people pray. My armies stand to arms, their guns are primed, my horsemen range the desert keeping watch and ward, and any intruder venturing within the precinct is beheaded. Alone, I walk forward to the tent, then lift the flap and sit down on the sand. And all is silence.

✕ 33

AND NOW THAT I am afflicted by this dull ache within my breast that my doctors cannot heal; now that I am like a forest tree under the woodman's axe and ere long God will lay me low like an outworn tower; and my awakenings are no longer the proud awakenings of youth, when limber are the sinews and every thought is buoyant—even now have I found my consolation, which is not to let myself be cast down by these portents of a failing body, nor overborne by infirmities which are base and personal, locked up within me, and to which the historians of my empire will not accord three lines in their chronicles. Little matters it that my teeth are loosening, my cheeks sagging—and indeed it were unseemly to crave the least pity on that score. Nay, anger wells up within me at the mere thought of it! For these flaws are in the vase alone, not in its contents.

They tell me that when my neighbor in the East was stricken with a palsy, and one side of him grew cold and numb, and he needs must drag with him everywhere that dead half of himself which smiled no more, even so he lost nothing of his dignity, but, rather, profited by this ordeal. To those who praised him for his strength of mind he answered scornfully that they forgot who he was, and bade them keep such eulogies for the tradesfolk of the city. For a ruler, if he begin not by ruling over his own body, is but a ridiculous usurper. I reckon it no loss but an amazing boon that today I have freed myself a little more from life's empery.

Thus is it with old age. True, all that awaits me on the downward slope is unfamiliar. But my heart is full of my dead friend and, gazing at the villages with eyes drained dry by my loss, I wait for love to flood through me again, like a returning tide.

✣ 34

AGAIN I GAZED DOWN at the city lighting up in the dusk; a pale face dappled blue by sudden gleams flashing forth from the houses. I marked the disposition of the streets. And the great silence setting in, a deep-sea silence like that which broods on the rocks of the abyss. Much as I admired the well-laid-out streets and squares, and the temples dotted here and there like spiritual granaries, and the hills encircling the city like a night-black garment—nevertheless a picture rose before me, despite the living flesh that filled it, of a withered plant that has been severed from its roots. Likewise I thought of empty granaries. For what I had under my eyes was no longer a living being whose every part throbbed in unison with the others; no longer was there a heart drawing up the blood and then pouring it forth through the whole body; no longer was the city one flesh, capable of rejoicing in happy fellowship on feastdays, wrapped in a unity of time and place. Far otherwise, these were but parasites ensconced in others' shells, each living for himself in his retreat and refusing to co-operate. No longer was there a city; but only the simulacrum of a city, and it was peopled by dead who

117

fancied themselves alive. As a tree that is dying of drought, a rotting fruit, or the body of a tortoise dead under its shell—thus did it seem to me, my city. Sorely it needed to be revived by a new uprush of sap. All those half-dead branches must be refastened to the parent trunk; granaries and cisterns replenished with their store of silence. And it was on me that this task fell; for who else was there to love and succor them?

✵ 35

THUS WITH THE MUSIC to which I listened—music which they could not understand. And the issue, I perceived, was simple: a choice of alternatives. *Either* you have them listen to songs they know, and they progress not; as when you teach them what they understand already and they are none the wiser. Likewise you may fence them in with the customs that have been theirs for a thousand years, and then there is not within them as it were a tree that waxes greater year by year, ever putting forth new flowers and fruit—but, replacing this, time-proved wisdom, calm devotion and repose in God. *Or,* on the other hand, staking your all on progress, you may hustle them on and brutally dislodge them from their customs; and presently you find that you are leading but a rabble of emigrants who have cast away their birthright. An army constantly pitching camp, but never consolidating its positions.

But all ascent is painful, every change of heart has its birth pangs; and I cannot force the secret of this music that I love unless, first, I have put forth a painful effort. Indeed I deem it the handsel of my pains, and no faith have I in those who take their delight in stores amassed by others. Thus if you would imbue them with the bliss and ecstasy of love it is not enough to plunge the sons of men in the flood tide of music, poetry and eloquence. Not love alone but suffering, too, goes to the making of man's plenitude. And likewise weariness of spirit and moods of irritation sullen as lowering skies. For even in those who enjoy the poem, the joy in the poem is not all; else never would you see them looking sad. Ravished by its beauty, they would have bliss untrammelled; indeed all men would share their rapture, without having any obligation to create. But such is man that he rejoices only in what he himself builds up, and, to enjoy the poem, he needs must undergo the toil of its ascent. For even as the scene glimpsed from the mountain-top lacks power to enchant the heart, and has meaning only if it is the meed of the climber's weariness, built up as it were by his effort—for presently, once you have rested and are eager to progress, the same landscape has no more to give, and merely makes you yawn—even so is it with the poem that is not begotten of your effort. For though the poem may be another's work, yet the joy it bestows is the fruit of your labors, of your soul's ascent; and well-stocked barns make but sedentaries, repletes, lacking the quality of Man. I use not love as a store kept in reserve; it is, above all, a generous activity of my heart. Nevertheless I do not wonder that there are so many men who fail to understand the poem, the temple, music, or the domain, and, contemplating them, say: "What are these but a diversity of things, more or less attractive? But none of them is worthy to rule my life." They who speak thus are, as we say, "knowledgable," sceptics, and prone to irony—which is the habit not of a man but of a dolt. For love is not presented to you as a gift bestowed by this face or that; even as a sense of plenitude comes not from the scene viewed from the mountain-top, but from the inner joy of having scaled and stormed the mountain, and won your foothold on the aery heights.

Thus with love. They err who think that they have but to learn about love, if they are to come by it. And that man hoodwinks himself who drifts through life hoping to be vanquished by love, learning by fitful fevers to enjoy brief stirrings of the heart, ever thinking to encounter that supreme fever which will enkindle his whole life; though, by reason of his pettiness of mind and the insignificance of the hill he has climbed, it can be but a short-lived exaltation of his heart.

Thus, too, love is no sure resting place if it does not transform itself from day to day, like a child in the womb. But you, my sedate friend, propose to loll in your gondola and to become the gondolier's song for all your days; wherein you dupe yourself. For all that is neither ascent nor a transition lacks significance. And when you halt on the way, you will have no joy of it; for the landscape will have nothing more to tell you. Then you will discard the woman; whereas you should have begun by discarding your old self.

Wherefore I have never been impressed by the reasonings of those miscreants and sophists who came to me and said: "Pray, show us the domain, the empire and the God of which you tell us. For stones and solid matter we can touch, and only in what we touch can we believe." Never have I sought to enlighten such a man by the disclosure of a secret paltry enough to be put into words. It would be vain for me to have him carried to the mountain-top, so that the truth of a landscape which he had not had to conquer might be revealed to him; no less vain than to seek to make him enjoy music that has not cost him any effort. Even as some men seek for a woman who will bestow love ready-made upon them, so such an one comes to me seeking to learn effortlessly. But this is not within my power to grant.

Therefore I called together my teachers and said: "Make no mistake. If I confide to you the little ones of my people, this is not in order that the sum of their knowledge may one day be weighed and measured up, but that I may see them climbing towards the summit, and rejoice in their endeavor. No joy have I in a pupil who, borne in a litter, has visited the summits of a thousand mountains and thus has viewed a thousand landscapes; for, firstly, he will not truly know a single one of them and, moreover, a thousand landscapes are but a grain of sand in the vastness of the sum of things. To him alone do I give thought who has spared himself no effort in the toilsome ascent of a mountain—though but a single

mountain—and is thus equipped to understand the myriad landscapes that will meet his eyes thereafter. Far better will he comprehend them than your would-be wiseacre with his thousand
mountains!

"And, given such a youth, if I wish to kindle the true flame of
love within him, I must stablish love in his heart by the discipline
of prayer."

For the teachers had been misled by seeing that he who has thus
been trained to love always discovers the face that sets his heart
aglow. They imagined that some mysterious power resided in that
face. And likewise that, because the heart of one who has mastered
the poem is set aglow by it, the power resided in the poem. But
again I tell you: When I speak of "the mountain" I signify the
mountain to him alone who has torn himself on its thorns, scram-
bled up its crags, sweated upon its rocks, picked its flowers, and
then drunk deep of the wind that sweeps the summit. I signify—
but I *grasp* nothing. And when I say "mountain" to a fat huckster,
the word takes no purchase on his heart. . . .

It is not because the efficacy of the poem is passing from the
world that there are no more poems. Or because that of the face
is passing that there is no more love. Or because that of God is
passing that men's hearts are now impervious to the call of the
great fertile spaces dreaming in darkness, whence a ploughshare
would call forth a host of cedar trees and flowers. . . .

For, having given much heed to men's converse and their disputations, I know well the perils of the intellect, whose dogma is
that words can *grasp*. It is not by way of language that I shall
transmit what is within me; for it is inexpressible in words. I can
but *signify* this in so far as you may understand it through other
channels than the spoken word; by love's miracle or because, born
of the same God, we are akin. Else I have to drag it out, laboriously
—that sunken world within me. And thus, as my clumsiness avails,
I display this aspect or that alone—as in the case of my mountain,
of which I may say merely that it is high. But it is far more than

that, and behind those weak words I have in mind the far-flung glory of the night when one stands on the heights, alone and shivering, amongst the stars.

✼ *36*

WHEN YOU WRITE to Man, you freight a ship. But few such ships reach port. They founder in mid-course. Few are the phrases that go echoing on their ways through history. Much, perchance, I may have signified, but little have I grasped.

Hence another quandary; for it is far more important to train men how to grasp than how to signify. They must be taught how to set about the act of capture. This knowledgable man you point out to me—little does it matter to me what he knows. A dictionary would serve as well. What matters to me is what he *is*. Thus with the man who has written his poem and filled it with his fervor, but has failed in his fishing in the open sea and brought back nothing from the ocean depths. He may signify to me the springtime, but he fails to build it up within me, so that my heart can thrive on it.

I heard much talk by my historians, critics and pundits, who had observed that when a work is powerful, its power is expressed by its plan; for all that is strongly built tends to shape itself into a plan. And if that which chiefly I see in the city is a plan, this means that my city has expressed itself and is complete. But it was not the plan that founded the city.

THEREUPON I TOOK THOUGHT of the dancers, courtesans and singers in my city. They had litters of silver made for them and when they ventured forth therein, they bade runners go before them to announce their coming and cause the crowd to gather. Then, when the applause of the multitude had wrought agreeably on their nerves and roused them from their fragile slumbers, they would draw aside the silken veils before their faces, and deign to pander to the desire of the crowd by yielding glimpses of their pale beauty. Demurely they smiled, while the runners did their task with all their might, for they were flogged at nightfall, if the crowd had not forced the dancer's modesty by the insistence of its desire.

They bathed in baths of solid gold, and the populace was invited to watch the preparations for the bath. First a hundred she-asses were milked—for they bathed in asses' milk; then were added divers perfumes and an attar of flowers which was of a great price, but of so discreet a fragrance that nothing remained of it.

Yet I was not outraged thereby for, all things considered, the time spent on the distilling of this attar impaired but little the work of the empire, and, as for the price it cost, that was mere fantasy. Moreover, it was desirable that somewhere in my empire things of great price should be esteemed; for what counts is not the use to which things are put but the fervor that goes to their making. Since this attar existed, what mattered it to me whether or not it perfumed my courtesans?

For it was ever my rule, when my logicians fell to arguing, to appraise the fervor of my empire; and I took notice of their homilies only when my people, being set too much on luxuries, disdained the getting of their daily bread. But I did not penalize a reasonable luxury, which indeed bespoke the quality of their work, and little cared I what purpose these ornaments, useless for daily life, might serve. For, to my thinking, such ornaments are better employed in decking a woman's hair than in embellishing a public statue or some tedious monument. True, you may say the statue is the common property of all—but a beautiful woman, too, is well worth gazing at, and a monument (unless it be a temple dedicated to God) has this defect, that its task is but to flaunt its gilding before men, but it asks nothing from them. Whereas a woman's beauty calls for sacrifices; and she ravishes you the more, the more you give her—not by what she gives you.

So these women bathed gorgeously in their attar; and they served as living emblems of beauty, if of nothing more. Moreover, they ate only rare yet little appetizing foods, and a fishbone was enough to cause their death. Also they owned pearls which they lost time and again; nor was I indignant, for it is well that pearls should be ephemeral. Listening to the story-tellers, they would swoon with ecstasy; but forgot not, in swooning, to choose for their fall a cushion matching to perfection the color of their veils.

At times they indulged in the luxury of love. Then they would sell their pearls for the sake of some young soldier whom they paraded about the town, and in whom they thought to see the handsomest, most dazzling, manliest yet most elegant of all young men.

And, often enough, the simple youth was bemused with gratitude, thinking a great favor was bestowed on him; whereas in reality he was but the creature of their vanity, the servant of their vulgar self-display.

❧ 38

THERE CAME TO ME a woman who shrilled in my ears: "He is a scoundrel, a foul, corrupt, ignoble creature! A pox on the earth's face! A wastrel and a liar!"

"Go and wash," I bade her. "You have befouled yourself."
Another woman came, with a tale of calumny and injustice.

"Seek not," I said, "to have your deeds understood. Never will
they be understood, and therein is no injustice. For justice is ever
chasing an illusion, which contains its opposite. My captains in our
desert warfare—have you not seen how noble they are, noble and
poor and wizened with thirst? Curled up on the sand, they sleep
in the great darkness of the empire's night. Alert, of prompt avail,
and leaping to arms at the least sound. Men who have answered my
father's summons: 'Arise, all such as are ready to face death, after
bundling all their worldly wealth into a wallet slung around their
shoulders! Of prompt avail, and therewith loyal in the hour of battle, and never sparing yourselves. Arise, and I will entrust to you
the keys of the kingdom. . . .' Vigilant as archangels, these men
keep watch and ward over the empire. Nobler by far are they than
the minions of my statesmen, or my statesmen themselves. Nevertheless, when they are recalled to the capital, they take the second
place at banquets, and have to wait in anterooms; and, being truly
great, they fret at being thus humiliated, treated like underlings.
Then, 'Bitter is the lot,' they say, 'of him who is not judged by
his deserts.'

"But I make answer: 'Bitter, rather, is the lot of him who is understood and borne aloft in triumph, thanked, honored and enriched. For soon he is puffed up with vulgar self-esteem and barters
his starry nights for things that can be bought and sold. Yet hitherto
he was richer than those others, nobler and more admirable.' Why
then should he who kinged it in his solitude truckle to the opinion
of the sedentaries? The veteran carpenter finds his work's reward
in a well-planed plank. The other in the perfection of the silence
of the desert. He is bound to be forgotten once he comes back to
the city and if thereby he suffers, this is because he was not pure
enough. For this I say to you: The empire is founded on the value
of the men within it; and that soldier is a fragment of the empire,
a sharer in the great central trunk. Were it your fancy to give such
a man the privileges of the merchant and, summoning him back,

send out the merchant to the desert to replace him—wait but a few years to see what has come of your handiwork! You will find your merchant now a man of mettle, facing the desert wind on equal terms, and the other will have dwindled to a mere huckster.

"I favor men who are noble, and this my favor is 'injustice.' Wax not indignant over words. If you take those blue fish with long lacy fins out of the water and lay them on the bank, lo, they are ugly—and unjust it is they should be ugly. But yours is the fault: they were made to preen themselves in the limpid depths and their beauty dies where the shore begins. Likewise it is only where the city ends, with its traffic and its buying and selling and its vanity, that these lords of the desert have their beauty. For there is no vanity in the desert.

"Let them console themselves. If they so desire they will become kings again, for I will not cheat them of their kingdom, nor shall I spare them suffering."

Another woman came before me.

"I am a true and gentle spouse, and not ill-looking. I live for him alone, I mend his cloaks and dress his wounds. Yet, cruel that he is, he squanders all his time on a woman who flouts and despoils him!"

Whereto I made answer: "Be not thus misled as to the nature of man. Who truly knows himself? Within oneself one may advance towards the truth, yet the spirit of man is like the ascent of a great mountain. You keep the highest peak in view and often and often you fancy you are reaching it, but then you discover that yet more peaks, more ravines, more rock-walls intervene. Who indeed gauges his own thirst? Some there are who thirst after the sound of rivers and will give up their lives in pursuit of it. And some men yearn to feel a little fox cub nestling to their breast and lie in wait for one, though the foe is perilously near. That other woman you tell me of was, perhaps, bred as it were of his secret self, and thus he is responsible for her. For a man owes himself to that which he creates. He seeks her company so that she may plunder him; that she may quench his thirst. He will not be repaid by a word of love from her; but neither will he be defrauded by her insults. For there is no question of striking a balance and setting off a tender word against a taunt. He is rewarded by his sacrifice and by the word she says, whatever it be, that brings enlightenment to him. Like that man who has come back from the desert and whom no honors can requite, for the same reason that acts of ingratitude cannot cheat him of his due. For how could there be any question of acquiring or possessing, when the one thing needful for a man is to *become*— to *be* at last, and to die in the fullness of his being. Bear this in mind: ever a man's recompense is death, which launches the ship on its last voyage. And happy is he who thus puts forth to sea, with treasure freighted.

"And you," I said to her, "why shed tears? Know you not how to rejoin him?"

But it was then I understood how different is that alliance linking two together from mere good-comradeship, and sharing in common. All of them, I told myself, accost each other using a half-fledged language, which though it hardly signifies professes to convey. Wherefore you see them busy plying their scales and measuring tapes. All have logic on their side, but too much logic; they are but right and therefore are mistaken. They make dummies of each other for their shooting practice.

But true alliance unites us even though I stab you.

❧ 39

LEARN TO DISTINGUISH constraint from love. A man who swears by me and never speaks until I first have spoken interests me not at all. For I go my way seeking my light amongst my fellow men. To join in a chorus is one thing; and to compose the song another. And who co-operates in creation?

For here too is a dilemma which must be squarely faced. There is no creation unless all join and seek together; unless love has knitted the trunk of the tree into oneness. Yet this does not mean that each is subordinate to all—far otherwise. For what I have in mind is the flow of sap which regulates and builds up the branches like a temple in the sky. Herein lies the same confusion as that of the logicians who, discovering a plan in that which has been created, assume that it originated the creative act; whereas it is by means of the plan that the creation reveals itself. It is not a matter of subordinating the One to the Many, but of harnessing each to the work in progress. Thus each man compels the others to grow greater; and this, perhaps, by the very fact that they are at odds. As for me, I constrain them to create, for were they to receive all from me, they would become poor and paltry. It is I who receive all from them; and thereby they are greatened, because they have in me, whose greatness they have enhanced, an expression of their creative brotherhood. And even as I fold in my arms their flocks and herds, their seed-grain and the very walls of their dwellings, and, having made them mine, restore these things to them, as gifts of my love—even so is it with the sanctuaries they build.

But just as liberty is not license, this order is not the lack of liberty. (Of freedom I will speak anon.)

I will indite a hymn to thee, O Silence! To thee, who art the musician of the fruits, warden of deep-delved cellars, of granaries and barns. Thou art the jar of honey gleaned by the patient bees. The stillness of the great sea-spaces.

In thy embrace I fold the city viewed from the mountain-top, whenas night has stilled its rumbling wheels and clanging anvils and the tumult of its streets, and all things float becalmed in a bowl of shadows. For silence is God's cloak spread out upon man's restlessness, and in silence He steeps and soothes their fretful hearts.

I will hymn the silence of the woman who has become the pulp wherein a fruit is ripening; the silence of woman beneath the plenitude of her heavy breasts; and that silence of woman which is the silence of the day's vanities, and of life which is a sheaf of days: a sanctuary and a preparation. Silence, wherein moves from dawn to dawn and from dusk to dusk the one voyage leading somewhere, when she feels the child stirring in her womb. That silence in whose keeping I have deposited my honor and my blood.

I will hymn the silence of him who muses, gazing into the middle distance, receiving without expending, and distilling the elixir of thought. The silence that enables him to know and also not to know—for it is sometimes well for him not to know. The silence that keeps mental tares and parasites afar, and shelters the unfolding of your thoughts.

The silence of thought itself. The repose of the bees, once their honey is made and become a treasure hidden in the darkness of the honeycomb. The silence of thoughts shaping their wings in tranquillity; for any unrest of the heart or mind is evil.

Silence of the heart and silence of the senses. Silence even of the still, small voice within yourself; for it is good that you should be atoned with God, whose silence is the silence of eternity; all having been said, all done.

Silence of God, like a shepherd's sleep than which no sleep is softer, though threatened seem the lambs and ewes; when both flock and shepherd cease to be, for who can tell one from the other in the starry night, when all is at rest, and a wan glimmer of sleepbound wool?

O Lord, I pray that some day in the fullness of time, when all things created are being garnered in, thou wilt open the great door of eternity's grange to the garrulous race of men and, like a good physician healing them of their sickness, expunge all meaning from their questions.

For it has been brought home to me that man's "progress" is but a gradual discovery that his questions have no meaning. Thus when I consult my learned men, far from having found answers to last year's questions, lo, I see them smiling contentedly to themselves because the truth has come to them as the annulment of a question, not its answer.

So true it is that wisdom is not a matter of finding answers to problems, but a cure for the vagaries and imperfections of language; and this holds good even for the lovers whom I see at sundown, sitting on the low wall skirting the orange groves. Well I know that no answer has been given to the questions they asked yesterday. Indeed that is what love means: an end of questionings.

Thus, overruling seeming contradictions one by one, I make my way towards that silence wherein all questions have died away, in a bliss that passes understanding.

Ah, what ruin has been brought on men by those who cannot curb their tongues!

A fool is he who looks to God for answers. If He accepts you, if He heals you, it is by effacing your questions with his Hand, as a fever is allayed.

When comes the day, O Lord, of garnering in all that Thou hast created, open wide to us Thy portal and let us enter that good place where there will be no more answers, but only bliss, keystone of questions and supreme content. Then he who enters will discover a lake of soft water, vaster than all the seven seas together, of whose existence he had intimations in the low sound of streams, when he drew her to him on the low wall beside the orange grove, though she was but a gazelle brought to bay after long pursuit, and panting a little as he pressed her to his heart.

Silence, the haven. God's silence, haven of all wave-worn ships. . . .

❧ *40*

GOD SENT TO ME that woman who lied so daintily, so simply, with a cruelty redeemed by the sweetness of her voice. I bent towards her as towards a cool sea-wind.

"Why do you lie?" I asked.

She fell to weeping and her face was hidden by a veil of tears. And I pondered on her tears.

She is weeping, I thought, for not being believed when she lies. For though men may seem to act a part, I cannot hold this true; indeed I know not what such play-acting could signify. This woman wishes to seem other than she is; but that is by the way. Her tragedy is that she has so great a yearning to be that other woman, the woman of her dream. Thus far oftener have I seen virtue respected by those who feign it than by those who practise it, and are as virtuous as they are ugly. She who feigns, longs with all her heart to be virtuous and beloved, but lacks the ability to control herself; or, rather, lets herself be controlled by others. Thus she is always up in arms against them, and lying for her good esteem.

Arguments which make play with words are never true arguments; I will say nothing against them save that they express themselves amiss. Therefore, confronted by her lies, I held my peace; for in the silence of my love I heeded not the vain sound of the words, but only the struggle going on within her. The struggle of the snared fox to free itself. Or of the caged bird beating its wings until they bleed. And I turned towards God and said: "Why hast Thou not taught her to speak a language that conveys her meaning; for, were I to listen to her words, far from loving her, I would have her hanged. Yet there is something pitiful about her, she is bruising her wings in the dark night of her soul, and frightened is she of me as were those sand-fox cubs to which I proffered pieces of meat and which trembled, bit and snatched the meat from me so as to carry it off to their lairs."

Then, "Sire," I heard her saying to me, "they will not understand that I am pure."

True, I knew well the confusion she was creating in my house, turning it upside down. Yet I felt wounded to the quick by God's cruelty, and I prayed Him: "Help her to weep. Let her tears flow, and make her weary of herself, leaning upon my shoulder; thus she will find the lassitude she lacks."

✄ 41

DARKLING I LEFT my mountain-top and went down the slope of the new generations. Strange were their faces, and weary was I of all the words of men, nor any longer did I hear the song of their hearts in the rumble of their traffic, the clang of their anvils. Yes, I was detached from them as if I had unlearnt their language; and indifferent to a future which henceforth concerned me not. Then, pent as I was behind the thick walls of my egoism, and despairing of myself, I prayed: "O Lord, surely Thou hast withdrawn Thyself from me, and this is why I am forsaking men." And then I fell to wondering what it was in their conduct that had disappointed me.

Not that I was minded to claim anything of them. Why should I crowd my palm groves with new herds, and why add new turrets to my palace when already I was laboriously trailing my garments from room to room like a ship laboring in mid-ocean? Why feed more slaves when already seven or eight were posted in every doorway, like pillars of my house, and in the corridors I passed others who shrank back against the walls at the first rustle of my robe? Why capture yet more women when already I enfolded in my silence the women of my house, having learned no more to listen so that I might hear the better? For often I had watched them sleeping, their gaze veiled in the dark velvet of their lowered eyelids. And ever I left them to their slumber, seized with a desire to climb to my highest tower, bathed in a pure sheen of stars, and learn from God the meaning of their sleep. For in sleep all untoward things are hushed: shrill voices, earthbound thoughts, ignoble trickeries and the vanities which return to them with the light of day, when all each thinks of is to gain a tawdry advantage of another woman and supplant her in my favor. . . . Yet, did I but forget their words, all that remained was a twitter of birds at play and the soft lapse of tears.

❧ 42

THAT EVENING WHEN, leaving my mountain-top, I trod the downward slopes where every face was a stranger's and I was like a man being borne to his last rest by silent angels, I perceived the consolations of growing old. Of being an old tree, gnarled and wrinkled, burdened by many branches; of being as it were embalmed by Time, that had drawn tight the parchment of my fingers; of having become at last myself and all but immune from scathe. For when a man has thus grown old, how should a tyrant strike fear into him by the smell of torture (which is like the smell of rancid milk) or change anything within him, now that all his life lies behind, trailing after him like a tattered cloak secured by but a single thong? Thus, I mused, am I already laid by in the remembrance of men, and no recantation on my part would now have any meaning.

There befell me, too, the consolation of being at last rid of my shackles; it was as though I had bartered that old, gnarled flesh of mine for a new, winged body soaring in the invisible. And born at last from within myself, I could wander freely in the company of the archangel I had sought so long and vainly. It was as though, by discarding my shell of flesh, I had become amazingly young; yet this youthfulness was not charged with desire or zest but with a shining peace. It was the youth of those who stand on the threshold of eternity, not of those who are entering the tumult of life's dawn; and in it Space and Time were merged. I had completed life's becoming and become eternal.

Also I was like a traveller who comes on a young girl lying on the wayside, stabbed with a dagger, and lifts her up compassionately. Like an armful of cut roses she lies drooping in his arms; a flash of sudden steel has put her to sleep and she is almost smiling as she rests her pale forehead on death's winged shoulder and is carried down to the plain where are those who may haply heal her.

"Surely," the traveller thinks, "I will fulfill this sleeping loveliness with my life; for I give heed no longer to men's vanities and angers and pretensions, the gains or the misfortunes that may befall me, but I give heed only to that for which I barter myself. And when I have carried down this my burden to the healers of the plain, I shall become as it were the light of youthful eyes, the strand of hair on a pure, pale brow; and if, after she is healed, I teach her prayer, a soul made perfect will hold her proudly straight, like the stem of a flower well rooted in the soil."

I am not prisoned in this body of mine which is cracking like the bark of an old tree. As I make my slow way down the mountain side, I feel as if I were trailing after me like a vast cloak all the slopes and all the plains, star-scattered with the twinkling lights of the dwellings of my people. And like a tree I droop, weighed down by my guerdons.

My blessing on you, my sleeping people. Sleep on and may the sun be slow to call you from the gentling arms of the night. May my city have the boon of resting yet awhile before it tries its pinions, in the glimmer of daybreak, for the day's work ahead. Let those who were visited yesterday by misfortune and are now enjoying God's reprieve wait yet awhile before they bear anew the brunt of the bereavement, poverty, disease or condemnation which has stricken their lives. May they rest in God's bosom, all forgiven, welcomed all.

It is I who will protect you. For I am watching over you, my people. Sleep on. . . .

"ARE YOU NOT ASHAMED," I said to them, "of your enmities and feuds and rancors? Brandish not your fists by reason of blood shed yesterday, for though you come out of the adventure renewed, like the winged, radiant creature that tears its way through the chrysalis, or a child breaking from the womb, what will it profit you to have fought, on the pretext of what happened yesterday, in the cause of truths now voided of their substance? For, taught by experience, I liken the battle between men who rend each other's flesh to love's red ordeal. And its issue comes neither from one nor the other alone, but from both conjointly, and in it they are reconciled.

"True, the pains of childbearing must be gone through; but once these are over, comes the hour of great rejoicing. And in the newborn child they find themselves at one again. Consider how, when the shadows of night have fallen and closed your eyes, all men are alike. Even he who sleeps in prison, wearing the iron collar of a man condemned to death, is nowise different from the rest of you. All that is needful for such a man is to find himself at one again with his fellows, in love regained. I would forgive all men who have killed, for I refuse to make distinctions based on the artifices of language. This man in prison killed for love of those who are dear to him; no man stakes his life on a throw except for love. Once you know this you cease to call error whatever contradicts your truths, and to call truth the opposite of error. For know well that the same reasons which prompted you to climb your mountain, prompted him, too, your enemy, to climb *his* mountain, and he is ruled by the same motives as those which made you rise in the night; or, if not the same, by motives no less compelling.

"But all you can see in that man is what rejects the man you are. And he, too, can discern in you only what negates him. Yet each well knows that in himself he is quite other than a bleak or hostile negation; rather, the sponsor of a vision so all-compelling, so simple and so pure, that gladly would you lay down your life for it. Thus if you hate each other it is because each has formed a vain, delusive picture of the other, his seeming enemy. But I who rule you tell you it is the same vision that you both adore, though you see it dimly, through a shadow of unknowing.

"Wash, then, your hands of blood; nothing can come of slavery but slaves' revolts. Nothing comes of severity if there be no leanings towards a change of heart. And if there be natural leanings towards a change of heart, what need for severity?

"Why, then, when the opportunity arises, use your weapons? What will you gain by the taking of life when you know not who he is, the man you slay? I scorn that half-fledged faith which is shared by jailers only.

"Thus I would have you refrain from wranglings—which lead nowhere. When others reject your truths on the strength of facts averred by them, remind yourself that you, too, on the strength of facts averred by you, reject their truths, when you fall to wrangling with them. Rather, accept them. Take them by the hand and guide them. Say, 'You are right, yet let us climb the mountain together.' Then you maintain order in the world and they will draw deep breaths of eager air, looking down on the plain which they, too, have conquered.

"For nothing is gained by saying, 'There are thirty thousand dwellers in this town,' and having another reply, 'No, there are only twenty-five thousand.' For all could come to terms about a number, and one of you two would be proved wrong. Better were it for you to say, 'This town is an architect's handiwork, and built to last; a ship conveying men across the sea of Time.' And the other: 'This town is a hymn of men sharing in the same task.'

"Or it may be said, 'Fertile is that freedom which permits a man to come into his own, and encourages the contradictories on which he thrives.' Whereto another may retort: 'Freedom spells decay, but fertile is constraint, which is a driving force within, the secret of the cedar's growth.' Then lo, they fall to wrangling, even to shedding each other's blood! Yet regret not overmuch; for these are birth pangs, a wrestling with the angel within—and an appeal to God's arbitrament. Therefore say to each man, 'You are right.' For they *are* right. But lead them higher on their mountain, for the effort of climbing (which, left to themselves, they would shirk, as asking too much of their hearts and sinews)—lo, their very suffering will constrain them to it, and hearten them for the ascent! For if hawks are threatening to swoop, you fly upwards, and if you are a tree you strain to rise towards the sun. And therein your enemies co-operate with you, for in truth there is no enemy in all the world. By limiting you the enemy gives you your true form and shores you up. Freedom and constraint are two aspects of the same necessity, the necessity of being the man you are and not another. You are free to be that man, but not free to be another. You have the freedom of a language, but are not free to mix another with it. You are free within the rules of the game of dice you elect to play, but not free to spoil it by importing the rules of another game. Free to build but not to pillage or destroy your heritage by misuse of it; like the man who, writing badly, makes his effects by the liberties he takes and thus destroys his power of expression, such as it is. For when once he has destroyed the sense of style amongst men, they soon will cease to get any joy of hearing him. Thus it is when I liken my governor to a jackass, rousing laughter so long as the governor is worthy of respect and respected. But there comes a day when he is identified with the ass—and then my witticism is trite and stale.

"And all know this; for those who extol freedom insist also on obedience to the voice of conscience—the policeman within us—so that a man is always ruled by something, however 'free' he seems. Whereas those who speak for discipline assure you that it spells freedom of the mind; for in your house you are free to cross the vestibule and go from one room to another as the fancy takes you, to open doors and move up or down the stairways. And the more walls and bolts and bars your house has, the greater your freedom in it. And the more duties the hardness of your stones has imposed on you, the greater is the range of acts lying open to you, between which you can choose. But if you camp chaotically in a huge, common room, you will have not freedom but disintegration.

"When all is said and done, the city of their dreams is the same for all. Only some there are who claim for man the right of acting as he chooses; while others claim the right of molding him so that he may *be*, and become capable of action. And both are extolling the same man.

"Nevertheless both are mistaken. The former thinks of man as if he were eternal and existing in himself. Failing to understand that twenty years of teaching, of constraints and activities have founded within him the man he is and not another. And that your faculties of love come to you above all from the practice of prayer and not from any inner freedom. Thus it is with an instrument of music, if you have not learned to play it; or with a poem, if you know no language. And the latter, too, are mistaken, for they believe in the walls and not in the man; in the temple but not in the prayer. For it is only the silence latent in the stones of the temple that avails; not the stones themselves. And that same silence in the souls of men; and the souls of men wherein that silence dwells. Such is the temple before which I bow down; but those others make of the stones their idol and bow down before the stones as such.

"Thus is it with the empire. I have not made a god of the empire so that it should reduce men to servitude; nor do I sacrifice my menfolk to the empire. But I stablish the empire so as to fulfill men and inspire them with it, and for me the empire counts less than the man. It is in order to stablish men that I subordinate them to the empire; I do not subordinate men so as to stablish the empire. But I would have you refrain from that language of yours which leads nowhither; which distinguishes cause from effect, master from servant. For only interrelations, structures, reciprocities exist. I who reign am more subject to my people than any of my 'subjects' is to me. For when I go on to my terrace and, hearing their disputes and murmurings and cries of pain or shouts of joy

138

welling up through the darkness, blend all these into a hymn to God, I am acting as their servant. I am but the messenger who gathers them together and conveys them; I, the slave who bears them in their litters; I am their interpreter.

"Thus am I their keystone; it is I who hold them together and shape them into the likeness of a temple. And how could they cast this up against me? Do stones feel themselves wronged when their function is to uphold the keystone?

"But engage not in controversies on such matters, for they lead nowhere. Nor on controversies regarding men and their ways. For always you confuse effects and causes. How should men know what is coming to pass within them, when there are no words to grasp it? How could the drops of water know themselves to be a river? Yet the river flows on. Or how could each cell of a tree know itself in terms of the tree? Yet the tree grows. How should each stone be conscious of the temple? Yet the temple enshrines its silence, like a granary.

"And how could men know the purport of their deeds if they have not made, each for himself, the toilsome ascent of the mountain, so as to seek to *become* in its high silence? It may well be that God alone can know the true form of the tree. But all that men know is that one man presses to the right, another bears to the left, and each would like to kill that other who molests him and jostles him off his path—though neither knows whither he is going. Thus in tropical lands the trees war on each other, each jostling the other, filching its share of sunlight. Nevertheless the forest spreads till it covers the mountain with a close black pelt, sending forth its birds at daybreak. How, then, should the words of men's daily use grasp the infinite complexity of life?

"Every year are born word-spinners who will come and tell you that wars are 'unthinkable,' since none desires to suffer, to leave his wife and children, so as to conquer lands that he will never dwell in, or die of an enemy's hand, his belly stuffed with stones. True, if you ask any man to choose between war and peace, he will choose peace. Yet, a year later, when once again the empire takes up arms, those selfsame men who would not hear of war (since war in their crude language was 'unthinkable') will unite, guided by principles for which they have no words, in that very adventure which had seemed to them mere folly. A tree is stablishing itself, which knows itself not; and that man alone knows it for what it is who has won the gift of seership on the mountain-top.

"For that thing greater than themselves, which stablishes itself and dies after its course is run—since men are concerned therein—runs its course through men, though they have no words to express it. Nay, their very loss of hope is a token of its presence. When an empire is dying, its dissolution is heralded by the waning, in this man and that, of his faith in the empire. You would be wrong in holding him responsible for the empire's death; he but signifies the disease which is sapping its vitality. Yet how can you draw the line between effects and causes? If morals are decaying you can read signs of this in peculations by officers of state. No doubt you can behead them, yet they were but the outcome of an underlying rottenness. And you do not fight death by burying corpses.

"True, they needs must be buried, and you bury them. I prune away those that are tainted. But I eschew controversies regarding men; for these lack human dignity. Blind men taunting each other with their infirmities—such men are odious. Why should I waste my time hearing them bandy their stupid insults? When my army retreats my general blames the men, the men the general, and all alike blame the quality of the weapons with which they are supplied. The army blames the suppliers, and the suppliers blame the army. And presently they join in finding other scapegoats. But I answer: 'Being tokens of death, the dead branches must be lopped off, I agree. But it is absurd to hold them responsible for the tree's death; when the branches die, it is the tree that is dying. The dead branch was but a symptom.'

"Thus, when I see them rotting away, I lop them off without compunction; but I look beyond them. It is not individual men who are rotting away; it is Man who is rotting away in them. And I bend my gaze upon the sickness of the archangel. . . .

"Well I know that the sole remedy lies in invocation, not in explanation. Have doctors' explanations ever recalled a dead man to life? All they say is, 'This is why he died.' And true it is that the man died for some ascertainable reason—let us say, a disorder of the bowels. But his life was more than a good order of his bowels. And when you have duly arrayed your 'facts' in logical order, lo, it is like an oil-lamp that you have made, filled and trimmed, but which sheds no light unless first you light it.

"Thus you love—because you love. There is no *reason* for loving. Nor can any remedy avail that is not creative, for in the fervor of men's hearts alone will you build their unity. And then the all-compelling motive for their acts will lie in that hymn which you have taught them.

"True, tomorrow it will harden into a motive, a chain of reasoning, a dogma. For your logicians will promptly set to analysing your statue and classifying its reasons for being beautiful. And indeed, since it *is* beautiful, how should they be mistaken? Yet its beauty is something to be apprehended otherwise than by way of logic."

❧ 44

THE ONE THING THAT MATTERS is the effort. It continues, whereas the end to be attained is but an illusion of the climber, as he fares on and on from crest to crest; and once the goal is reached it has no meaning. Thus, too, there is no progress without acceptance of that which is, the Here and Now—that from which you are ever setting forth. No faith have I in repose. When a man is in an agony of indecision, caught in a dilemma, it is ill for him to seek a makeshift, precarious peace of mind by blindly choosing one of the two alternatives. What would the cedar gain by shunning the wind?

The wind rends its branches but, by the same token, stablishes it, and skillful indeed were he who could weigh the loss against the gain. You go seeking for a meaning in life, when life's lesson is, above all, man's need to fulfill himself and not to gain the spurious peace that comes of sterilizing conflicts. If something opposes you and hurts you, let it grow; for this means that you are taking root, engendering a new self, and welcome are these pangs if they enable you to bring yourself to birth. For no truth is proved, no truth achieved, by argument, and the ready-made truths men offer you are mere conveniences or drugs to make you sleep.

I scorn those who deliberately dull their wits so as to forget, or by diminishing themselves stifle an aspiration of the heart so as to live in peace. For bear in mind that every conflict of ideas without solution, every irreconcilable dilemma, forces you to wax greater so that you may absorb it within yourself. Thus with your tangled roots you clutch the earth, with its flints and loam, and build up a cedar tree to God's glory. For alone wins through to glory that pillar of the temple which has slowly shaped itself, by the wear and tear of its contact with men, through twenty generations; likewise, that you may have life more abundantly, submit yourself unflinching to the wear and tear of inner conflicts, for they lead Godwards. There is no other road. Thus it is that suffering greatens you, when you accept it.

But in the cities there are trees which the wind of the desert never buffets; and weaklings there are who cannot rise above themselves. They have aborted their true selves and make a lifelong habitation of an inn. Little care I what such men may become, or even if they live. Happiness for them is but to molder, ekeing their lives out with the sorry stores they have laid up. Such men will admit no enemies within or without themselves. As for the voice of God enjoining an endless quest, a yearning and a thirst ineffable, they shut their ears to it. They aspire not sunwards like the trees in the thick forest, ever thrusting up towards the open day that never will be theirs (for each is smothered in the shadow of the others); nevertheless valiantly they climb aloft, soaring slim and stately as pillars, transmuted into power by their ascent towards the sun whom they will never see. Thus though God is not to be attained, He proffers himself, and man builds himself up in Space, like the branches of the tree.

Wherefore I bid you mistrust the opinions of the multitude, for they force you back into yourself and hinder you from growing in stature. According to them, what is the opposite of truth must needs be error; and thus, to their thinking, your quandaries can easily be solved, since all the divers thoughts that crowd in on you in your ascent, being the fruits of error, must be summarily dismissed. They wish you to be anchored to the stores you have laid up, a self-parasite, battening on yourself, like one whose course is run. But then what would remain to spur you on to seek after God, to indite your own hymn and climb ever higher up the mountain, so as to impose order on the scene below and to preserve that inner light which cannot be acquired once for all, but is an endless striving sunwards?

Let them talk! They mean well and voice a certain kindliness which would have you, above all, happy. They would fain bestow on you before its time that peace which comes with death alone, when at last the stores which you have laid by avail you. For they were not laid by for use in life, but as honey for the winter of eternity.

Thus if you ask me, "Should I rouse that man or let him sleep on and be happy?" I would answer that happiness signifies nothing to me. "Yet," I would add, "if an Aurora Borealis kindled in the skies, would you let your friend sleep on? Surely none should sleep when such a wonder may greet his eyes. True, that friend of yours is enjoying his sleep, nay, wallowing in it; yet you would be kinder to wrench him from his happy torpor and hale him out-doors, so that he may *become.*"

FOR THE SAKE of her home the woman plunders you, and sweet indeed these are: the love that makes the fragrance of the house, the water-music of the fountain, the tinkling silver of the ewers, and the benediction of children coming home one after the other, their eyes flooded with the hush of twilight.

But seek not to contrast and appraise in the common coin of speech the splendor of the warrior battling in the desert and the happiness his love bestows. It is but a vain distinction, foisted on us by words. No greater love is there than that of the warrior steeped in the vastness of the desert spaces; nor in the forays round the wells can there be any nobler offering up of life than that of the great lover whose heart is filled with his love. Else that offering up of his life were not a sacrifice, nor gift of live. For if he who fights is not a man but a mere fighting-machine, wherein lies the greatness of the warrior? His deeds are no better than the blind lashings-out of an angry insect. And if he who caresses his woman is but a well-fed stalled beast, how can there be any greatness in his love?

I see greatness only in the warrior who gladly lays down his weapon to rock his child to sleep; in the husband and father who gladly goes to war. Here there is no question of a swinging to-and-fro, pendulum-wise, between two truths; or of something that holds good for a time and then of something else. Rather it is a matter of two truths which have meaning only when interlocked. It is as a soldier that you make love and as a lover that you make war.

Perchance that woman who has won you for her nighte, inured to the soft pleasure of your bed, speaks to you, her king of lovers, saying: "Are not my kisses sweet, is not our house cool even at high noon, are not our nights happy?" And you yeasay her with your smile. "Then," she says, "stay with me always and be all my world. When desire comes you need but stretch forth your arms and I will bend under your embrace like a young orange tree laden with its fruit. Oh, stay with me, beloved! For when you are afar you lead a brutish life that teaches no caresses and your heart's yearnings are like a sand-choked spring that has no green fields on which, flowing, to *become*."

And indeed often and often you have known, in those long, lonely nights out in the desert, a desperate craving for the woman whose picture shapes itself in your mind's eye; for all women wax more beautiful in silence. Nevertheless, the truth is that you learn the lore of love only when your love is out of reach; and the lore of the blue landscape seen from your mountain-top only when you are struggling up a rock wall on your long ascent; and you learn of God only in the exercise of prayer that remains unanswered. For the one satisfaction that time cannot wither, the one joy that never knows regret, is that which is granted you when your course is run and in the fullness of time it is given you to *be,* having finished with *becoming.*

How easy it is to be misled into pitying him who launches his appeal through the indifferent darkness and deems that time is flowing uselessly for him, robbing him of all he most desires in life! And well your heart may bleed for this thirst for love unsatisfied, if you forget that love is, in its essence, but the thirst for love—as indeed is well known to men and women weaving the pattern of a dance, who build their poem on the *approach,* though they might begin by an embrace.

But this I say to you: it is the missed opportunity that counts, and in a love that vainly yearns from behind prison bars you have perchance the love supreme. Prayer is fruitful so long as God does not answer. And it is on the flints and stones of the wilderness that love thrives.

Therefore confuse not fervor with the putting to use of stores that have been laid up. Fervor that seeks aught for itself is not fervor. Thus the fervor of the tree goes into its fruit, which gives nothing back to it in exchange. Thus, too, with me, as regards my people. My fervor flows towards the shepherds, from whom I expect nothing in return.

Therefore wrap not up yourself in a woman, seeking of her what you have already found. You can but return to her and retrieve her now and again, like the mountain dweller who sometimes comes down to the seashore.

❧ 46

Now I would speak to you again of fervor. For you will have many a reproach to overcome. Thus the woman will ever be reproaching you for what you dispense otherwhere than with her. For, to the mind of the majority, whatever is given in one place is stolen from elsewhere; it is their dealings in the marketplace and their forgetfulness of God that have thus shaped their minds. Yet, in reality, what you give does not lessen your store; far otherwise, it augments for you the riches you can distribute. Thus he who loves all men, by grace of his love of God, loves each man vastly more than he who, loving but one of them, extends merely to his partner the paltry field of himself. Even as he who, far away from his beloved, is braving the hazard of life and death gives more to her—for he gives her a man who *is*—than he who gentles her day and night, yet *is* not.

Beware of parsimony in this respect, for where the heart is in the giving, there is no question of goods that are being traded thriftily. In giving you are throwing a bridge across the chasm of your solitude.

And, when you give, stay not to discover what manner of man is he who receives. There will always be some to tell you, "This man was unworthy of your gift." As though there were any question of goods you might be squandering! That very man who could do you no service as regards gifts you might desire of him may be of service in respect of the gifts you grant him; for you are serving God through him. And well do they know this, they who feel no mawkish pity for the blains and boils of flunkeys, yet none the less will risk their lives and undertake a hundred days' march across a savage desert with the sole aim of healing a flunkey of their flunkey of a boil. They alone prove their baseness and truckle to the flunkey-dom of their flunkeys who expect of such a man some token of his gratitude; for, even did he strip himself to the bone, he would still not have enough to repay a single look of yours. But that which you have done is to make a gift to God through this man who is God's depository, and it is you who should go down on your knees for that he has deigned to accept it.

❦ *47*

How EAGERLY in my youth I awaited the coming of the beloved who was being brought to me, to be my wife, in a caravan that had set out long since, and from a land so remote that men had grown old in their long wayfaring across the desert! Have you ever seen a caravan grow old? The men whom my watchmen challenged on the frontiers of my empire had never set eyes on their homeland. For such as might have told their memories of it had died on the way and been buried, one after the other, in the sand. Thus they who came to us had but memories of the memories of others. And the songs that they had learned from their elders were but legends of legends. What miracle could be more wonderful than this land-fall of a ship that men had built and rigged far out on the high seas? Or than that young girl who landed from this desert ship, in a shrine of gold and silver; and, having learned our language, could utter the word "fountain," whereof all she knew was that once upon a time, in some golden age and happy clime, such a thing had existed. Thus she would murmur the word "fountain" like a prayer to which no answer can be given—and indeed 'tis often thus, by reason of men's memories, that you pray to God. Stranger yet was that she had learned to dance, and this dance had been taught her amongst the rocks and briars of the wilderness. Moreover, she knew well that a dance is a prayer tempered to win the hearts of kings, though in the harsh life of the desert it can hope for no response. (Thus with your prayer, so long as life is yours; it is a dance you learn to dance so as to win God's favor, when you enter his Presence.) And no less wonderful was that she brought with her all that might bestead her at her journey's end. With her young breasts, soft and warm as doves, and her smooth belly apt for giving sons to the empire, she came to us all ready, like a winged seed wafted across the ocean. So well molded and knit together, so rich was she in enchantments she had innocently woven and never put to use (as you, too, are endowed with the successive merits of your deeds and the lessons you have learnt, which will bestead you only in the hour of death, when at last you have *become*); and so little use had she made of dances apt to woo kings' favor (I speak not of her breasts and belly, which were virgin), or of fountains sweet to parched lips, or of the lore of garlands (for she had never seen a flower)—so innocent yet so *complete* was she that when at last she came to me, in her supreme perfection, she could but die. . . .

❧ 48

I HAVE SPOKEN to you of prayer which, by reason of God's silence, is an exercise of love alone. Had your prayer availed, and had you discovered God, you would have merged yourself in Him, having fulfilled yourself, and then what need were there for you to grow in stature, so as to *become*?

Thus, gazing upon that woman pent within the triple rampart of her pride, he who stood beside her sorrowed bitterly for the seeming injustice of man's estate on earth.

"O Lord," he said, "I understand tears and I await their coming, for when they fall like a gentle rain in which the menace of the storm is quenched, pride is subdued, and pardon granted. Let that woman but relax herself and weep—and I forgive. But, like a wild beast fighting tooth and claw against the injustice of Thy creation, she cannot bring herself to make an end of lies."

And again, pitying her for her great fear, he said to God, regarding men: "Thou hast struck fear into them, and struck it deep, with all the spines and teeth and claws, the venoms, barbs and thorns of Thy creation. Much time is needed for them to shake off their great fear, and to come back to Thee."

For well he knew how far away she was, that woman who lied, how dark was her perdition, and how long the road that she must travel to come back. And he pitied such unfortunates for the vast distances they have within them, measureless to man.

Some there were who wondered at his seeming indulgence for the grossest laxities. But well he knew that there was no indulgence in his heart.

"O Lord," he said, "I am not here to sit in judgment. There are times and there are men for judging, and perchance I, too, may be called on to play the judge of others. But as for that woman, I called her to me because she was afraid; not to deal harshly with her. Has one ever seen a rescuer, deeming the man who owes his life to him unworthy of it, cast him back into the sea? Nay, we save a man regardlessly, for it is not he whom we are saving, but God through him. Only when once he is saved may we take thought to punish him. Thus if a condemned man is sick, we cure him first; for it is lawful to punish a man in his body, but not to misprise the body of a man."

To such as say, "There being such slender hope of saving this woman, what prompts you to act thus?" I would reply that a civilization does not rest on the using of its inventions, but solely on the fervor that goes to the making of them. Nor do you ask a doctor to justify his care for his patient by a reference to the man's deserts. The one thing that matters is the performance of his task. For "ends" are mere appearances, landmarks strewn haphazard along a path whose issue is hidden from you. Beyond yonder mountain height is another mountain height. And beyond that individual life there is something else that you are serving, though it be but the plain bounden duty of saving life. But if you do it for the sake of gain and begin, as though a contract were involved, by asking him you save to pay you, you are a tradesman, not a man.

You can know nothing of the stages on the way, which are mere verbal distinctions; only the direction has a meaning. It is the going-towards that matters, not the destination; for all journeys end in death.

Thus in her laxity I saw but anguish and despair. For when you let all things slip through your fingers, it means that you no longer try to grasp. And laxity is but a giving-up of being. Soon you despair of acquisitions which wear out and perish, one after the other. True, the flower withers, but it becomes a seed; yet you, who believed in the flower as other than a passing phase, are filled with despair. For, mark you, the sedentary is not he who, loving a maiden, takes her to wife, then rocks the child to sleep, then shapes his manhood, and, lastly, in a ripe old age dispenses wisdom—thus faring ever forward. Sedentary is he who seeks to make of the woman an abiding place and have his joy of her as of a unique poem or a store laid by; and such an one soon learns the vanity of his hopes, for no hoard on earth is inexhaustible, and the blue landscape you glimpse from the mountain-top is but an adjunct of the triumph of your climb.

Then he puts away the woman; or else, now that her hopes are frustrate, she takes another lover. Yet the folly of their comportment was the sole cause of their failure. For there is but one way of loving, and that is loving not so much the woman herself as what lies beyond the woman. Not the poem, but what lies beyond the poem. Beyond the landscape seen from the mountain-top. Laxity comes of the anguish of having failed to *be*. Thus the man harassed by sleeplessness tosses about on his bed trying to find a coign of coolness, but hardly has he touched it than it grows warm and repels him. So he proceeds to seek elsewhere for a lasting source of coolness; but there is none, for no sooner has he touched it than its store of coolth is spent.

Thus is it with the man or woman who can see but the hollowness of their fellows, for hollow indeed they are unless they serve as casements opening on God. This is why in the common way of love you love only what eludes you; for else you soon are sated and sicken of your conquest. Well they know this, the dancing-girls who play the play of love before me.

Therefore I would fain have gathered her together, that woman who was preying on the world and feeding on thistles; for the fruit that truly nourishes lies ever beyond the individual and no being can move you once you have warmed your hands at his flame and taken the measure of what he has to give. It is at the moment when you give up hoping aught from him, and only then, that he moves your heart. Or when he is hardly more than a wraith, a lost sheep, a child unknowing; or like that poor, frightened fox cub which snaps at your finger when you feed him—and would you bear him malice for the terror and aversion that possess him? Would you take such or such a word or gesture for an affront, when so easy is it, overlooking the words and the futile meaning they convey, to perceive God beyond them?

I am the first to have a head fall when my justice has ordained this; when it is I who am reviled. But I stand too far above that poor snared fox, not indeed to forgive him (for at that lonely eminence to which I have condemned myself there is nothing to forgive), but not to hear beyond his wildering cries the voice of his sheer despair.

This is why it well may be that a woman who is perfection's self, fairer, nobler than the mean of women, may nevertheless fail to give you a nearer glimpse of God. In her there is nothing for you to solace, to bind together and reunite. And when she asks you to give your time wholly to her and immure yourself in her love, she is inviting you to that selfishness of two-in-one which in their blindness men call the light of love, though it is but a sterile blaze, a wastage of your garners. I did not lay up my stores to house them in a woman and gloat over them.

And so this woman, with all her treachery, her lies and waywardness, asked more of me, more of my heart's largesse; and by forcing me to dwell in that silence which is a token of veritable love gave me the savor of eternity. For there is a time for judging, but there is also a time for becoming. . . .

49

CONFUSE NOT love with the raptures of possession, which bring the cruellest of sufferings. For, notwithstanding the general opinion, love does not cause suffering: what causes it is the sense of ownership, which is love's opposite. Thus when my love of God sends me footsore along the highways of the world, this is above all that I may bring Him to other men. I do not make a chattel of my God; I am nourished by what He gives to others. Thereby I can recognize the man who truly loves—by his inability to be wronged. Thus the empire wrongs him not who dies for the empire. You may hear talk of the ingratitude of this man or that, but who would talk to you of the empire's ingratitude? The empire is built with your gifts, but how sordid were your stocktaking, did you reckon on the homage it might pay you! He who has given his life to the temple, bartered himself for the temple—this man has truly loved; yet in what way could he feel wronged by what the temple has got of him? True love begins when nothing is looked for in return. And if the habit of prayer is seen to be so important for teaching a man to love his fellow men, this is because no answer is given to his prayers.

Your love is based on hatred when you wrap yourself up in a certain man or woman on whom you batten as on a stock of food laid by and, like dogs snarling at each other round their trough, you fall to hating anyone who casts even a glance at your repast. You call it love, this selfish appetite. No sooner is love bestowed on you than (even as in your false friendships) you convert this free gift into servitude and bondage and, from the very moment you are loved, you begin to fancy yourself wronged. And, so as the better to enslave your victim, to flaunt your suffering. True enough, you suffer; and it is this very suffering that displeases me; how, indeed, could I admire it?

Doubtless in my young days I sometimes paced my terrace, raging under the baleful stars because some slave girl in whom I thought to see my anodyne had fled the palace. Gladly would I have led forth armies to recapture her, and to possess her I would gladly have flung provinces at her feet. But, God is my witness, I did not travesty the meaning of things; never did I name as love, even though I were ready to risk my life in it, this hunting down of my prey.

By this I recognize true friendship—that nothing can disillusion it; and likewise the quality of true love is that it cannot be wronged. Thus if someone comes to you, saying, "Put away that woman, she is doing you wrong," hear him out indulgently, but change nowise your conduct—for who has the power to wrong you? And if another says, "Put her away, for all your solicitude is wasted on her," hear him out indulgently, but change nowise your conduct—for you have chosen once for all.

And if yet another comes to you, saying, "Here you owe somewhat. There you owe nothing," or, "Here your gifts are welcomed. There they are mocked at," shut your ears to such arithmetic. To all alike will you reply: "To love me is, above all, to collaborate with me."

50

BEAR WELL in mind that your whole past was but a birth and a becoming, even as was all that has taken place in the empire up to
the present day. And if you regret anything you are as foolish as
would be one who laments his not having been born in another
country, or in another age, or of a different stature, and embitters
his life with such idle daydreams. Mad is the man who is forever
gritting his teeth against that granite block, complete and change-
less, of the past. Then take today as it is given you, and chafe not
against the irreparable. "Irreparable" indeed means nothing; it is
but the epithet of all that is bygone. And since no goal is ever attained, no cycle ever completed, no epoch ever ended (save for the
historian, who invents these divisions for your convenience), how
dare you affirm that any steps you have taken which have not yet
reached, and never will reach, their consummation, are to be regretted? For the meaning of things lies not in goods that have been
amassed and stored away—which the sedentaries consume—but in
the heat and stress of transformation, of pressing forward, and of
yearnings unassuaged. Thus the man who, defeated and under his
conqueror's heel, builds himself up anew—I would call him more
victorious, by reason of the effort he puts forth, than he who complacently enjoys the fruits of victory, like a sedentary enjoying the
goods he has laid by, and already treading the downward path to
death.

Then, you may ask me, whereto must I shape my course—since
goals are meaningless? And I would answer you by imparting that
pregnant secret, hidden under simple, common words, which I have
learned little by little in the long course of my life: to wit, that preparing the future is but stablishing the present. Those who are for
ever pursuing phantoms of the mind, bred of their imagination, do
but fritter themselves away in utopian dreams and vain conceits.

The Wisdom of the Sands

For the true use of the imagination is to decipher the present under its teeming incoherency and the anomalies of language. But if you let yourself go whoring after those will-o'-the-wisps, your idle dreams of an imagined future, you are like a man who thinks he can build newfangled temples and invent their pillars merely by giving free rein to his pen. Yet, sitting at his drawing table, how could he come to grips with his enemy, and, having no enemy to contend with, by whom could he be stablished? Against whom would he shape his pillar? The pillar stablishes itself, generation after generation, by the wear and tear of its contact with life, and though it be but a form, you do not invent it. All you can do is to polish it in an unaccustomed way. Thus are born great works and empires.

Never is there anything but the Here-and-Now to set in order. What is the good of fretting against this heritage? As for the Future, your task is not to foresee, but to enable it. And surely you have enough work to your hand when you are given the Present as your raw material. I, too, when I contemplate this assemblage of mountains and dwelling places, barley-fields and herds of sheep and goats, existing at this present moment, and I name it an empire, I make of it something that was not there before, something which I might call a single, simple entity; for anyone who touched it with the scalpel of the intellect would destroy it, before even he had known it for what it is. Thus I stablish the Present, even as the effort of my limbs when I climb the mountain crest marshals the landscape and reveals in its oneness that soft blue expanse in which, like eggs in a wild bird's nest, the towns repose—which similitude is neither truer nor falser than likening these towns under my eyes to ships or temples; but only different. And thus it lies in my power to make of man's estate a nourishment for my serenity.

Know then that all true creation is not a prejudgment of the Future, not a quest of utopian chimeras, but the apprehending of a new aspect of the Present, which is a heap of raw materials bequeathed by the Past, and it is for you neither to grumble at it nor to rejoice over it, for, like yourself, all these things merely *are*, having come to birth.

Therefore let the Future unfurl itself at leisure, like a tree putting forth its branches one by one. From one present moment to another the tree will grow, and, when its days are numbered, cease to live. Feel no qualms, then, for my empire. Now that I have fulfilled my task—that of the sculptor hewing a block of stone—and now that men have perceived that graven face in the diversity of things, I have given a new trend to their destinies by the majesty of my creation. They will advance from victory to victory, and henceforth my singers will have a brave theme for their songs, since instead of extolling dead gods they will extol life.

Observe my gardens, where the gardeners start work at daybreak so as to create springtime in them; they do not discourse of stamens and corollas, they sow the seed.

Therefore I bid you, the desolate and defeated, lift up your hearts. You are an army marching on to victory. For this very moment that is Now is your beginning, and how good is it in this dawn to be so young!

But believe not that it is an easy thing to *think the Present*. When you do this, the very raw material you must put to use resists you—whereas your speculations as to the Future meet with no resistance. Thus a man who, prone on the sand, beside a dried up well, is already parching in the furnace of the sun, can give free course to his fancies. And then how easy they seem to him, those vast strides that will bring him to deliverance, how simple it were to quench his thirst in that dream-world where sleek brown slaves bring him water galore and no briars impede! . . . But, alas, that future wherein enemies are none comes not into being; presently the death agony sets in, he grits his teeth on the burning sand, and gradually the palm grove, the great river and the women singing as they wash their garments on the banks, melt away like vapors in the sun.

But he who walks a real path, tearing his ankles on the stones, forces his way through the brambles and rasps his nails till they bleed on the rough boulders. For all these are degrees of his ascent, obstacles he must surmount one by one. As for water, slowly he is bringing it into being with his flesh, his blistered hands and the wounds on his feet. By the sheer effort of kneading together realities that conflict with each other, he draws water from the stony desert, like the baker who, kneading the dough, feels it hardening little by little, growing sinews that resist him, forming in knots that he must break—and it is thus that he begins creating bread. Thus is it with the poet or sculptor who begins by working on the poem or the stone with a freedom in which he risks to lose his way, being at liberty to make the face he is working on smile or weep, and lean this side or that; and such is his freedom that he succeeds not in *becoming*. But a moment comes when the fish bites and the line tautens. A time when you have not said what you meant to say, by reason of another word that you wish to retain and because you want to say that word also; thus you encounter a resistance, a conflict of two truths. Then you begin to erase, even as you begin molding your clay into a smile that was holding out against you. It is not that you choose one or other alternative (as the logic that concerns itself with words would have it); what you are devising is a keystone that will link together your conflicting truths, so that nothing may be lost. Thus you discern that your poem is taking form, or a face is about to emerge from the stone; for behold you are now surrounded by friendly enemies!

Therefore hearken not to those who seek to help you by bidding you renounce one or another of your aspirations. You are conscious of a driving force within you, the thrust of your vocation. If you play false to it, you are mutilating yourself; yet bear in mind that your truth will take form slowly, for it is the coming to birth of a tree and not the finding of a definition, and therein Time plays an essential part. The task before you is to rise above yourself and to scale a difficult mountain. That new thing which is an unity wrested from the world's diversity does not reveal itself to you as the solution of a puzzle, but as a quelling of dissensions, a healing of wounds. But as for its potency, you will judge of this only when it has become. This is why I have always revered—as gods too often forgotten—slowness and silence.

❧ 51

A FRIEND IS, above all, one who judges not: he of whom I have already spoken, who opens his door to the vagabond, to his crutch and the staff he deposits in a corner of the room, and does not bid him dance, so as to prove his skill in dancing. And when the wayfarer tells him how spring is breaking into flower along the roads, the friend is he who welcomes in the spring whereof this tattered man is harbinger. And if he tells of the ravages of famine in the village whence he comes, suffers with him the pangs of famine. For the friend within the man is that part of him which belongs to you and opens to you a door which never, perhaps, is opened to another. Such a friend is true, and all he says is true; and he loves you even if he hates you in other mansions of his heart. And the friend in the temple, he whom by God's grace I meet and stand beside, is one who turns towards me the same face as mine, illumined by the same God. And there we are at one, even if elsewhere he be a huckster and I a captain; or he a gardener and I a seaman. For beyond and above our differences we meet on common ground, and I am his friend. And, when we are together, I can keep silence, having nothing to fear from him for my inner gardens, my mountains and my ravines—for he will not trample them. That which you receive from me with love, my friend, is as it were an envoy from the empire within me; an envoy whom you will treat hospitably, bidding him be seated and listening to his words. And thus we shall have joy of each other. Have you ever seen me, when I give audience to an ambassador, holding him aloof, or spurning him because in the heart of the empire whence he comes, a thousand days' march from mine, they eat food that I abhor, or their manners are alien to mine? Friendship is a truce of God; a free intercourse of minds on a level far above such petty differences. When a man sits at my table, nothing exists for which I would reproach him.

Know, then, that hospitality and courtesy and friendship are meetings of the man within the man in each. Never would you see me frequenting the temple of a God who took heed of the outward aspect of His worshippers, a man's fatness or his leanness; and why frequent the house of a man who refused to countenance his guest's crutches and insisted on his dancing, so as to judge of his skill?

You will find quite enough judges scattered about the world. If need there be for molding yourself anew and toughening yourself, leave this task to your enemies; you may rely on them to see to it, like the storm that molds the cedar tree. It is for your friend to welcome you, as you are. And, likewise, be sure that when you enter His temple, God judges you no more, but receives you as His guest.

❦ 52

I MUSED ON VANITY, which has always seemed to me not a vice but an ailment. Thus with that woman whom I saw swayed by the opinion of the crowd, falsifying her voice and deportment when she knew she was observed, drawing vast satisfaction from being talked about, and glowing with pleasure when men gazed at her admiringly—in her I saw something other than mere stupidity; rather, a sickness of the soul. For how derive satisfaction from one's fellow men save by way of love and the gift of oneself to others? Nevertheless the satisfactions her vanity procured for her seemed

159

to her the best of all, for she was ready to pay for them even at the cost of forgoing other pleasures.

A scurvy joy, like that which comes of a sore—the pleasure you get from scratching where it itches! Whereas a caress is a protection and a refuge; when I fondle a child I am shielding him from the world, and he feels the sign of this ruffling the soft bloom of his cheek.

But the vain woman is—a caricature!

Of all vain persons I would say that they have ceased living. For who can barter himself for something greater than himself, when he begins by insisting on receiving? Stunted for eternity, such men will never grow to human stature.

True, when I commend one of my men-at-arms who has proved his courage, I see him greatly moved and quivering a little, as the child quivers when I fondle him. But therein is no vanity.

You, the vain, know not the gentle quivering of the flower that scatters on the wind its seeds, which will not be given back to it.

Never will you know that joy abounding of the man who bestows on the world his work, which will not be given back to him.

You will not know the fervor of the dancing-girl weaving for others the patterns of a dance, which will not be given back to her.

And thus it is with the warrior who withholds not his life. If I commend him for this, it is because he has built his bridge, and I make him understand that by his self-renunciation he has made himself at one with all men. Thus he is pleased, not with himself, but with his fellow men.

Like the woman, the vain man, too, is a caricature. Not that I extol modesty; rather, I value pride, which spells awareness of existence, and permanence. If you are modest you are ever blown about by the wind like a weathercock, since your neighbor has more weight than you.

I bid you live not by what you receive but by what you give; for that alone augments you. But this means not that you should despise what you give; you must shape your fruit, and it is pride that sponsors its permanence. Else you would change its color, savor, fragrance, as the winds list. But, for you, your fruit serves nothing; it acquires its value only if it cannot be given back to you.

I hear the voice of her who, lolling in her sumptuous litter, lives by popular applause. "I give them my beauty and my grace, the lustre of my presence. And the onlookers admire my progress, the passing of a majestic ship of destiny. Surely I need but *be,* to give."

Your gift is spurious, the fruit of vanity. For you can give only that which you transform, as the tree gives the fruits of the earth which it has transformed. The dancer gives the dance into which she has transformed her walking steps; the soldier, his blood, transformed into a temple or an empire.

But the bitch in heat is nothing—though dogs flock around her and solicit her. For she has not transformed what she gives, and her joy is stolen from the joy of creation: effortlessly she lavishes herself on those lusting dogs, her courtiers.

Likewise with him who rouses envy and sniffs its subtle fragrance —deeming himself happy if only he is envied! A caricature of giving! You see him rise to speak at banquets, bending over the guests like a tree bowed down by its fruits. But the guests get nothing of him. True, there are always some who, being yet more foolish than the man himself, imagine they are plucking fruit and feel honored by his condescension. And if that vainglorious man knows this, he fancies he has given, because the other has received. But they are like two sterile trees bending towards each other.

Vanity bespeaks a lack of pride, a truckling to the mob, ignoble humbleness. For you woo the populace so as to convince yourself your fruit is good.

Thus with him who is favored by the King's smile. "It proves he knows me," he will say complacently. But if love for the King were in his heart, he would blush and hold his peace. For that royal smile would have but one meaning for him, to wit: "The King accepts the sacrifice of my life." And then it would be as if his whole life were given and bartered for a king's majesty. "I have contributed," he might say, "to the beauty of the King, which beauty comes from his being the people's pride."

But the vainglorious man envies the King. And when the King smiles on him he struts about, a parody of royalty, wrapping that smile about him like a cloak, so that he, too, may be envied. The King has lent him his purple. Yet he is but a mummer, and his soul an ape's.

❦ 53

I FELL TO MUSING on the great example given by courtesans and their commerce with love. For if you believe in worldly goods for their own sake, you are deceived: even as there is no landscape to see from the mountain-top except in so far as you have built one up for yourself by the long effort of your ascent, thus it is with love. Nothing has meaning in itself, but the true meaning of each thing lies in its structure; thus a face carved in marble is not the sum of two ears, a nose, a chin, a mouth and so forth, but the musculature of the head comprising them. Like a fist clenched on something other than itself. And the vision of the poem lies not in the stars or the number seven or the water in a pool, but solely in the harmony I make when I set my seven stars dancing in the mirror of the pool. True, for the nexus to operate we must first have objects to be linked together. But its efficacy lies not in these separate objects. The efficacy of the fox-trap lies not in its wires or frame or any part of it, but in the interlocking of these things into a whole, which is a creative act—and presently you hear a fox howling, for he has been trapped. Thus I, the singer, the sculptor, or the dancer, can snare you in my nets.

So, too, with love. What may you hope to get of the courtesan? Only a tranquillizing of the flesh after your battles in the oases; for, asking nothing of you, she does not constrain you to *be*. But when you are all aflame to hasten to the help of your beloved, your love is charged with gratitude because the archangel sleeping in it has been roused up by you. It is not the easy access of the one that makes the difference, for if you are loved by your beloved you have but to open your arms and she will press herself to you. The difference lies in the giving. For no gift can be made the courtesan; whatever you bring her, she regards it perforce as tribute money.

And since this tribute is enforced you will question its amount. (This is the only meaning of the dance which here is danced.) Thus when at nightfall the soldier is allowed to roam the houses of ill fame and has in his pocket but his meagre pay—which he must eke out to best advantage—he bargains for love, buying it like food or drink. And even as food makes him capable of enduring another long march across the desert, so this bought love gives him an appeasement of the flesh, enabling him to endure another spell of isolation. But the man himself, having been changed into a huckster, feels no fervor.

To give to the courtesan you would need to be richer than a king; for, whatever you may bring her, she thanks herself first, flattering herself on her adroitness and admiring her skill and her beauty, which have won from you this tribute. You might pour a thousand caravan-loads of gold into that bottomless pit, and yet you would not have even begun to *give*. For there must be someone to receive.

This is why my men when dusk is gathering on the desert fall to stroking behind their ears the sand-foxes they have caught, and feel a vague thrill of love. For each has an illusion that he is *giving* to the little wild creature and experiences a rush of gratitude when trustfully it nestles to his breast. But in the district of the stews far must you seek before you find a woman who nestles to your bosom by reason of her need of you.

Nevertheless, it sometimes happens that one of my men, neither richer nor poorer than the others, treats his gold like the seeds that the tree scatters on the wind; for soldier-like he despises hoarding. Clad in the splendor of his magnanimity, he makes his progress through the stews; as the man who is about to sow his barley walks, taking long strides, towards the red loam worthy of receiving it. And then he scatters abroad his little store of wealth, having no wish to keep it to himself; and he alone knows what love is. Indeed it may be that he wakens love in one of these women, and thus a different dance is danced—a dance in which the woman receives.

But, mark my words, the man who cannot see that receiving is very different from accepting is blind indeed. Receiving is, above all, a gift, the gift of oneself, and I would not call him a miser who refuses to ruin himself with presents; the miser is one who bestows not the light of his countenance in return for your largesse. And miserly is the soil which does not clothe itself in beauty when you have strewn your seed upon it.

Thus even courtesans and drunken soldiers sometimes shed light.

⚓ 54

I FELL TO MUSING on the savor of the things men make. Thus those in a certain camp made pottery which was good to look at; and those of another camp, pottery that was ugly. And it became clear to me that no laws can be laid down for the embellishing of pottery. Neither monies spent on apprenticeship, nor awards and competitions, would avail. Indeed I even observed that craftsmen who worked for the sake of an ambition other than the excellence of their workmanship, even though they toiled night and day, never sparing themselves, ended by producing vulgar, pretentious, over-complicated work. For those sleepless nights of theirs were put to the service of their venality, their vanity or a taste for luxury—to the service of themselves, in other words—and they no longer bartered themselves, under God's guidance, for a work of art which thus became a source of sacrifice and an intimation of His presence; a work wherein their sighs and wrinkled brows and heavy eyelids and hands that trembled after daylong molding of the clay could merge into the satisfaction of a task well done, the aftermath of fervor. For I know but one act which is fertile, and that is prayer; and I know also that every act is a prayer if it be a free gift of oneself in order to *become*. Then you are like the bird that builds its nest, and the nest is warm; the bee that makes its honey, and the honey is sweet; the man who shapes his urn for love of the urn and behind that love is prayer. What belief can you have in a poem written for sale? If a poem be an article of commerce, it ceases to be a poem. And if your urn be an article of competition it ceases to be an urn and a likeness of God; rather, it is in the likeness of your vanity or your vulgar appetites.

✄ 55

THERE WAS REVEALED to me another truth concerning man: to wit, that neither his happiness, nor even self-interest, means anything to him. The only interest that stirs him to action is that of achieving permanence, of continuing. Thus the rich man's concern is ever to heap up wealth; the mariner's to sail the sea; the robber's to continue keeping stealthy watch under the stars. But as for happiness, I have seen all men flouting it without a second thought when it meant the mere absence of worries and security. Even in this murky coastal city, this sewer flowing seawards. . . .

There came a time when my father was grieved by the lot of the prostitutes who were rotting away in their stews like lumps of livid, tainted fat, and tainting likewise sojourners in the city. And he bade his men-at-arms lay hands on some few of them, as one traps insects to observe their ways. So one night a patrol tramped down the narrow streets of nighttown, between the oozing walls of those houses of decay. Here and there, in a booth from which there issued like viscous slime a smell of rancid cooked meat, the soldiers saw a woman sitting on her stool under the bleak glare of a lamp, herself forlorn and wan as a lantern in the rain, the clumsy ox-face gashed by a red smile. Like those jellyfish that spread their clinging filaments around them, these women had a way of chanting a monotonous refrain, endlessly repeated, so as to draw in the passers-by, and all along the street one heard these plaintive litanies of lust. When a man was taken by the lure the door closed hastily behind him and his desire was glutted in a room dreary beyond imagining, while for a time the litany gave place to another sound, the hurried breathing of the creature in her lair, where in sullen silence the soldier was buying from a wraith a respite from dreams of a love beyond his reach. It was to allay their ache that the man had come, haunted perchance by memories of the palm-groves and the smiling girls of his homeland. For little by little, in the course of marches and countermarches in the desert, these memories had put forth leaves and branches in his heart—until the burden of them was no longer to be borne. The music of the stream had changed to a tocsin, and the girls' smiles, the small breasts pouting beneath silken shifts, the rippling shadows of their half-glimpsed forms— all these had changed to an ever fiercer flame preying on his heart. Because of these he had come here to squander his humble pay and call upon the harlots' street to purge him of his dreams. When the door opened again he stepped forth sullen, hard and bitter, now he had tarnished his dearest treasure, whose lustre had become more than he could bear.

So my father's men-at-arms brought to him their catch of polyps, dazzled by the harsh light of the guardroom. And my father bade me observe them.

"Now I will show you," he said, "what chiefly rules our hearts."

He had them clad in new garments, and each woman was given a clean, cool house with a fountain playing in the courtyard, and, by way of work, fine laces to embroider. Moreover they were paid so lavishly that they now earned twice what they had earned before. Nor would he permit the keeping of any watch on them.

The Wisdom of the Sands

"So now," he said to me, "we see them happy, this sorry jetsam of the deep. Clean, contented, freed from fear."

Nevertheless, one after the other, they slunk back to the stews.

"For," my father said, "they missed their infelicity. Not by reason of a foolish preference for infelicity instead of happiness, but because each of us is drawn ineluctably towards that which weighs heaviest in himself. Now bright houses, dainty lacework and fresh fruits are as it were a pastime, the toys of leisured ease, and these women, being what they were, could not make their lives of them. What wonder if they soon grew weary? For light and cleanliness and needlework need a long schooling if they are to be more than a recreation, agreeable while it lasts, and to become part of life's texture, strands in a chain of obligations and requirements. Those women received, but they gave nothing. Thus it was that they missed (not because they were bitter, but despite their bitterness) those tedious hours of waiting and watching the dark rectangle of the door wherein ever and again a form loomed up, gift of the night, sullen, full of hatred. They missed that little thrill of apprehension, coursing like a subtle poison through their veins, when the soldier flung the door open and gazed on them as a man gazes at a beast marked down for slaughter, his eyes fixed on its throat. Sometimes indeed it befell that a man slashed the throat of one of them with his dagger, as one slits a waterskin, so that he might unearth her little hoard of silver hidden between bricks or under a heap of tiles.

"Also they regretted the squalid brothel room where they were wont to forgather when struck the hour appointed by authority for the bolting of their doors; and where, drinking their tea or reckoning their gains, they would hurl foul words at each other or have their fortunes read upon their tainted palms. And perhaps the fortune teller promised them a house like one of those that I provided, gay with climbing flowers and dwelt in at that time by someone worthier than herself. For the wonder of a house built with the stuff of dreams is that it shelters not one's present self but a self transformed. Thus it is with travel, which can transform you into another man. But if I coop you up in this my palace it is ever your old self that goes its ways therein, dragging with it the desires and rancors and distastes that have taken root in you; it is your old self that limps about it, if you were wont to limp—for there is no magic rune that can transform you in the twinkling of an eye. I can only, by dint of constraints and suffering, slowly make you slough your skin and teach you to *become*. But she has not sloughed her skin, the woman who, fresh from the brothel, wakes up in a bright, spotless room, and yawns, and, when there comes a knock at the door, makes a little shrinking movement, though no longer has she blows to fear; and when there follows another knock feels a wild thrill of hope, likewise bootless, since to her the after-dark brings no more gifts. Being no longer fordone by their fetid nights, these women can no longer savor the release that daybreak used to bring. Preferable may seem their present lot, but they have lost the promises, changing from night to night, their fortune tellers gave them, of a great change in store, enabling them to live in fantasy a life more wonderful than any life has ever been. And, behold, they now are ravaged by those sudden waves of passion, outcome of their sick and sordid lives, which return to them, irresistibly, ever and again; as to creatures that have long ceased to live upon the foreshore there still return, timed to the tidal ebb and flow, certain movements that seal them up upon themselves, though the sea is far away. When these fits of rage come over them these women have no longer any injustice against which they can make shrill protest; they are like the mother of a dead child, in whose breasts the milk wells up in vain.

"For true was my saying that ever a man seeks after what is weightiest in him; and not for happiness."

⚘ 56

THERE CAME TO ME a craving for my last end, and I prayed God: "Grant me that peace which dwells in garnered harvests, in things set finally in order, in folded flocks. Let me now *be,* having done with *becoming.* Weary am I of my heart's bereavements, and too old to put forth branches anew. One by one I have lost my friends and foes, and the path of melancholy pleasures that lies before me is all too clear. After long wanderings I have come back to mine own place and, when I look around me, I see all men worshipping the golden calf, not out of self-interest but out of sheer stupidity. And the young folk of today are more alien to me than young barbarians without a God. Laden am I with useless treasure, as with a music that has lost its potency for ever.

"Reveal Thyself to me, O Lord; for all things are hard to one who has lost touch with God."

After the tumult and the shouting a dream came to me by night.

For I had entered the city as a conqueror and, surging around me with a great sheen of banners, crowds greeted my progress with shouts and song, and underfoot was strewn a path of flowers for my triumph. Yet the sole feeling God sent me then was one of bitterness; meseemed I was the prisoner of a horde of weaklings.

This multitude, I told myself, for all the glory it is showering on you, leaves you utterly alone. Even those who seem most lavishly to give themselves remain aloof from you; for there is no bridging the gulf between man and man save by way of God. They alone are my true companions who bow down with me in prayer; grains of the same ear of wheat and mingled in the same measure of flour for the making of bread. But these people bowing before me in my triumph make a void within me. I cannot respect those who fuddle themselves with applause, nor accept such adoration of myself. I wave away their incense, for I refuse to judge myself by others' esti-

169

mation; rather, I am weary of myself, as of a cumbrous burden and, to enter into the House of God, I must first divest me of myself. Thus they who glorified me made me sad at heart, like a dried-up well above which men bend, seeking to quench their thirst, in vain. Since I had nothing worthy of the giving to bestow, and nothing more to receive from these men who were prostrating themselves before me.

For the man I need is one who is a casement opening on the sea, and not a mirror, gazing whereat I yawn. In all that multitude the dead alone, who no longer make ado of vanities, seemed worthy of my respect.

Then it was, wearied by the plaudits of the crowd—an empty hubbub of voices from which I had nothing more to learn—that I dreamt my dream.

A rugged, slippery path overhung the sea. A rain storm had broken and the wet darkness was flowing like a split waterskin. But ever doggedly I clomb upwards and on towards God, for I desired to ask of Him the wherefore of things and to have explained to me the issue of the bartering of myself that He had thought fit to enjoin on me.

But when I reached the summit of the great crag all I found was a huge block of black granite—which was God. Was it not thus indeed, I asked myself, that I had prefigured Him: immutable and incorruptible? For I still hoped not to be doomed to solitude.

"O Lord," I prayed, "enlighten me. For my friends, my companions and my subjects have come to seem to me like gibbering puppets which I have well in hand, moving them as the mood takes me. But it is not this obedience of theirs that grieves me, for it is good that my wisdom should enter into them. My grief is that they have diminished to reflections in my mirror, thus making me lonelier than a leper. When I laugh, they laugh; when I keep silent, they are glum. They are hollow men whom my words fill with a semblance of life, like a gust of wind swelling out the branches of a tree. Thus I am no longer bartering myself for something other than myself, for in all that teeming concourse I now hear only my

own voice, which they cast back at me like the defunctive
in a temple. What can I hope to get from a love like this, w
but a multiplication of myself?" But, gleaming darkly under the
rain, the huge block of granite remained impenetrable.

"O Lord," I said to it, seeing a black crow perched on a branch
near by, "well I understand that silence befits Thy majesty. Nevertheless, I seek a sign from Thee. When I end my prayer, bid that
crow take wing, and this will be as it were a nod from another man
than myself and I shall no longer feel alone in the world. I ask
nothing save that a sign may be given me that there is perhaps something to understand."

And I watched the crow. But it moved not. Then I bent towards
the looming blackness.

"Lord," I said, "Thou art right. It would ill befit Thy majesty
to hearken to my bidding. Had that crow taken wing I would have
been yet sadder. For such a sign was one I could have received
only from an equal—and therefore, yet again, from myself; as being but once more a reflection of my desire. Thus again would I
have been thrown back on my solitude."

Therefore, having bowed down, I retraced my steps.

But now a strange thing befell me; my despair gave place to an
unlooked-for tranquillity. Though I sank deep into the mire on
the downward path, tearing myself on brambles and buffeted by
the storm, a light serene flooded my whole being. I had learned
nothing, but there was nothing I could have learned without regret
and disillusion. True, I had had no access to God, but a God who
suffers access to Him is a God no longer. Nor if He is swayed by
prayer. And for the first time I perceived that the whole greatness
of prayer lies in the fact that no answer is vouchsafed it, and into
this exchange there enters none of the ugliness of vulgar commerce.
And that the lesson of prayer is a lesson of silence; and love begins
there only where no return may be expected. Thus love is, primarily, the practice of prayer, and prayer the practice of silence.

I came back amongst my people folding them for the first time
in the silence of my love. And thus evoking their gifts, even unto

171

death, the greatest gift of all; thus bound were they by the spell of my closed lips. For now I was their shepherd, tabernacle of their hymns and guardian of their destinies, lord of their chattels and their lives; yet poorer than they and humbler in my pride, that unbent not. Knowing well that there was nothing for me to receive from them, but in me they *became,* their hymns melting into my silence. And thus both they and I were but a single prayer, melting into God's silence.

✿ 57

BEING NEITHER lax and lukewarm nor intransigent, I refuse alike to compromise and to reject peremptorily. Thus I am ready to accept a man with all his faults, yet on occasion to display severity. I do not treat my adversary as a living symbol of the ills that befall us, a scapegoat whom it were well to burn to ashes in the market place. I accept him wholly as he is; nevertheless I have no truck with him. For clear water is an excellent thing, and so is pure wine. But their mixture is, to my mind, a drink for eunuchs.

No one in the world but is absolutely right. Save those who argufy, chop logic, demonstrate and, by dint of using an abstract language that has no content, are incapable of being either wrong or right. Their talk is but a foolish noise; nevertheless, when they wax over-proud—as too often befalls—they may cause men's blood to flow for many a long day. As for such, I merely lop them off the tree and thus am rid of them.

That man is right who submits to the destruction of his urn of flesh if this will save the treasure shrined in it. How both to befriend the weak and to fortify the strong—that is the dilemma which impales you. It well may happen that your enemy, as against you who fortify the strong, befriends the weak. Then there is no help for it; you twain must join issue, you to save your empire from the corruption of those demagogues who extol the ulcer for the ulcer's sake, and he to deliver his territory from the cruelty of the slave-drivers who, with the lash of their constraint, hinder man from becoming. Sometimes life forces these dilemmas on you with an urgency compelling a recourse to arms. For when it prospers like a plant growing alone in a fat soil, a single aim—if it has no enemy to counterbalance it—becomes a growth of lies and infests the world.

This comes about because the field of your awareness is so limited, and, even as when a highway robber waylays you you cannot simultaneously think out the tactics of the fight and feel the blows, and likewise as on the high seas you cannot at one and the same time feel the fear of shipwreck and the heaving of the billows—so that he who is appalled ceases to vomit and he who vomits forgets to feel afraid—even so (unless you be seconded by the enlightenment of a new language) it is impossible for you at one and the same time to think and to live two conflicting truths.

❧ 58

PRIMED WITH ARGUMENTS, a certain man came before my father and thought fit to harangue him.

"The happiness of men . . . ," he began.

My father cut him short.

"Utter not that word in my presence. I relish words which have living flesh in them, but I reject dead husks."

"Nevertheless," the man replied, "if you, the ruler of our empire, take no thought for men's happiness . . ."

"I take no thought," my father said, "for capturing the wind, so as to store it up; for once I hold it motionless, the wind ceases to be."

"Yet, speaking for myself," the other said, "were I the ruler of an empire, I would wish men to be happy."

"Ah," my father answered, *"now* I understand you better! *That* word does not ring hollow. I have, indeed, known happy men and unhappy men. As I have seen fat and thin men, healthy men and invalids, living men and dead. I, too, would have men happy, as I would rather have them alive than dead. Though needs must be that generations pass away."

"Why then," exclaimed the other, "we are in agreement!"

"No!" After taking thought my father added: "For when you speak of happiness, either you are speaking of a state of man, the state of being happy—like that of being in good health—and then I have no power of acting on what is a mere effluence of the senses; or else you are speaking of something tangible, which I can aspire to implement. But where, I ask you, is it to be found?

"One man is happy in peace-time, another in warfare; one man needs solitude for the uplifting of his heart, another needs the throngs of feast days; one man takes his pleasure in poring on the laws of nature (which are answers to man's questions), and another finds his joy in God (in whom all questionings cease to have a meaning).

"Did I wish to illustrate happiness with examples, I might say that the sailor's is to sail the sea, and the smith's to shape iron on his anvil, and the rich man's the getting of more wealth—but my words would have taught you nothing. But also a rich man's happiness might sometimes be to sail the sea, the blacksmith's to acquire wealth, and the sailor's to do nothing. Thus this fleshless phantom which you seek to grasp ever eludes you.

"For rightly to understand that word you must regard happiness as a reward and not an end in itself, for as such it is meaningless. Thus I can know that a certain thing is beautiful, but I cannot regard beauty as an end in itself. Have you ever heard a great sculptor saying, 'I shall wrest beauty from that block of stone'? Those who bemuse themselves with such poetic vaporings are but artists of the trumpery. Whereas you will hear the true sculptor saying, 'I am trying to draw forth from the stone the likeness of that which is prisoned in my breast, and I cannot set it free without chiselling the stone.' And whether the face that emerges be old and heavy-featured, or even misshapen, or bodies forth the grace of a young girl asleep, you will say, if it is the work of a great sculptor, that it is beautiful. For beauty, too, is not an end to be sought after, but a reward.

"Moreover, when I said that for the rich man happiness means the piling up of more wealth, I lied to you. For if we have in mind the blaze of triumph that a conquest brings, this means that his toils and struggles have been rewarded; and, if he is elated by the golden vista of the years ahead, he rejoices for the same reason that you rejoice in the landscape seen from the mountain-top, when it is built up by your long ascent.

"Likewise when I tell you that when the thief finds his happiness in the vigils he keeps under the stars, it is because there is a part of him worth saving and this part has its reward. As for the gold he covets, he covets it as a means whereby a man may be trans-figured in the twinkling of an eye into an archangel; for, vulner-able and earthbound now, he pictures him who will make his way through the thick darkness of the night, hugging a cruse of gold to his breast, as uplifted, soaring on unseen wings.

"In the silence of my love I have given much time to watching those of my people who seemed happy. And ever I learned that happiness came to them as beauty comes to the statue—by not hav-ing been sought after. And I also saw that it was a token of their perfection and the quality of their hearts. Open your house for life to the woman who can say to you, 'I feel so happy!' for the happi-ness shining on her face is a sign of her quality, since it flows from a rewarded heart.

"Ask not, then, of me, the ruler of an empire, to procure happi-ness for my people. Ask not of me, the sculptor, to roam the streets in quest of beauty—for, knowing not where to go, I would but sit down. Beauty *becomes;* and likewise happiness. Ask me only to build up souls in men, wherein these fires can burn."

❧ 59

A GREAT WEARINESS descended on me. And simpler it seemed to me to say that I was forsaken of God. I felt as though my keystone were lacking; no longer anything resounded in me; hushed was the voice that speaks in the silence of the soul. Then, having climbed to the summit of the topmost tower, I mused, "Why those stars?" and sweeping my domains with my gaze, I wondered, "Why these domains?" And, when I heard a murmurous lament welling up from the sleeping city, I asked myself: "Why that lament?"

Like a stranger in a noisy crowd speaking not his language, I felt lost, forsaken and alone. Like an undwelt-in house. For true indeed it was that I had lost my keystone, and nothing within me could serve a purpose any more. Yet surely, I told myself, I am the same man, having the same knowledge, stocked with the same memories, watching the same scene—only drowned henceforth in the futile diversity of things. Thus even the noblest fane, if there be none to view it as a whole, to bask in its silence, and to build up its significance in his heart, is a mere aggregate of stones. Thus was it with me, with my wisdom, memories, the perceptions of my senses. I was like a scattered heap of cornstalks, not a sheaf. And I knew the weariness of spirit that comes of being estranged from God.

I was not tortured—a man's predicament—but unmanned, perverted. Easily could I have grown cruel as I paced my garden languidly, like someone vainly awaiting another's coming, half alive in a makeshift universe. I prayed to God, but mine were not true prayers, for they rose not from a man but from the semblance of a man, a taper made ready but unlit. "Would that my fervor might return to me!" I sighed. For I knew that fervor comes only from that heaven-made knot which binds things together. And then it is like a ship that answers to its helm. Or a shrine seen by all. Yet what is the shrine but raw material disposed at random, if you no longer glimpse behind it the architect and sculptor?

Then it was I perceived that when a man truly comprehends the statue's smile, the temple's silence or the beauty of the landscape, it is God he is discovering. Since he then is going beyond and behind the thing itself, so as to reach the key; beyond the words, so as to hear the hymn; beyond the star-hung curtains of the night, so as to commune with eternity. For God is the supreme meaning behind men's language, and your words take meaning only when they show you God. If a little child's tears move you, they are windows opening on the vastness of the sea; for not those tears only, but the whole world's tears, are quickening your compassion, and that child is but one who takes you by the hand and shows you the sorrows of mankind.

"Why, O Lord," I prayed, "impose on me this journey through the desert of despair? I am struggling amongst thorns. Yet a sign from Thee would be enough to make the desert blossom like a rose; then the golden sand and the great open spaces and the wind sweeping the desert would be no more a jumble of incoherencies, but one vast empire wherein I lift up my heart, perceiving Thee beyond it."

And it became clear to me that God is pertinently revealed by His very absence, when He withdraws Himself. For, to the sailor, He is the significance of the sea, and to the husband love's significance. But times there are when the sailor asks himself, "Why the sea?" and the husband, "Wherefore love?" And then the world seems empty, and life a tedious tale. Nothing is lacking but that divine knot which holds things together—and then all is lacking.

If, I mused, God withdraws Himself from my people as He has withdrawn Himself from me, I shall make them like the dull, mechanic ants of the antheap, all fervor being drained out of them. Thus when the dice signify nothing, no game is possible.

Herein, I learnt, intelligence can serve you not at all. You may discourse about the order in which the stones that make the temple are arranged, but you will not touch on the essential thing that lies behind the stones. And you may discuss the lips and eyes and nose of the statue, yet you will not light on that essential thing which lies beyond them. The sculptor aimed at capturing a god, and a god must needs be taken in traps that are not of his essence.

❧ 60

THERE CAME TO ME an indefeasible desire to build up souls; and therewith a loathing for the worshippers of everyday realities. For, if you make a fetish of reality, you will find that, in the last resort, you have nothing but food to give men; and the quality of food changes little with the advance of civilization.

Thus whatever joys you get from being the governor of a province, you owe them to the structure I have built up, though this be of no immediate use to you, but serve only to uplift your heart by grace of the vision of the domain that I have planted in it. Your pleasures, too, even the gratifications of your vanity, owe nothing to material objects which, at the moment, render you no immediate service: all that delights you in them is the hue that they acquire when bathed in the radiance of my empire.

Thus with the woman whose body has been anointed daily, for fifteen years, with precious oils and perfumes; who has been schooled in poetry and grace and the silence that is as a shrine or a vale of wellsprings behind the smooth dome of her forehead— will you tell me that because another woman's body may resemble hers, the glamor she bestows on your nights is like that of the paid harlot? And if you discriminated not between them, on the pre-text that you enrich yourself by making your conquests easy (for clearly it costs less effort to shape a prostitute than to perfect a princess), in reality you would be impoverishing yourself.

It may be that you lack ability to appreciate the princess—for a poem in itself is neither a gift nor something you can amass, but a challenge to scale the heights of yourself. It may be, too, that you are not held by the grace of her gestures (there being music to which you have no access, because too great an effort would be needed on your part); nevertheless this is not because she is of no account, but because *you* do not exist.

In the silence of my love I listened to men's colloquies, I heard their voices raised in anger and I saw the flash of knife-blades. And however sordid they and their lusts might be, never did I see them stirred to passion (save when their appetite for food came into play) except by things that had a meaning vaster than the words they used conveyed. Thus the woman for whose sake you wish to kill means to you more than a mere thing of flesh and blood; she is as it were your homeland, banished from which you would feel an exile, drained of significance. And, if this befalls, lo, even the pot in which the evening tea is brewed is a reminder of your loss, for the significance it once derived from her is gone.

But if, misled by the dullness of your perception, and observing that men cherish the pot in which the evening tea is brewed, you esteem the utensil for its own sake, as something of intrinsic sanc-tity, and force men into shaping these things—then there will soon be none to esteem them, and all will be the losers. Likewise would it be if, having observed the tender charm of young children, and the reverence surrounding a childbed and the rite of motherhood, you thought fit to dissociate this aspect of life and, with a view to mere numbers, you set to building barns and stables and lodged a herd of women in them, like cattle, so that they might breed and multiply. Then, too, you would have lost for ever that very thing which you were seeking to promote; for little would it mean to you or to your people, the motherhood of stall-fed cattle.

I HEAR YOU ASKING: "Where does slavery begin, and where does it
end? Where begins, where ends, the universal? And where do the
rights of men begin?"

True, I know the rights of the temple (which is the meaning of
its stones) and those of the empire (which is the meaning of its
denizens) and those of the poem (which is the meaning of its
words). But I cannot acknowledge the "rights" of the stones as
against the temple, of the words as against the poem, of the rights
of the individual man as against the empire.

True egoism exists not; only abstention. He who goes his solitary
way, mouthing "I . . . , I . . . , I . . . !" is as it were an absentee
from the kingdom. Like a loose stone lying outside the temple, or
a word of the poem stranded high and dry, or a morsel of flesh
not forming part of a body.

"But surely," a man once said to my father, "surely we might do
away with empires and unite men in a single temple? Thus their
meaning would accrue from a temple wide as the world."

"Nay," my father answered, "this but shows your lack of understanding of the matter. For consider these stones which you begin
by seeing as forming part of an arm and drawing their meaning
from it; and those other stones which make a wing, and the others
that make a neck. Together they make an angel. Then if you gather
together the stone angels, arches and pillars, lo, you have a temple!
And then if you gather the temples together you have a Holy City
by which you set your course when faring across the desert. Dare
you say that, instead of subordinating the stones to the arms, wings
and neck of the statue as a whole, then the divers statues to the
temple, then the divers temples to the Holy City—dare you say that
you would gain anything if, instead of acting thus, you were to
start out by subordinating the stones directly to the Holy City and

thus making it a huge, uniform mass? Does not the splendor of the Holy City, which is one, emanate from the very diversity of its component parts? Does not the splendor of the pillar, which is one, emanate from the base, the shaft and the capital, which are diverse things? For the higher is the truth, the higher you must soar to discern and grasp it. Like a long slope stretching down from a highland to the sea, life is one, yet diverse on each successive level, and transmits its power, stage by stage, from Being to Being. Mark that seagoing ship, of how many different things it is compounded. As you first approach it, you perceive its sails, masts, hull, bowsprit and stempost. Then, drawing nearer, you see ropes and rigging, planks and nails. And each of these can likewise be split up into smaller parts, if you scan it closely.

"My empire has no significance or true life, nor do parades of troops presenting arms mean anything, unless these be more than a mere pageant, an array of uniformities; even as a town means nothing if it be but an array of stones laid in a certain order. But in the beginning is the home, then homes merge into a family, then families into a clan, then the clans into a province; and, finally, the provinces compose my empire. And then you see the empire full of fervor, throbbing with life from north to south and from east to west—like a ship at sea that is nourished by the wind and turns it to account on a course that never changes, though the wind often shifts and though the ship itself is an assemblage of diverse things.

"Only when this has been accomplished can you continue your task of pointing men towards the heights, and gather empires in, so as to make therewith a still vaster ship which, drawing the other ships unto itself, bears them ever onwards on a single course, nourished by winds that veer and fall and rise again, but ever heading towards the selfsame star. To unify is to bind in an ever firmer knot the diversities of sundry things, not to efface them for the sake of a symmetry leading nowhere."

❧ 62

NEVERTHELESS, herein a doubt may well assail you, for sometimes we have seen an evil tyrant trampling men underfoot; and the usurer holding them in thrall; and on occasion even the builder of temples serving not God but himself, and turning man's toil and sweat to his own advantage. And thereby men are not raised above themselves.

This happens when you set about it in the wrong manner. For it is not a question of your climbing the steep ascent and making of the stones that chance throws in your way the arms and limbs of a statue. And, after that, as chance has supplied you with your angels, arches and pillars, erecting the temple. For, following this procedure, you are at liberty to call a halt at any stage of the work that suits your fancy. It is no better to subject man to the temple than to the mere arm of the statue. For like the tyrant and the usurer neither the arm nor the temple is endowed with the faculty of merging men into itself and enriching them in return for its own enrichment.

The divers particles of earth do not amalgamate as chance has brought them together and, rising sunwards, build a tree. To create the tree, you had first to cast the seed in which it lay dormant into the earth; and the life force came from above, not from below. . . . Your pyramid has no meaning unless it culminates in God.

THIS WOMAN has but to depart, and behold everything is changed, the meaning has gone out of it! What avails the good thing you acquire today if it no longer serves to beautify the morrow? You dreamed you could employ it to grasp—and now there is nothing left to grasp! What good to you is your ewer of pure silver if it no longer serves the little rite of drinking tea together, preceding the hour of love? Of what use is the wooden flute hung on the wall if it no longer makes melody for her? What avail the palms of your hands if they serve not to clasp her sleeping face between them? Now she is gone, you feel like a shop filled with objects marked for sale—things that have been assigned no place in her and, by the same token, none in you—each with its tag, forlornly waiting to come to life.

Thus, too, with the hours of the day never more preluding a light footfall, then a sudden smile on your threshold, a smile that is the honeycake which love has made afar from you in silence, and of whose sweetness you are soon to take your fill. Hours which are no longer hours of leavetaking when needs must come̅ an absence; nor of the slumber in which you refresh your desire.

And now the temple is no more: only a huddle of stones. And you, too, are no more. Yet loth are you to abandon hope that one day she will return to that silver ewer, this deep-piled carpet, and once more give a meaning to the morning, midday, evening hours, to your triumphs and your toils, and once again make of you a man who is near her or afar, approaching or departing, losing or regaining something. For now that she serves no longer as a keystone, your life is emptied of concern; you neither draw near or recede, neither lose nor regain anything whatever in the world.

For when you imagine you are in touch with things, grasp or desire them, hope for or relinquish them, shatter or broadcast them, conquer or possess them, you are deluded; for you can neither grasp nor keep, neither lose nor retrieve, neither hope for nor desire anything other than the light that is imparted to them by their sun. Between things-in-themselves and you there is a gulf impassable; the only bridge is between you and those aspects of things which are unseen visages emanating from God, from the empire, or from love. Thus when I see you embarking as a sailor on a long voyage overseas, I know this is by reason of a face that consecrates your absence for you and of the prospect of that radiant voyage of return whose spell the old travellers' tales, with their lore of magic islands and pink coral reefs lost in a southern sea, have cast on your imagination. For in your fancy those old songs of golden galleons mingle with the song of the waves, even though the days of galleons are no more; and those coral reefs, though never your sails waft you thither, lend their effulgence to the evening glow spreading across the sea. And, though never shipwreck befalls you, all the old wrecks of which you have heard tell add to the waves' lament along the cliffs, dirges for the unburied dead. Else what could you do but yawn as you tug at the stiff ropes, instead of nourishing your heart with visions vast as the sea. For nothing matters that is not primarily a vision, a civilization, a temple built for your heart's contentment.

This is why prison walls cannot confine him who loves, for he belongs to an empire that is not of this world, being made not of material things but of the meaning of things; and thus he mocks at walls. Even though you build them thick as the walls of strongholds, and though he knows she is sleeping, dead to the outside world and for the moment unavailing for him, nevertheless in the secret places of his heart she nourishes him. And no man-made thing can sunder them.

Thus is it with all visions emanating from the divine knot which binds things together. For if the woman of whom you are deprived is one whom you desire but in the flesh and memories of whose body only haunt your sleepless nights, you will be no better off than your dog if he tries to devour a pictured piece of meat. For the god who, being of the spirit, can pass through walls has not been born within you. But already have I told you of that man who is lord of a domain and walks forth in the dews of daybreak. At that moment he is not making use of anything in his domain, and can see nothing but the sunken road in which he is walking. Nevertheless he is no ordinary man, and there is greatness in his heart. Thus, too, is it with my sentinel, who is in touch with nothing of the empire he serves save the sentry path he paces hour after hour, a ribbon of granite glimmering in the starlight. Whose lot could seem more wretched, pent as he is in a narrow prison a hundred paces long, and in constant peril of death? Bowed down by heavy weapons, visited with imprisonment if he sits down even for a moment, and with death if he falls asleep; drenched by rain, numbed by frost, or burnt by the sand-wind—and having nothing to look forward to, save, this night or another night, the flash of a gun in the shadows and a bullet through his heart. What lot indeed could seem more abject? What beggar is not more favored, being free to go where he lists, to gaze his fill at the crowd and to mingle with it in the marketplace, and to take what amusement comes his way?

Nevertheless my sentinel is part of the empire. The empire sustains him and in him is a vastness that the beggar lacks. His very death will be profitable, because thereby he barters himself for the empire.

I send out my prisoners to break stones. And the stones they break are void of meaning. But if you are building your house, is it not quite otherwise with the stones you break? You are setting up a wall, and your gestures bespeak not a punishment but a hymn.

A change of perspective is all that is needed for the understanding of these matters. True, you deem a man enriched if, when at the point of death, his life is saved and he goes on living. Yet, were you to move to another mountain-top and thence observe his life's task fulfilled and bound together like a sheaf, it well might be that you would judge him the happier for a death that had a meaning.

Thus, too, with those whom I took prisoner on the eve of battle so that they might disclose my enemy's plans. "I am a man of my own land," one of them answered me, "and your torturers cannot prevail against this." And I could have crushed him between mill-stones without extracting the oil of his secret, for he belonged to his empire.

"You are a poor man," I told him, "and at my mercy."

He laughed at my word "poor," for he possessed something I could never wrest from him.

Herein lies the significance of that training of the mind which makes the man. For your true riches are not material things which are of service only when you are putting them to use—as with your ass when you are riding it, or your dishes when you are eating off them—and have no significance when they are laid aside. Or when you are separated from them by the force of things—as with a woman whom you merely lust after, but love not. True it is that the animal has access only to material things, and not to the nuances they emanate by way of language. But, being a man you are nourished by the meanings of things and not by the things themselves.

Therefore I build you up and shape you, showing you in the stone that which is not stone but the sculptor's inspiration, the majesty of a dead warrior. And thus you are the richer because somewhere there exists that warrior hewn in stone. Thus too, in creating a domain with my sheep and goats, dwellings and mountains, I am building on your behalf. And though nothing therein may be of immediate service to you, nevertheless it completes your being. I take common words and, weaving them into the poem, enrich you with them. I take mountains and rivers and, binding them together in my empire, exalt you with them. And on days of victory even the prisoners in their prisons, the dying on their truckle-beds, the debtors beset by bailiffs—lo, all are aglow with pride, since there is no hospital nor prison which can hinder you from receiving; from all these diverse raw materials I have drawn forth a god who laughs at walls and triumphs over suffering.

That is why I build Man up and, breaking down walls and wrenching out prison bars, I set him free. For I have brought into

186

being one who communes, and mocks at jailers and dungeons; nay, even at the torturer's red irons, which cannot break his spirit.

For clear it is that you do not commune directly one with the other; but each of you communes with the empire, which indeed means something different to each of you. Thus, if you ask me how to reach her whom you love, when sundered from her by walls or seas or death, I answer that useless it is to cry out for her presence; it is enough for you to cherish that from which no wall can cut you off—the picture in your mind of the house, of the tray with a tea-urn on it and the deep-piled carpet, whose keystone is the beloved one sleeping afar from you; inasmuch as your love for her abides though she is absent and asleep.

Wherefore I say that your chief aim in the building up of Man is not to give him learning, which serves no end if he be but a walking book, but to lift his eyes and point him to those higher levels on which there are no more things-in-themselves, but only aspects of that divine bond which binds things together. For material things have nothing to give you unless, reverberating on each other, they yield the only music that can touch the heart.

Thus, too, with your work, whether it be the getting of bread for the children or bartering yourself for what is vaster than yourself. Thus, too, with your love, if it be some other loftier thing than the quest of a body to embrace; for the joy you have of loving is immanent in love itself.

Wherefore I will speak first of the *quality* of woman. When, after long wandering in the desert, you come to the city and visit the street of brothels and choose a certain woman so as, in her, to forget love; and when you fondle her and hear her murmuring soft words in your ear—however great her beauty, once love's act has been accomplished, you depart divested of yourself and without having shaped a memory to treasure.

Yet, if by some miracle it happened that under the very same appearance, using the same words and gestures, she were that island-born princess who, after journeying in many a slow-moving caravan across the wilderness, and having been steeped for fifteen years in music, poems and wisdom, has become like finely tempered steel, aglow with anger at the least affront and with resolution in the hour of peril, rich with the treasure of herself that none can take from her, and dedicate to gods whom for nothing in the world would she abjure; ready to proffer her young grace to the headsman's axe if bidden pronounce but one word that she would disdain to utter, and so noble in her bearing that her last steps would be more moving to behold than the gracefullest of dances—if by some happy chance it were she who opened her young arms to you, when you entered the moonlit hall paved with gleaming flagstones where she awaited you, and said the very same words as that other woman, which coming from her would voice a perfect soul, then be assured that at daybreak you would go back to the wilderness with its sand and thorn bushes, not the same man, but a hymn of thanksgiving incarnate. For it is not the man we see, with his sorry husk of flesh and his farrago of ideas, who weighs in the scale of things; it is his soul, more or less vast as may be, with its climates and its mountain ranges, its oases of silence, its flowery slopes and melting snows and slumbrous pools—that territory unseen yet boundless wherein he proves his seigniory. From this secret source you draw your happiness, and once you know this there is no more turning from your course. For your navigation on a shallow river—even if you close your eyes and, letting its wavelets rock your boat, you picture vastness—is not the same as a voyage across the fathomless sea. Nor, though they may look alike, do you get the same pleasure from a false as from a real diamond. And the woman who merely holds her peace in your presence is not the same as she whose silence is deep as the sea. Nor can you fail to perceive this.

Therefore I refuse to lighten your task and, because women are a sweet pasture for your body, to make it easier for you to capture them, by withdrawing from them the woman's apanage: aloofness and nobility. For in so doing I would be destroying the very things which you aspire to capture.

Thus, in your commerce with whores, all you will ever get of them is a brief forgetfulness of love in their embraces. Whereas the only act I sponsor is one which enriches for you the act that is to follow and incites you to persevere in your climbing of the mountain, thus training you for the conquest of another, still loftier peak; wherefore, that you may stablish and perfect your love, I would have you ever aspiring to scale a soul cloud-girt and inaccessible.

✖ 64

A DIAMOND is the fruit of a people's sweat; yet the diamond that a people's sweat has brought forth is neither divisible nor consumable, nor of any service to those who toiled for it. Should I then forgo the capture of that earthborn star, the diamond? As well ask me to abolish my workers in the goldsmiths' street, who carve golden ewers (which, like the diamond, are indivisible) because each ewer absorbs a man's life and, while the man is carving it, I must feed him on wheat grown elsewhere; and because, if I send him to work the land, instead, though there will be no golden ewer, there will be more wheat to share amongst my people. But will you, on these grounds, maintain that it were better for man's dignity never to wean the diamond from the earth and nevermore to shape gracious forms in gold? Wherein would man be the better off thereby? And what care I about the use to which the diamond is put? So as to humor the jealousy of the multitude I might, if needs were, consent to burn once a year all the diamonds I had harvested, and make that day a public festival. Or I might well appoint a "queen" whom I would clothe in their effulgence—and then my people would have a bediamonded queen. Thus all would share in her brilliance or the merrymakings of a festival. How indeed would they be the richer if these precious stones were buried in a museum, where likewise they did service to none save some idle loiterers, and ennobled but some vulgar, dull-witted attendant?

For it cannot be denied that those things have value which cost men time and toil (as does the temple). And that the glory of my empire, in which each man participates, comes from the diamonds I have them delve for and from the queen whom I bedeck with them.

❧ 65

I KNOW BUT ONE freedom and that is the freedom of the mind. As for any other freedom, it is but a mockery and a delusion, for however free you may think yourself, you have to use the door when you go out of the room, nor are you free to make yourself young at will or to profit by the sun at night. Yet if I oblige you to use one door and not the other, when there are two, you will complain of my high-handedness, forgetting that, were there one door only, you would undergo the same constraint. Likewise if I deny you the right to wed a certain woman whose beauty has caught your fancy, you will denounce my "tyranny," having failed to notice (because you have never seen one otherwise) that every woman in your village squints.

But when you wed her who is as I have constrained her to become and when for you, too, I have shaped a soul on my anvil— then both of you will enjoy the only freedom which has a meaning, that which is an activity of the mind and soul.

For license whittles you down to nothingness, and, as was wont to say my father: "Not-being is not freedom."

Well I remember how when my dead father had become as it were a mountain looming on the horizon of men's minds, our logicians, historians and pundits, bloated with the windy words he had thrust back down their throats, reared their heads again and trumpeted their marvellous discovery—that man is beautiful.

And beautiful he was—because my father had built him thus.

"Since man is so beautiful," they argued, "we must liberate him. Then he will blossom forth in happy freedom, and all he does be wonderful. But, as things are, we are frustrating his splendor."

Thus I, when I walk in the cool of the evening in my orange groves, whose trunks are trained to straightness and the branches pruned, might likewise say: "How beautiful are my orange trees, how rife with fruit! Why, then, have lopped off those branches which also would have borne fruit? Were it not better to leave the tree its liberty. Then it would blossom forth in happy freedom. But, as things are, we are frustrating its splendor."

They had their way and set man free. And straight as a tree he held himself, for he had been pruned and trained to straightness. And when came the police officers seeking to control him, not from respect for that mold which once broken cannot be replaced, but from a mere lust for domination, those whose splendor was frustrated broke into revolt. Like a flame their ardour for freedom swept ahead, till the whole land was ablaze. The freedom they sought was the freedom to have beauty and, in dying for freedom, they died for their beauty, and beautiful were they in death. And the voice of freedom rang clearer, purer, than a bugle call.

But I remembered my father's words: "Such freedom is the freedom of not-being."

For in the process of time they lapsed into a mere rabble; since if you decide for yourself and your neighbor does likewise, his acts and yours cancel out and come to nothing. Thus if many people take a hand in painting a certain thing, each according to his taste, one daubs red, another blue, another yellow, and so on—till in the end the thing painted is a dingy grey. If, after a procession has formed up, each man goes the way his fancy chooses, all are as dust before a wind of folly and the procession breaks in pieces. If you split up your power and share it out, far from augmenting the power, you lay it waste. And if each man chooses the site of the temple for himself, and places his stone wherever he thinks fit, you will never see a temple, only a huddle of stones. For creation requires oneness; your tree is the uprush of one seed alone. And truly you may call the tree "unjust," for other seeds have been frustrated by it.

True, power, if it comes but of a lust for dominance, is, to my mind, a fool's ambition. But I praise that power which, wielded by a creator, sponsors a creative act and goes against those natural inclinations which tend to mix things in a formless mass, causing the glacier to melt into stagnant ponds, temples to crumble into dust, the fires of noon to lapse into a tepid warmth, the message of a book to grow dim as the pages fall apart with use, languages to lose their purity and degenerate, efforts to tell against each other, and every structure issuing from that divine knot which holds things together to disintegrate into a mass of incoherencies. True power is like the cedar tree which draws its nurture from the stony waste and, delving in barren, thankless soil, traps the sunlight in its branches, and in the eternal sameness of the desert, wherein all is shared out and slowly levelled down, rears up its "injustice," transcending stones and rocks, building a green temple in the sunlight, singing harp-like in the breeze, restoring movement to the moveless. For all life is a building-up, a line of force—and injustice. Thus, if you see a group of children growing listless, you need but impose on them constraints—the rules of a game—and presently you will see them playing merrily together.

Thus came a time when, there being no more new goods to be had, freedom meant but a sharing out of stocks amassed, in an equality shot through with hatred. For when you exercise your freedom you hamper your neighbor and he hampers you. And when repose is achieved it is but the repose of marbles when they have ceased rolling. Thus freedom leads to equality, and equality to stagnation—which is death. Were it not better for you to be ruled by life; to endure the lines of force of the growing tree, like so many obstacles to overcome in a day's march. The only constraint which cramps you, and needs must you resent, stems from your neighbor's malice, your equal's jealousy, and an equality like that of animals. And these will engulf you in a morass of not-being; yet so foolish are the words men use that, if your life goes to the rhythm of a growing tree, they speak of "tyranny."

Thus came a time when man's freedom meant no more his right to grow in beauty, but an expression of the multitude into which man had been absorbed perforce—and the multitude is never free, since it has no directive movement, but merely holds its ground, like a dead weight. None the less this right to stagnate was called freedom; and justice, this stagnation.

But, as time went by, that very word "freedom," though it still aped the sound of a bugle call, lost its appeal; for men began dreaming, dimly albeit, of another bugle call summoning them to wake and set to building.

For that call alone has beauty which summons you from sleep.

The only discipline that is worth while is one which subjects you to the temple, according to your relative significance; for the stones are not free to place themselves as they think fit—else there is nothing to which they give themselves, nothing whence they derive significance. Its function is to make you obey the bugle call when it rouses up within you something greater than yourself. They who died for freedom, when it was an aspect of themselves yet greater than themselves, giving an outlet to the beauty immanent within them, these men gladly submitted to that beauty's bidding and to the disciplines imposed on them. Thus when at night the bugle shrilled, they were not free to go on sleeping or fondling their wives, for they were *governed;* and little reck I, since constraint there must be, whether it came from within them or from without.

For, if it came from within, I knew that it must have come from outside them, to begin with; even as you owe your sense of honor to your father, who trained the child you were to obey its rules.

Though by discipline or constraint I mean the opposite of licence (which is a kind of cheating), I seek not to enforce it by way of

193

pains and penalties; for, walking amongst my people in the silence of my love, I have seen the children of whom I spoke obeying the rules of their game and blushing for shame if they cheated. For they knew the visage of the game (and by "visage" I mean what emanates from the game, its aura). To its shaping go their fervor, the joy of solving problems and the glad temerity of youth—and all these things have a special savor deriving from the game alone and, as it were, a certain god presiding over it, who thus makes them *become*. But if it happens that, though proficient at the game, you take to cheating, you will soon find that you have lost those very things which held your interest in it—your excellence and probity and skill. Thus the love of a visage acts on you as a constraint.

For all that the rigors of the law can do is to make you resemble your neighbor. How indeed could the policeman look beyond this? Order for him is the order of the museum, where all is neatly ranged and docketed. But I do not base the empire on your being like your neighbor, but on the merging of your neighbor and yourself into a unity which is the empire.

Thus my constraint is a rite of love.

✼ 66

IF YOUR LOVE has no hope of being welcomed do not voice it; for if it be silent it can endure, a guarded flame, within you. It gives you a direction in the maze of the world, and you are augmented by being given your bearings, when these enable you to approach and to retreat, to enter and go out, to find and to lose. For your function is to live, and there can be no life unless some god has established lines of force for you.

If your love is not returned and—sad reward for your fidelity!— it becomes but vain entreaties because you lack the strength of mind to keep it secret, then, if there be a doctor, have yourself cured. For love must not be confounded with a bondage of the heart, and while a love that pleads its cause has beauty, love that entreats is beggarly.

When the outside world sets up a barrier against your love—drastic as a monastery wall or the ban of exile—then thank God if she loves you in return, even though you have neither sight nor sound of her. For love has lit a candle for you in the dark forest of the world. And little matter that you put it to no immediate use; he who dies in the desert possesses his dear home none the less for being far away from it.

It may seem that when I build up great souls and, choosing the most perfect of them, set walls of silence round it, none is the gainer. Nevertheless it ennobles my whole empire. And whoever passes makes obeisance; and born are signs and wonders.

Thus if there be love for you, though distance makes it unavailing, and love on your part in return, you walk in light. For prayer that has but silence for its answer is strong to save, if so be that the god to whom you pray exists. But if your love is accepted and her arms open to welcome you, then pray God to save your love from over-ripeness and decay; for I fear for hearts that have their uttermost desire.

✤ 67

I TRUST NOT HIM who tends to judge from a set point of view; as I mistrust him who, being the ambassador of a worthy cause, lets it master his discretion and puts himself in blinkers.

When I speak with him, my task is to awaken the man within. But I am wary of his approaches. They are full of sleights and stratagems and he seizes on my truths only to twist them to the service of his empire. Yet why should I reproach him for so doing, when the great cause he is defending invests him with its greatness?

Whereas the man who hears me out and with whom I can converse on an equal footing, and who does not seize on my truth merely to make it his and use it against me when this serves his purpose—such a man I might call thoroughly enlightened. Yet this is all too often because he neither works nor acts; neither struggles nor solves problems. Like a lamp pinkly gleaming in a garden as a mere adornment, such a man may well be the finest flower of an empire, yet sterile for being too pure.

Herein lies indeed the problem of my relations and my converse with others; of bridging the gulf between that ambassador of a cause other than mine, and myself. And of the meaning of the language we use.

For there is no true converse between men save by way of the god who is revealed to them, their mediator; even as I can communicate with my soldier only by way of the vision of the empire, which has meaning for us both. And as the lover can communicate across distances and walls with her alone who is the woman of his house and whom it is his to love though she be afar and sleeping. Likewise as concerns the ambassador who comes to me from a foreign land to voice his cause; if we aspire to match our wits against each other on a higher level than a game of chess—on that level where subterfuge is ruled out and on which, even if we join fierce issue, we esteem each other and breathe freely in each other's presence (as it was with that king who reigned beyond my eastern marches, my well-loved enemy)—if I aspire to meet the foreign ambassador on this level, I can do so only by conjuring up a new vision which will be our common measure.

Thus, if he believes in God as I do, and subjects his people to God as I do mine, we can meet on common ground in that tent of truce pitched far out in the desert, and while our armies kneel apart, commune in God and pray together. But if you have no God whose sovereignty you both acknowledge, no hope is there of communing, for the same raw materials have different meanings in his vision of the world and yours; even as according to the architect's vision different temples rise from stones that are alike. How indeed could you impart your meaning when victory for you is his defeat and, for him, your defeat spells victory.

68

THEY PESTERED my father with their self-importance.

"We and we alone should hold the reins of power. For we alone know the truth."

Thus said the spokesman of the geometers of my father's empire.

"So you know the truth?" my father answered. "You mean, the truth of the geometers?"

"What then? Is it not the truth?"

"No," replied my father.

When these men had left him, "They know," my father said to me, "the truth of their triangles. As others know the truth of bread—that if you knead too feebly it will not rise. Or if your oven is too hot, it burns; or, if too cold, the bread is sodden. Yet though our bakers know their craft well and make bread whose crispness is a pleasure to our teeth, they do not come to me and ask to be made rulers of the empire."

"Perhaps," I answered, "that holds good for the spokesmen of the geometers. But what of our historians and pundits? They have explained the ways of men. Surely they know what man is."

"Personally," my father said with a smile, "I would entrust the government of the empire to him alone who believes in the devil. For so many ages have gone to perfecting him that by now he certainly is skilled in unravelling the tangled ways of men. But obviously the devil can give us no help at all in explaining relations between lines, nor do I expect my geometers to locate him in their triangles. Thus nothing in their triangles can help them to direct the ways of men."

"Your words are dark," I said to my father. "Do you then really believe in the devil?"

"No," my father answered. "Yet what do we really mean by that word 'believe'? If I 'believe' that summer makes the barley ripen, I say nothing pregnant or open to discussion, for I have begun by giving the name 'summer' to the season when the barley ripens. And similarly with the other seasons. But if I ascertain such seasonable relations as, for example, that deriving from my knowledge that the barley ripens before the oats, I can believe in these relations since they *are*. But the objects brought into relation mean very little to me; I use them but as a net to snare a prey."

Furthermore my father said: "In these matters it is as with the statue. Think you that the sculptor making it seeks merely to reproduce a nose, a mouth, a chin and so forth? Nay, what he seeks is a correlation between these separate things, a correlation which will (for example) spell grief. And one which, moreover, it is possible to convey to you, for you enter into communication not with things but with the knots binding them together.

"A savage thinks that the sound is *in* the drum. And so he worships the drum. Another thinks the sound is in the drumsticks, and reveres the drumsticks. Yet another that the sound lies in the might of his arms, and you may see him strutting proudly, holding up his arms for all to admire. But you know better; you know the sound is not in the drum, nor in the drumsticks, nor in the man's arms; what you call the 'truth' in this respect is the drumming of the drummer, no more and no less.

"Therefore will I not deliver the reins of power within my empire to the spokesmen of the geometers who revere, as if it were an idol, what has served to build, and because a temple uplifts their hearts, worship its stones. Soon would I see them using the 'truths' that hold good for their triangles for the governing of men."

But I felt sad at heart.

"So there is no truth?" I said.

198

My father smiled.

"Could you succeed in telling me in good set terms to which desire of the mind athirst for knowledge an answer is denied, I too would lament the infirmity which hinders us from knowing. But I perceive not what it is that you would have one grasp. For one who reads a love letter his cup of happiness is full, no matter what the paper or the ink employed; for it is not in the paper or the ink that he discovers love's message."

69

THUS I PERCEIVED that, misled by the illusions of their speech and having observed that taking a thing to pieces may further knowledge and having learned the devastating efficacy of this procedure, men laid waste their inheritance. For what is true of the material world (though even there not wholly true) is false as regards the mind. Thus you, being a man, are so built that all things are dead and void for you unless they pertain to a spiritual kingdom; and likewise, however crass and slow-witted you may be, you deem a thing more beautiful than others and desire it only in virtue of the meaning that it has for you. Gold, for example, you desire because it is pregnant with unseen treasures; and when your wife desires a gold ornament, it is not so that she may cumber her tresses with it but because this ornament, being consecrated by use and wont, and in men's eyes esteemed, vouches for an hierarchy, conveys an unspoken message and is a token of supremacy.

Thus was revealed to me the one and only wellspring where mind and heart can drink. The only nourishment that meets your need and the only heritage worth saving. And likewise I saw that where you have laid waste you must rebuild. But now, lo, you are in the midst of your ruins, dispersed at random, and though the animal in you is glutted, the man within is starved, though he knows not what it is he hungers for. For man is so built that his appetite is the outcome of the food he eats and thus, if a part of you is always undernourished and half asleep for lack of a certain kind of food or exercise, you never think to ask for that food or exercise.

Therefore, unless someone comes down from his mountain-top and enlightens you, never will you know which path of the divers paths before you leads to your salvation. Even as you will never believe, however learned may be the arguments advanced, in the man who can and will be born of you, or awaken within you, since he has not yet come into being.

Therefore my compulsion is as the might implicit in the tree, thrusting it up to freedom from the stony ground that is its womb.

✼ 70

THUS WAS IT when I found my sentry sleeping at his post.

That such an one should be punished with death is but fitting. For so much hangs on his wakefulness: the safety of so many men whose breathing has the slow cadences of sleep while life replenishes them, pulsing in their bosoms like the throbbing of the far-off sea in the recesses of a landlocked creek. And the safety of closed temples full of sacramental treasure slowly gathered in like honey, to the making of which have gone men's sweat and hammerings and chisellings; and of precious stones unearthed, and the toil of eyes worn out with long poring over needles as they make the cloth-of-gold blossom with flowers, and delicate devices wrought by devoted hands. And granaries so well stored that none dreads winter's durance. And sacred books which are the granaries of wisdom and the handsel of man's best. And the sick whose last end I make so peaceful according to the ancient customs of their kind that they hardly see the darkness fall, for it is but a passing-on of the heritage from hand to hand.

Sentinel, my sentinel, you are the very meaning of the ramparts enwrapping like a sheath the city's frail body lest it should pour forth its life; for when a breach is made, drained is its lifeblood. To and fro you pace, straining your ears to catch the least sound from the desert which is mustering its forces, and you feel its unseen menace breaking on you like billows, pounding you and hardening you withal. For there is no distinction between that which ravages and that which stablishes you; it is the selfsame wind that carves the dunes and rubs them out; the same waves that shape the cliff and crumble it; the same constraints that shape your soul or deaden it; the same toil that makes you live and hinders you from living; the same love fulfilled that crowns your cup and drains it. Thus your enemy serves as your mold, forcing you to take form within your ramparts; even as we may say of the sea both that it is the enemy of the ship—since it is always seeking to engulf it and the ship's whole life is one long struggle with the sea—and also that the sea is the wall and mold and shaper of the ship; since, through countless generations, it is the prow's cleavage of the waves that has been tapering the hull, which has become ever more graceful so as to glide more smoothly in its element, and thus the sea has stablished and beautified the ship. Thus, too, we may say it is the wind, which rends the sails, that has designed them, as it designed the wing—and that, lacking enemies, you can have no form or just proportion.

But what would the ramparts be, were there no sentry?

That is why this man's sleep lays the city naked to her enemies; and why, when he is found sleeping, he is haled away and drowned in his own sleep. . . .

But when I gazed more nearly at him I saw that his face was like a child's as he lay there, his head resting on a stone slab and his lips a little parted. And he was still hugging his rifle to his side, like the plaything that a child takes with him to his dreamland.

And gazing at the young face, I pitied him; for I have pity in these fiery nights of the desert for men's lapses.

When sleep the sentinels, 'tis the barbarian at the gate who strews their eyes with dreams. Then are they vanquished by the desert, leaving the gates free to turn noiselessly on their well-oiled hinges, so that the city may be fecundated when she has become exhausted and needs the barbarian.

Sleeping sentry, you are the enemy's advance guard. Already you are conquered, for your sleep comes of your belonging to the city no more, and being no longer firmly knotted to the city, but waiting for new life to enter and laying yourself open to the sower of new seed.

Thus a vision rose before me of the city undone all because of one young soldier's sleep, *your* sleep, my sentinel; for it is you who bind all together, or unbind, within yourself. How fair to see you are, my sentinel, when you keep faithful watch—my city's eye and ear! And how noble is your understanding, by far outdoing with your simple love the vaunted intelligence of my pundits, for they understand not the city but divide it. For them the city means: here a prison, there a hospital, yonder a friend's house—and even this last they split up in their thoughts, into this room and the next room, and so on room by room. And not content with this, they list the various objects in each room. And, lastly, dissect each object into its component parts. But what avails them all that rubble, refusing as they do—as is the way of pundits—to build anything therewith?

But you, sentinel, when you keep watch, are in communion with the city made over to the starry night. Not with this house or that, not with the hospital or the palace, but with the whole city. Not with that dying man's lament, nor those cries of a woman in travail, nor the whisperings of lovers, nor the whimpers of the new-born babe—but with the manifold exhalation of a single, sentient body. With the whole city. Not with this man's sleeplessness or that man's sleep, not with this man's researches or that man's poems, but with the dark fires of mingled sleep and fervor that are smoldering under the white ashes of the Milky Way. With the whole city. Sentinel, O sentinel, your ear is pressed to the very bosom of her you love, measuring the silences, the murmurous tides within her, that must not be divided if you would hear aright; for these sounds are the beating of a heart and it is her very life you hear.

Sentinel, when you keep your watch unsleeping, you are my equal. For the city rests on you, and on the city rests the empire. True, I condone your kneeling when I pass by, for thus things are ordained and, as the sap rises from the roots towards the leafage, your homage should ascend. Such is the circulation of the empire's blood, as is the mother's milk flowing towards the child, and youth's respect towards old age, and the love of the bridegroom towards the bride. Yet much would you err in saying that one gives and the other receives. I, too, serve; and it is you I serve.

Thus it is, when I see you leaning on your rifle, I hail you as my equal in God, for who can discriminate between the foundation stone and the keystone, or deem the lot of the one or of the other the more enviable? So when I look at you, my heart thrills with love, though there is nothing to hinder me from having you arrested by my men-at-arms.

There you lie before me, asleep. A sentry sleeping; a sentry dead. And when I see you thus I tremble; for in you the empire, too, is sleeping, dying. You are but a symptom of its mortal sickness, for ill betides when it gives me sentries who fall asleep.

True, I told myself, the headsman will do his work and drown this young man in his sleep. . . . But then, in my compassion, a new, perplexing thought waylaid me. For only strong and healthy empires behead sleeping sentries; whereas empires that give their rulers sentries but for them to sleep have lost the right of cutting off anything whatever. It is well to understand the uses of severity. Not by cutting off the heads of sleeping sentries are empires awakened; but when empires are awake, then fall the heads of sleeping sentries. Here, also, you confuse cause and effect. When, because you see strong empires cutting off heads, you try to renew your strength by putting men to death, you are but a bloodthirsty buffoon.

Stablish love and you stablish the wakefulness of your sentries and the due punishment of those who fall asleep; for they have already, by behaving thus, cut themselves off from the empire.

You, my sentry, have nothing guiding you but the discipline which comes from your corporal, who keeps watch over you. And if the corporals have doubts of themselves, they have no discipline save that which comes to them from their sergeants, who keep watch on them. And the sergeants get theirs from the captains, who keep watch on them. And thuswise, stage by stage, up to myself, who have but God to rule my ways; and if I doubt myself I am out of plumb, a broken reed.

And now I would impart to you a secret—which is that of permanence. When you sleep your life is in abeyance; but it is likewise in abeyance when those eclipses of the heart befall you which are the causes of your weakness. For around you nothing is changed, yet all has changed within you. So here you are, my sentinel, confronting the city, but no longer pressing your ear to the bosom of your beloved and hearing her heartbeats merge with her silence and soft breathing; for still all things are signs of her and she is one, though invisible amongst the scattered objects which you have lost the power of gathering into oneness, now that you are at the mercy of all the drifting sounds of the night that contradict each other: the drunkard's song gainsaying the sick man's lament; the voices keening in the death chamber gainsaying the cry of the newborn babe, the silent majesty of the temple gainsaying the tumult of the crowd. So it is you ask yourself: "What am I to make of all this disorder and diversity signifying nothing, for all that I can see?" For if you no longer know that here a tree stands, then the roots, trunk, branches, leafage have no common measure. And how can you be faithful when an object for your fidelity is lacking? Well I know you would not sleep were you watching at the bedside of her you love. But that which should have been the object of your love is dispersed into fragments strewn at random, and you know it no more. Unloosed for you is the God-made knot that binds all things together.

But I would have you faithful to yourself, knowing that you will find the homeward way. Not that I ask you to understand and feel at every moment, for too well I know that even for the most passionate love there are moments when it traverses the waste places of the heart. Even when you are with her whom you love dark thoughts sometimes beset you. "That voice is her voice. That brow is hers. And, lo and behold, she has said a foolish thing! She has stumbled. . . . How can I love her?" For her oneness is disintegrating and can sustain your love no longer; soon you come to think you hate her! Yet how should you hate, when you are not even capable of loving?

But you keep silence, for dimly you are conscious that all this is but a dream hovering above your sleep. What at such a moment is true of the woman holds good for the poem you might chance to read, or for the domain or the empire. A power has left you, the power of being suckled and even of perceiving—this, too, calls for love and understanding—the God-made knots that bind things together. But, my sleeping sentry, you will regain the objects of your love; they will be restored to you as your due—not one or another of them, but all. Therefore it is incumbent to respect in you, when the plight of being unfaithful befalls you, the momently abandoned house which presently will be replenished.

Far be it from me to claim that all my sentries are fervent when they go their rounds; many are listless, their minds full of their next meal. For while the gods are asleep within you, the animal craving for satisfactions of the belly persists; indeed your bored man always thinks of eating. Nor do I claim that my sentries' souls are awakened (by "soul" I mean that which within you enters into communion with those outer forces which are the God-made knots binding things together; that part of you which mocks at walls). I simply claim that now and then the soul of one bursts into flame; that now and then one of them feels his heart beating faster, and conscious of his vastness drinks in the starshine, while, like a shell full of the murmurs of the sea, he enfolds within him the uttermost horizons of his world.

It suffices me that you have known such moments, the vision of the plenitude of being a man, and that you hold yourself in readiness for such visitations; for with them it is as with sleep or hunger or desire, which come back to you at intervals. Thus if at whiles you are uncertain, your uncertainties are wholly pure, and I would not have you grieve over them.

Thus, if you are a priest the vision of God will come back to you in His good time; if you are a sculptor, the vision of the perfect face; if you are a lover, the vision of love; and if you are a sentry, the vision of the empire, provided you are true to yourself and keep your house clean and bright, though deserted for the moment it may seem. You cannot know the hour of the coming of that blissful visitation, but this you know, that come it will, and nothing else can satisfy your heart's desire.

Therefore I build you up, through long, toilsome hours of study, so that the poem, as by a miracle, can thrill through you like a tongue of fire; and, with the rites and customs of the empire, I make you such that the empire can grip your heart. For no gift comes to you unprepared-for. And that visitation comes not, if there be no house ready to receive it.

Sentinel, O sentinel, it is by brooding on the doubts that assail you as you pace the ramparts in the long, sultry nights; it is by listening to the sounds of the city when the city has no word for you; it is by watching over men's dwellings when they are but a mass of clotted darkness; it is by breathing in the surrounding desert when it is but an empty waste of sand; it is by forcing yourself to love without loving, to believe without believing, by being loyal when none remains to whom you can be loyal—it is thus alone that you prepare yourself for the sudden glory of that vision which sometimes comes to the sentry on his round, the gift and recompense of his love.

Being true to yourself is not hard when someone is present on whom you can bestow your loyalty; but what I ask of you is that your memories should conjure up an inner voice at every moment, saying: "Let my house be visited. Lo, I have built it and I keep it pure and bright!" My discipline is there to aid you. Thus I compel my priests to make sacrifice, even though the sacrifice has no longer any meaning; and my sculptors to carve figures, even though they be unsure of themselves; and my sentries to go their rounds on pain of death; for else, having cut themselves off from the empire, they would be dead men already. And so by my severity I save them.

But as for you, my sleeping sentry—sleeping not because you have failed to stand by the city but because the city has failed to stand by you—I grow conscious, gazing on your young, pale face, of the precariousness of the empire if it can no longer keep my sentinels awake.

Yet assuredly I err when I seem to hear in its plenitude the nocturne of the city and to see as bound together in a knot that which, for you, has fallen asunder. And well I know the long hours you had to wait, holding yourself erect like a lonely taper in a shrine, before there came to you that inward gleam, your recompense, and then in an ecstasy you went your round and it was like the figure of a strange dance under the stars, in the dark immensity of the universe. For yonder in the blackness of the night are ships unloading cargoes of ivory and precious metals, and it is your privilege, my sentry on the ramparts, to help in guarding them, and thereby to embellish with gold and silver the empire that you serve. Somewhere, too, lovers are keeping silence before they dare to speak, gazing at each other with the words hovering on their lips— for if one speaks and the other shuts his eyes, the whole world is changed. And you are the guardian of their silence. Somewhere, too, a man is breathing his last. They bend over him to glean that word from the dying lips which is like a benediction that will endure for ever and be treasured up by them. And thus you are the guardian of a dead man's last word.

Sentinel, O sentinel, none can assign the bounds of your empire when God gives you that illumination of the soul which is the sentry's prerogative, and the clear-eyed gaze enfolding vast expanses that is yours. Little care I that at other times you are a young man who grumbles about his duties and is always thinking of his next meal. It is good that you should sleep and that you should grumble; but it is ill if through unmindfulness you let your dwelling fall into ruin. For loyalty is being loyal to oneself.

My wish is to save not you alone but your comrades. And to obtain of you that inner permanence which comes of a well-built soul. For I do not destroy my house when I go away from it; nor burn I my roses when I am done with looking at them. They will remain for when I look at them again and will flower in the light of my eyes.

Therefore will I send my men-at-arms to arrest you, and you shall be condemned to that death which is the death of sentries who sleep at their posts. All that remains to you is to take heart of grace in the assurance that, by the example of your punishment, you are bartering yourself for something greater than yourself, the vigilance of my sentinels keeping watch and ward over the empire.

✣ 71

LAMENTABLE INDEED it is that she whom you see gentle and simple-minded, truthful and so modest, should be so vulnerable to the wiles of selfishness, to brutality or low cunning which take advantage of her fragile grace and innocent trust; and it may be you would wish her more versed in the world's ways. Yet there can be no question of desiring that the maidens of your house should be warier, versed in the world's ways, and chary of their gifts; for, by training them to be thus, you would have ruined that very thing you set out to safeguard. So true it is that every virtue has in it the seed of its own destruction. Generosity contains the risk of the parasite who will gnaw its heart out; modesty, the risk of the grossness which will soil it; kindness, the risk of the ingratitude which will turn it sour. Thus, in sheltering her from all life's natural risks, you would be aspiring to a world already dead. Forbidding the building of a temple beautiful, for fear of the earthquakes which might destroy a thing of beauty.

I cannot have too many of them in my land, these maidens who are trustful; though it is they alone who can be deceived and betrayed. True, if the woman-stealer filches one of them, I shall grieve. But, if I desire to have a mettlesome fighter, I must run the risk of losing him in war.

Desist, then, from your contradictory desires.

Know well that it is for no idle cause that I love what is threatened; nor need we regret that such is the lot of all precious things. For therein I discern a condition of their quality. I love the friend who, in the midst of temptations, keeps his loyalty. For, unless temptation come, there is no loyalty, and I have no friend. And I am willing that some should fall on the way so that the others may make good their work. I love the brave soldier who never flinches under the enemy's fire; for if courage ceases to be, I cease to have soldiers. And I am willing that some should die, if by their deaths they stablish the valor of the others.

Thus, if you bring me a treasure, I would it were so fragile that a gust of wind could waft it away. And what I love in a young face is that it is threatened with age; and in its smile, that a word from me could change it so easily into tears.

✼ 72

THEN WAS MADE CLEAR to me the solution of the difficulty whereon I had often pondered; which was the quandary that afflicted me so cruelly when I, the king, was gazing down at my sleeping sentry. The cruelty of taking a youngster lost in happy dreams and pitchforking him, as it were, into death, aghast during those last terrible moments at being made to suffer thus at men's hands.

For as I gazed at him he awoke and drew his hand over his brows; then, not yet having recognized me, proffered his face to the stars, with a little sigh at the effort of picking up again his heavy weapons. And then it was revealed to me that here was a soul I had to win.

Standing beside him, I, his king, gazed down upon the sleeping city, breathing-in seemingly the same effluence—and yet it was not the same. And I thought: There is no means of making clear the tragic import of this moment. No course that would avail is open to me, save to convert him, and disclose to him not these things which he sees, breathes in, appraises and possesses even as do I, but rather the vision shining across these visible things—that God-made knot binding them all together. Thus, too, I saw that we must distinguish between conquest and constraint. To conquer is to convert; to constrain is to imprison. If I conquer you, I set a man free, but if I use constraint on you, I crush you out. For my conquest is a building up of yourself, through you and within you. Constraint is but the heap of stones aligned and all alike—from which nothing will be born.

And I saw, too, that all men should thus be conquered and won over. Those that watched and those who slept, those who went their rounds on the ramparts, and those who were guarded by my sentries' rounds. Those who were rejoicing over a newborn babe and those who mourned their dead. Those who prayed and those who doubted. What I name "conquest" is building up for you the structure that befits you, and opening your mind to a fullness of understanding. For lakes there are to slake your thirst, so but you be shown the way to them. Thus will I instal in you my gods, so that they may enlighten you.

And assuredly it were best that in your childhood and betimes you should be conquered; else we shall find you casehardened and no longer capable of learning the language of the spirit.

THE TIME IS COME to speak to you of that wherein you err most grievously. For I have found those men fervent and known them for happy men, appearances notwithstanding, who, in the desolation of those arid lands where under a fiery sky the dead soil gapes and crumbles, sift and puddle the stony matrix. Bruised by the sun, like overripe fruit, their limbs torn on the rocks, they delve daylong into the clayey depths and, coming up, sleep naked in their tents—and their whole life goes to the getting but once a year of a diamond of the first water. Whereas I see those men unhappy and embittered, who, after procuring diamonds galore to glut their luxury, find that they have but useless flakes of glass at their disposal. For what you need is not an object, precious though it be, but a god.

True, the possession of a thing may be lasting; but not so the nutriment you get from it. For it has no meaning save inasmuch as it augments you; and you greaten yourself in the winning of it, not by possessing it. This is why I praise him who sets you to scaling a mountain peak, or to the studious effort needed for a poem, or to the winning of a soul that is inaccessible—and thus constrains you to *become*. But him I despise who is but a hoard amassed, for you have nothing to receive from it. And once the diamond won, to what use will you put it?

I restore to you the meaning of the festival, which meaning men had forgotten. The festival is the consummation of the preparations leading up to it, the summit of the mountain after the ascent; it is the capture of the diamond when it befalls you to win it from the earth, the victory that crowns a war, the sick man's first meal on the first day of his recovery, the dawn of love when you entreat her and she lowers her eyes. . . .

Wherefore, for your instruction, I devised this parable.

If I so wished, I could create for you a civilization full of joy and fervor, with teams of workers merrily laughing as they come home from work, urged on by a great zest for life, eagerly awaiting the morrow's miracle or the poem that will echo the golden music of the stars. And yet this life would be but an incessant digging of the soil to win from it diamonds which, after long gestation in the womb of earth, have been transmuted into solid light. (For having come from the sun, then become giant ferns, then clotted darkness, lo, they have retrieved the light of their beginning!) Thus it lies in my power to ensure for you a life of high emotion if I condemn you to this drudgery of delving, and summon you to the city once a year for that great festival whose climax is the consecration of the diamonds which, in the presence of the sweating crowd, are burnt and vanish in a haze of broken lights. For the heart's emotions are not quickened by the using of the prizes you have won; your soul is nourished by the significance of things and not by things themselves.

True, I might equally well delight your eyes by decking a princess with that diamond instead of burning it. Or I might seal it up in a coffer in a temple treasury and thus make it shine the brighter for your mind's eye alone which, unhindered by seals and walls, could feast on it. But assuredly I shall be doing you no vital service if I *give* it you.

For I have discerned the underlying meaning of all sacrifice, which mulcts you of nothing, but, rather, enriches you. For if you try to grasp the object, when in truth your heart is set on its significance, you are, as it were, nuzzling the wrong breast. Did I devise an empire where every evening diamonds harvested in other lands were handed out to you, you might as well be given pebbles; for you would no longer be getting aught of that on which your heart was set. Richer is the man who toils, year in, year out, battering the rock, and once a year burns the fruit of his work that light may flash forth from it—far richer is such a man than one who every day receives the fruits of others' toil in some far land, which have cost him no effort.

Thus with the ninepin—your pleasure lies in toppling it over. And you make merry. But you can get no joy of a fallen ninepin.

Therefore sacrifices and festivals are bound up together. For in them the meaning of your deeds and efforts is displayed. How indeed aver that a festival is other than a great bonfire kindled, once the firewood has been gathered, for men to feast their eyes on the leaping flames? Or other than the joy of your relaxed sinews, after the long climb to the mountain crest? And the gleam of the diamond in the light, once it is won from the earth's womb? And the wine harvest, once the grapes are ripe? How then could it be possible to see a festival as a laying-up of stores? A festival is your journey's end after the long day's march and a consummation of the march; but nothing have you to hope from your transformation into a sedentary. And this is why no lasting repose is to be got from music, or a poem, or the winning of a woman, or your glimpse of the landscape from the mountain-top. I lay you waste if I disperse you along a level line of days, and if I fail to order them and steer their course like a ship bound for a certain port. For the poem is a festival, on condition that you make its arduous ascent, and the temple is a festival only if it sets you free from your petty cares of every day. Day after day you have suffered by the city which has driven its traffic over you, and been tormented by the fever and the fret of earning the daily bread, curing diseases, solving problems, roving hither and thither, laughing here and weeping there. But then comes the long-awaited hour assigned to silence, the bliss of contemplation. You climb the temple steps and enter by the portal; and, lo, here is the open sea, the vastness of the Milky Way above you, a treasure-house of quiet, a victory over the daily round. And all these your soul needed, as your body needs food; for daylong you had been fretted by so many things and objects which served you nowise. Here it was good for you to come and to *become;* so that a visage might take form from the diversity of common things, and a plan emerge, giving all a meaning. Yet what service would my temple render you, did you not dwell in the city, had you not struggled and suffered, and had you not borne on your back the load of

stones that you must now build up within you? Thus did I tell you
concerning my soldiers and love; if you are a lover and no more,
the woman yawns when she is with you, there is no love to warm
you; for only the fighting man knows the art of loving. Yet if he
be a fighting man and no more, he who falls on the battlefield is but
an insect carapaced in scales of metal. Only he who has loved can
die a man's death. And herein lies no contradiction save in the terms
of language. Thus, too, the fruit and the roots have a common
measure, which is the tree.

❧ 74

BUT THINK NOT that in any way I scorn your natural desires; nor
even that they are adverse to your true significance. Indeed, to make
my meaning clear, and illustrate it, I use words that seem to stick
out their tongues at each other, like quarrelling children; such as,
for example, "necessary" and "superfluous," "cause" and "effect,"
"the kitchen" and "the ball-room." But I have no faith in these
antitheses which derive from a flaw of our language and the choice
of an unsuitable mountain whence to observe the deeds and ways
of men.

Thus with the meaning of the city; my sentry has access to it only
when God has endowed him with that clearness of vision and of
hearing which beseems the sentry; and then the cry of the newborn babe no longer seems discordant with the wailing round a
deathbed, nor the marketplace with the temple, nor the street of
harlots with the faithful loves elsewhere. Rather, he perceives that
it is from this diversity that the city arises, which absorbs, weds and
unifies; even as in the tree the divers elements are made one, and
within its silence the temple embraces and dominates its diversity of
statues, pillars, arches and altars; even as I approach to you only

on that level where there is an end of petty disputations; whereon I no longer contrast the singer with the winnower of corn, or the dancer with the sower of the seed, or the stargazer with the nail-smith. For thus to divide you up would mean I had not understood you—you have slipped through my hands!

Thus it was that, wrapped in the silence of my love, I went into the city to observe the people therein; for I wished to understand my city.

As for the relationship between the diverse activities of man, no appraisal can be made according to any set idea—of this am I convinced. In such matters reasoning is of no help. For you do not build up a body starting with a completed whole; but you sow the seed, and it is the only whole that you perceive. It is only the nature of the love bestowed that gives birth to the true proportions, and these are undisclosed in the beginning—save in the foolish jargon of logicians, historians and pundits who will direct your notice to the individual parts and point out how you might have encouraged the growth of one of these at the expense of the others, finding words easily enough to prove that this favored one is worthier than the others. Yet, with no less plausibility, they might have proved the opposite, had they been so minded; for, to revert to that simile of the kitchen and the ball-room, you have no scales wherein to weigh the importance of the one as against the other. For your language loses all meaning once you begin to prejudge the future. Building the future means building the Here and Now. It means creating a desire that centers on today; and thus throws a bridge from today to tomorrow. It does not concern acts that have meaning only for the morrow. For when your being makes a break with the Here and Now, it dies; life, which is an adaptation to the present and a continuance in the present, depends on innumerable relationships beyond the reach of language, and its due equilibrium hangs on a myriad delicate adjustments. And if you tamper with one of these in the course of demonstrating some abstract theorem, life ceases; even as it is with the elephant, enormous as he is: if you sever even one tiny blood vessel, he dies. Think not that I am asking you never to change anything. For you may well change everything. With a barren plain you may create a forest of cedars. But your task is not to build up cedar trees, but to sow seeds; and then, at each moment, the seed itself, or that which rises from it, will achieve its due equilibrium in the Here and Now.

Yet many are the angles from which these matters can be viewed. If I choose to scale that mountain, which affords a view enabling me to sort men out according to their deserts, for their sharing in the common stock, it is probable that I shall dispense justice accordingly, and it will work amiss. For it is no less probable that, had I scaled another mountain, that sorted men out differently, my justice would have been different. But I would have my justice comprehensive. And to this end I studied men under their various aspects.

For justice fulfills itself in many ways, and not in one alone. Easy would it be to sort out my generals according to their age and reward them accordingly, increasing their dignities and duties as the years went by. But equally well I might accord them spells of rest increasing with the years, and, lifting their burdens, call on younger men to shoulder these. Or I could base my justice on the empire. Or else on the rights of the individual; or, beyond him and against him, those of Man.

And when, reviewing the hierarchy of my army I sought to judge its equity, lo, I was enmeshed in a tangle of issueless contradictions! For I had to take into account the services rendered, the differing capacities of the servants of the empire, and the well-being of the empire itself. And whenever I found a scale of merit seemingly incontestable, it proved that another, likewise seemingly incontestable, must be erroneous. Thus little care I when men prove to me that there is a code self-evident, in terms of which my decisions are outrageous; for I know in advance that, whatever I do, thus will it ever be and that the one thing needful is to weigh the facts and to let the truth mature in silence, if I am to ensue it, not in hollow words, but with verities that turn the scale.

I MIND ME of that sour-faced, cross-eyed prophet who one day came to visit me, in high and gloomy dudgeon.

"It were best," he said, "to destroy them root and branch."

Thus I saw he had a craving for perfection. For death alone is perfect.

"They are evildoers," he said.

I held my peace. I seemed to see under my eyes that steely soul of his shaped like a sword. And I thought: This man lives but to war on evil. It is on evil that he thrives. Without it where would he be?

"What," I asked him, "would bring you happiness?"

"The triumph of virtue in the world," he answered.

But I knew he was lying. For this "happiness" he wanted would mean the idling and rusting of his sword.

And then was revealed to me, little by little, a strange yet patent truth—that he who loves good is indulgent towards evil. For though the words seem at cross-purposes with each other, good and evil interlock; your bad sculptors are a forcing-bed for your good sculptors, tyranny tempers valiant souls to fight against it, and famine leads to the sharing of bread between neighbors—a sharing sweeter than the bread itself to hungry lips. Thus those men who had hatched plots against me and, hunted down by my police, cut off in secret lairs from the light of day, and, ever carrying their lives in their hands, had sacrificed themselves to something other than themselves and willingly faced danger, durance, and injustice by reason of their love for freedom and justice—those men always seemed to me invested with a special beauty and a radiance that glowed on the very scaffold, like a flaming cloud above them. Therefore never have I cheated these men of their death. What were a diamond but for the hard rocks that must be bored and broken before it can be won? What is the value of a sword, if there be no foe; of fidelity, if there be no temptation; of homecoming, if there be no absence? That prophet's "triumph of virtue" were but the triumph of the stall-fed, docile ox tied to his manger. And I count not on the stall-fed and the sedentaries.

"You are struggling against evil," I told him, "and every struggle is a dance. You get your pleasure from the dance; in fine, from evil. But I would rather see you dancing for love of love.

"For if I stablish for you an empire in which men's hearts are stirred by poems, a day will surely come when the logicians fall to arguing thereon and wordily apprising you of the peril to which the poem is exposed, from its opposite—as if there were the 'opposite' of anything whatever in the world! Then will you see police officers arising who, confusing the love of the poem with hatred of its 'opposite,' will now devote themselves to hating instead of loving. As though love of the cedar tree meant the destruction of all olive trees! Then will you see them haling off to prison musicians, sculptors or astronomers, invoking absurd arguments, built of words that weave the wind. And thus will perish my empire; for the cult of the cedar need not involve the ruin of the olive groves or an embargo on the fragrance of the rose. Instill in a people's heart the love of sailing ships, and it will draw into itself all that is fervent in your land and transmute it into sails and rigging. But you, my man, would wish to take the activities of the sailmakers in hand and foster these by denouncing, persecuting and wiping out as heretics all who do not see eye to eye with you. And you will have logic on your side, since by logic you can prove anything you like, and all that is not a sailing ship can be shown to be the opposite of the sailing ship. Thus, from purge to purge, you will exterminate your race; for you will find that each of us loves something else as well. Nay, more, you will end by exterminating the sailing ship itself, for the hymn of the ship becomes on the nailsmith's lips the hymn of nailmaking. And once you have thrown him into prison, no more nails will be forthcoming for the making of the ship.

"Thus is it with him, too, who thinks to favor the great sculptors by exterminating the bad, whom in his foolish parlance he denounces as the 'opposites' of the former. And then, my friend, surely you yourself would be the first to forbid your son to choose a calling whose prospects looked so black!"

"If I have understood you aright," snarled my cross-eyed prophet, "you would have me tolerate vice!"

"Not so," I answered. "You have understood . . . nothing!"

✼ 76

FOR IF I do not wish to wage war, and it so happens that my limbs are stiff with rheumatism, I may well find in my infirmity a reason for abstaining from war; whereas, if I am set on making war, I will hope to cure my rheumatism in the exercise of battle. Thus a simple desire for peace would have assumed the guise of my rheumatism, as it might have taken on that of love of the home, or respect of my enemy—or anything else at all. If you would understand men, begin by never listening to them. For the nailsmith talks to you of his nails; and the astronomer of his stars. And both forget utterly the sea.

✼ 77

MISLED BY REASONING run wild, these numskulls believed that contraries exist. Whereas life is a network of relations so complex that if you destroy one of your two seeming contraries, you die. For bear

219

this well in mind: the only contrary of anything whatsoever is, and is but, death.

Thus with the poet who racks his brains, tracking down and erasing whatever is the contrary of perfection. Soon will you find that, from deletion to deletion, he has brought his whole script to dust. For nothing can be perfect. But one who loves perfection never tires of embellishing his work.

Thus with him who is ever tracking down the contrary of virtue. Soon will you find him making a holocaust of all; for no man is perfect.

Thus with him who destroys his enemy. But he used to live by him, and by his death he dies. The contrary of the ship is the sea. But it was the sea that shaped and tapered the stempost and the hull. And the contrary of fire is ash, but the ashes nurse the fire.

Thus with him who fights against human bondage, fanning the flame of hatred in men's hearts, instead of fighting for freedom and quickening their love of it. And since everywhere, in every hierarchy, you can find some trace of servitude, you may think fit to describe as servile the task imposed on the foundations of the temple, whereon rest the nobler storeys which alone soar heavenwards. And, lo, borne forward on a tedious tide of logic, you will find yourself constrained to destroy the temple!

For the cedar tree stands not for hatred and disdain of all that is not cedarwood; it is a creature of the rocky soil tapped by the roots and changed into the growing tree.

If you fight *against* anything whatsoever, the whole world will fall under your suspicion, for in every nook and corner your enemy may lurk or find assistance. If you fight *against* anything whatsoever you can but end by destroying yourself, for always within you is a trace, however slight, of that which you combat.

The only injustice known to me is the injustice of creation. Yet in creating you did not destroy the juices of the earth, which might have nourished brambles, but you built up a cedar which took these juices for itself—unjustly, if you will—and thus the brambles came not into being.

Once you become a tree of a certain kind, never can you become a tree of another kind; and thus you have been "unjust" towards the others.

✣ 78

I WOULD NOW SPEAK for the lonely woman who is you; for I desire to make yours the illumination I have won. Having discovered that it is possible to bring you the nourishment you need, in your silence and your loneliness.

For the gods make light of walls and seas. And you, too, are enriched by the knowledge that somewhere in the world there exists a homely fragrance of beeswax; even though it will never be for you.

But I have no means of judging the quality of the nourishment I bring you, save by judging you yourself. After receiving it, what do you become? I would wish to see you folding your hands in silence, while your eyes grow dark and pensive like those of a child to whom I have given a new toy which gradually absorbs him. And this gift is more than the mere material thing he falls to playing with. Just as with a few pebbles he can build a fleet of warships, so when I give him a single wooden soldier, he makes a whole army of it, with its captains and oaths of loyalty to the empire and strict discipline and deaths of thirst in the desert. Thus is it with the instrument of music, which is indeed far more than a machine for making sounds; rather, a snare in which you may capture something on which your heart is set and which is of a different essence from the trap itself. Thus would I illuminate you also, so that your little attic room may be bright and gay, and tenanted your heart. For when once I have told you of the fire undying under the ashes, it is not the same sleeping town that you look down on from your casement window. Even as it is no longer the same dull familiar sentry's beat for my sentry, once he feels himself to be a headland of the empire.

When you give yourself, you receive more than you give. For, after being nothing, you *become*. And little I care if these words seem at cross-purposes with each other.

For you, the lonely woman, will I speak; for I wish to make you my abode. Perhaps, by reason of a sprained limb or an affliction of the eye, it is distasteful for you to welcome a flesh-and-blood spouse under your roof. But there are stronger presences than those of flesh and blood and sometimes have I seen one who is lying on a truckle-bed, dying of a cancer, become another man when tidings of a great victory were brought and, though thick walls shut out the blare of the trumpets, his room seemed echoing with it. And surely what had permeated from the outside world into that sickroom was nothing other than the knot holding things together which is implicit in the name of Victory and makes light of stone walls and sundering seas. And why should there not exist a divinity still more fervently compelling—who will mold you into a woman faithful, dowered beyond all telling, her heart aflame with love?

For true love is inexhaustible: the more you give, the more you have. And if you go to draw at the true fountainhead, the more water you draw, the more abundant is its flow. That homely fragrance of beeswax exists for all and, if another woman also savors it, its fragrance is enhanced for you yourself.

But as for that flesh and blood spouse, if he bestows his smiles elsewhere, he will be plundering you and will make you weary of loving. That is why I shall enter your dwelling, and no need have I to make myself known to you. For I am the knot binding the empire together, and I have devised a prayer for that lonely woman who is you. I am as it were the keystone of a scheme of life that gives things their full savor. I can bind you, too, together—and then your days of loneliness are over.

How then should you not follow where I point the way? For I am none other than yourself. Thus is it with music which builds up its own pattern within you, setting your heart aflame. As for the music, it is neither true nor false; only, by its immanence you are enabled to *become*.

I would not have you isolated in your perfection—isolated and embittered. Rather, will I awaken you to fervor, which gives all and takes nothing; for fervor seeks neither ownership nor even the presence of its object.

But the poem has beauty for reasons lying beyond all logic, since they pertain to another level. And the wider are the vistas it lays open to you, the more it quickens your emotion. For dormant in you are many melodies that can be conjured forth, but all are not of the same quality. Thus bad music opens up paths that lead along the lower levels of the heart; and then the god who manifests himself to you is but a demigod.

Wherefore I have devised this prayer for the lonely woman who is you.

❧ 79

THIS IS THE PRAYER of loneliness.

Have pity on me, O Lord, for the burden of my solitude is more than I can bear. Nothing have I to look forward to, and no voice comes to me in this room where I sit alone. Nevertheless, it is not human presences I crave, since I feel myself even more derelict when I plunge into the crowd. Yet many another woman there is like me, alone in a house like mine, who none the less feels contented with her lot, if those whom she loves are going about their tasks elsewhere in the house. She can neither hear nor see them. For the moment she is receiving nothing from them. But in knowing that these others are in the house—unseen, unheard albeit—she finds her happiness.

O Lord, I, too, ask for nothing that may be seen or heard. Thy miracles touch not the senses. If Thou willst but enlighten my spirit as to this my dwelling, surely I shall be healed of my distress.

The wanderer in the desert, if he belong to a house that is dwelt in, has joy of it, even though it lie at the world's utmost rim. No distance can prevent him from being sustained by it, and, should he die in the desert, he dies in love. Therefore, O Lord, I ask not even this, that my dwelling place should be anear.

If, walking in a crowd, a man sees all of a sudden a face that thrills him, lo, he is a man transfigured, even though that face be not for him! Thus it was with the soldier who loved a queen. He became the soldier of a queen, and all his life was changed. Therefore, O Lord, I ask not even this, that the dwelling place whereof I dream be promised me.

Far out on the high seas rove fervent men who give their lives to seeking an isle existing only in their dream. Now and again they hymn, these happy mariners, that island of the blest, and their hearts swell with joy. And it is not the hoped-for landfall that crowns their cup of happiness, but the hymn they sing. Therefore, O Lord, I ask not even this, that somewhere in the world there should exist the dwelling place I crave. . . .

Loneliness is bred of a mind that has grown earthbound. For the spirit has its homeland, which is the realm of the meaning of things. Thus is it with the temple, when it bespeaks the meaning of the stones. Only in this boundless empyrean can the mind take wing. Not in things-in-themselves does it rejoice, but only in the visage which it reads behind them and which binds them into oneness. Grant me but this, O Lord: that I may learn to read.

Then for ever will be lifted from my shoulders the burden of my solitude.

Low DEEDS enlist low souls as their vehicles; noble deeds, noble souls.

Low deeds are conditioned by low motives; noble deeds, by noble motives.

When I have an enemy betrayed, I have him betrayed by traitors.

When I have a house built, I have it built by masons.

When I make peace, I have it signed by cowards.

When I cause men to die, I have war declared by heroes.

For evidently when one of two opposing tendencies gains the day, it is he who has shouted loudest in favor of that course who takes command of it. And if the course in question be humiliating, though necessary, it is he who was in favor of it even before it became necessary (out of the mere baseness of his mind) who will take the lead. It is as hard to have a surrender agreed to by heroes as to have cowards opt for a last stand.

If, though humiliating from one point of view, a certain act is necessary (since nothing in the conduct of life is simple), I bring to the forefront him who, because he himself smells foul, will be least nauseated. I choose not for my scavengers men with dainty nostrils.

Thus it is when my enemy has won the day and I must open negotiations. For conducting them I choose one who is friendly with the enemy. But malign me not by deeming I esteem the former, or submit to the latter voluntarily.

For it may well be that were you to ask my scavengers to voice their feelings, they would tell me that they empty the refuse bins because of a liking for the smell of ordure. Likewise my headsman would confess he has a taste for blood.

But greatly would you err, did you appraise me, who set them to these ugly tasks, in terms of what these men say. It is my loathing for refuse and my love for clean, bright door-sills that lead me to enlist the services of scavengers. And it is my hatred of the shedding of innocent blood that has forced me to appoint an executioner.

❦ *81*

"I HAVE WRITTEN my poem. All that remains to do is to correct it." But my father waxed wroth.

"So you write your poem first, and then correct it! But what is writing but correcting? What is the sculptor doing, if not correcting? Have you watched him modelling the clay? Correction by correction the face emerges; nay, the very first thumb-stroke was a correction of the primal lump. When I found my city, I 'correct' the barren wilderness. Then in the making I 'correct' my city. And correction by correction I follow the path that leads to God."

❦ *82*

Now WILL I SPEAK of the mirage of the happy isle, and lift the mist from your eyes. For you fondly think that in the glorious solitude of open spaces, the natural freedom of fields and flocks and trees, the fervor of a love going its own wild way, you best can shoot up straight and shapely as a tree. But the trees that I have seen shoot up the straightest were not those that grew in freedom. For such trees, being in no haste to grow, loiter in their ascent and their trunks are gnarled and twisted. Whereas the tree that rises in the virgin forest, being hard pressed on all sides by enemies bent on robbing it of its share of light, drives sunwards with a steady up-thrust, peremptory as a clarion call.

In that "happy isle" of yours you will find neither freedom, nor love, nor exaltation.

If you bury yourself in the desert for a long time (for I speak not of a brief respite from the tumult of the city—which is another matter), I know but one means whereby I can quicken it in your behalf, brace you to strive your utmost, and make the sands of the wilderness a hotbed for your fervor. And that is to score it with a network of lines of force—whether these pertain to nature or to the empire.

Thus I string out the wells so sparsely that each calls for a full day's march and there can be no halting on the way. Moreover, towards the seventh day you well may find yourself compelled to use sparingly what little water remains in your waterskins and to strain every nerve to reach a well yet more remote—but what triumph in the winning of it! True, in your besting of distance and the desert you may lose many a camel on the way; but your victory will repay the sacrifices undergone. And the caravans sunk in sand that failed to make the well bear silent witness to its glory, and its radiance seems hovering upon the bones that lie bleaching under the desert sun.

Thus at the hour of setting forth, when you inspect the loads, tugging at each rope to make sure that the weight is well distributed, and next you check the store of water—you are summoning forth what is best in you. And presently you set out for that far-off land blessed by many waters, beyond the sands, and one by one you climb the intervals between the wells spaced out like the steps of a staircase; and, because there is a battle to be won and a dance to dance, you are gradually caught up in the ceremonial of the desert. Thus it is, while strengthening your bodily endurance, I build up a soul for you.

Moreover, if I would still further enrich you, and if I wish the wells to attract or repulse you with intenser force, like electric poles, making the desert serve as a whetstone for your mind and heart, I people it with foes. Thus when you find them holding the well you needs must feint and fight and conquer, if you are not to perish of thirst. And according as the tribes encamped there are fiercer or less fierce, akin to you in their ways of thought or speaking some outlandish tongue, better or less well armed—your steps are nimbler or less nimble, stealthier or louder, and the length of each day's march will vary, though the ground to cover is, to all appearances, the same. Thus a vastness which at first seemed uniform, a featureless waste of sand, becomes as it were a huge magnetic field, sparkling with divers colors and different everywhere. Indeed, to your mind's eye it well may seem yet more diversified than those happy lands where are blue mountains, smiling valleys, green meadows and fresh-water lakes.

For at one place your steps are those of an outlaw under sentence of death; at another, those of one set free. Here, those of a man trapped in an ambush; there, those of a man who has got the better of a surprise attack. Here, your steps are rapid, as of one in gay pursuit; there, prudent as when you enter on tiptoe the room where she is sleeping, and her sleep must not be disturbed.

True, it well may happen that no high adventure befalls you in the course of most of your journeys; none the less they serve their purpose, for they bring home to you these aspects of the changing scene, and the ceremonial of the desert which you learn from them becomes justified—nay, necessary and absolute—in your eyes, and thus the quality of your dance is ennobled and enriched. And then you may discover a strange thing. If I foist on your caravan a man who knows not your tongue and shares not your hopes and fears and joys, and if nothing be asked of him but to copy the gestures of the drivers of your beasts to burden—this man will see nothing whatever save an empty desert, and will yawn his days away throughout the journey, which will seem to him interminable, tedium without end! For him the well will mean but a smallish hole which has to be cleared of sand before it serves its purpose. How indeed could that wayfarer have learned what lay behind the seeming monotony, being of its very nature invisible? For all you see is a handful of grains of sand blown to and fro by the winds; though for one who is attuned to their significance, they can transmute his whole world, as salt transmutes a banquet. Thus my desert, if only I show you the rules of the game pertaining to it, can become so fraught with magic potency that even if you on whom my choice has fallen are selfish, commonplace, sceptical and half-blind, a dweller in the suburbs of my city or moldering your life away in an oasis, I have but to force on you a single crossing of the desert and, like a seed from its sheath, the man within you will break loose and your heart and mind blossom forth like a flowering tree. Then you will return to me having sloughed your skin, newborn, rejoicing in your goodlihead, and built to live the life of the strong. And though all I have done was to make you hear the secret voices of the desert—for that which is essential lies not in things but in the meaning of things—the desert will have made you germinate and wax in splendor like the ascending sun.

That crossing of the desert will be like a swimmer's crossing of a lake. And when you scramble up the further bank, laughing, comely, a man for all to admire, be sure the women will know you for what you are—the very man on whom their hearts were set—and then you will need but to scorn them, to make them yours.

But how flagrant is the folly of him who avers that men's happiness comes from the satisfaction of their desires! Seeing them going their various ways, he fancies that what counts, above all, for a man is to attain his end. As if there ever were an end attainable!

Therefore I say that what counts first and foremost for a man is the tension of the lines of force that weave their net around him and, resulting from these, the cohesion of his inmost self; and that likewise count for him the attraction of the well, the resonance of his steps, and the steepness of his climb towards the mountain-top. For you need but look at one who has scaled the highest pinnacle, tearing his knees on the crags and straining his wrists to breaking point, to perceive that this man's joy is far above the mean joy of the sedentary who, after having dragged his flabby self there on a day of rest, lies sprawling in the grass on the comfortable dome of an easy foothill.

In your blindness you have undone that God-made knot which binds things together, and now no current flows through your ruined world. For, having seen men striving eagerly towards the wells, you thought that the wells were everything, and accordingly had more wells bored for them. Likewise, having seen men eager for the seventh day's rest, you have multiplied their days of rest. And, having seen that men desire diamonds, you have broadcast diamonds amongst them. And, seeing that men fear their foes, you have crushed out their foes. And, seeing that men want love, you have built a whole town of brothels, where all the women are for hire. And in so doing you have shown yourself yet crasser than that old skittle-player, who in his folly sought to take pleasure in a cataclysm of skittles that he had his slaves bowl over.

But think not I am counselling you to belittle your desires. For where nothing stirs there are no lines of force. True, when you are dying of thirst, the thought of a near-by well quickens your desire. But if for some reason the well is quite inaccessible to you and you can neither receive aught from it or give it aught, then surely it is as if this well had no existence. Thus is it with a woman whom you chance to see as you walk by, and who cannot be for you; near though she be at that moment, she is farther from you than if she dwelt in another town and were married to another. Yet I transfigure her for you if I make you feel her as an element in a world invisible, a structure woven of tight-drawn lines of force. If, for example, you can dream of making your way to her house by night, placing a ladder at her window, carrying her off, swinging her upon your horse and having your pleasure of her in the darkness of the desert. Or, if you are a soldier and she is a queen, you can hope to die for her.

But weak and paltry is the joy you get from false structures, which you invent as a mere playground for your fancies. Thus, if you love a certain diamond, it is enough for you to move towards it taking deliberately short steps and walking ever more slowly, for you to have a banquet of contrived emotion. But how much better if your progress towards the diamond is part of a ceremonial that grips you and forbids your hastening, and if, thrusting forward with all your might and main, you have to struggle against the brakes that I impose and which check your speed. If access to the diamond is not absolutely denied you (which would annul its significance for you, making it a mere show piece empty of concern), nor made easy (which would call out nothing in you), nor made difficult by some foolish artifice (which would be a travesty of life), but simply part of a structure closely knit and rife with implications —then indeed you are enriched thereby. Indeed I know nothing that can better stablish you than your enemy—and these words should nowise surprise you; for they mean simply that, to make war, you must be two.

It is in boring wells, in achieving a day of rest, in winning the diamond from the earth and in earning love that your true riches lie. But not in owning wells, in having days of rest, or diamonds, or love at will. Even as you are none the better for merely desiring these things, without striving towards them.

And if you contrast desire and possession as being one of those pairs of words that clash against each other, nothing you understand of life. For the fact of your being what you are, a man, governs them both, and there is no antithesis between them. Thus, if you seek the plenary expression of desire and you encounter obstacles which are not frivolous but the resistances set up by life— which is the other dancer, your partner and your rival—then the dance begins. Else you are as futile as a man playing pitch-and-toss against himself.

Were my desert too rich in wells, an order would needs come from God, forbidding some of them.

For the lines of force that stretch across the world should act upon you, so that you derive from them your trends and tensions and your courses of action; nevertheless, since all are not alike beneficent, they form part of something which it is not given you to understand. And this is why I say there is a ceremonial of the desert wells.

Hope nothing, therefore, from that happy isle wherein you picture a store laid up for you of never-failing joys—like that harvest of skittle-pins of which I spoke. But if I wish to invest the treasures of that happy isle, once you have made your landfall in the darkness, with the glamor of your dream—then I will create a desert for you and scatter them along its length and breadth, in the pattern of a visage of that something behind everything which is not of the essence of things-as-they-are. And if I desire to give you lasting joy of it, I will provide you with a ceremonial of the treasures of the island.

❧ 83

FORGET NOT that your phrase is an *act*. There is no question of bandying arguments if you wish to make me take action. Think you that I will let my conduct be decided by your arguments? Surely I could think of better ones to counter them!

When have we seen a cast-off wife regain the lost ground by a lawsuit in which she proves her case? The lawsuit merely stirs up more ill feeling. She could not reconquer you even by being or seeming to be the woman you once loved, for you no longer love that woman. Thus I have seen an unhappy woman, who, by grace of a sad sweet song she sang, had won her husband, fall to singing it again on the eve of the divorce. But that sad sweet song exasperated him!

Perchance she might regain him by reawakening in him the man he was when he loved her. But, for that, a woman needs creative genius; for her task is to impose a certain bias on the man—as I might impose on him a bias towards the sea, which would make him a builder of ships. Then it will be with him as with a tree that grows and, in growing, changes. And he will ask again for that sad sweet song.

To stablish love towards me I bring to birth within you someone who is all for me. I will not prate of my distress, for that would disgust you with me; nor will I ply you with reproaches, for, justly, these would vex you. Nor shall I enumerate the reasons you have for loving me; for you have none, and the only reason for loving is —love. Nor shall I seek to appear such as you once liked me to be; for now you no longer would have me so; else you would love me still. But, rather, I shall train you to grow towards me, if I have the ability, and will reveal to you a landscape that will make you become my friend.

It was like an arrow piercing my heart when she whom I had forgotten said to me: "Hear you your lost bell?"

When all is said and done, what words of mine can avail? Often have I climbed to my mountain-top and gazed, musing, at the city. And, walking in the silence of my love, I have listened to men's words. True, I have heard words that led to acts, as when a father said to his son: "Go to the spring and fill this pitcher;" or the corporal to the soldier: "Be at your post at midnight." But ever has it seemed to me that such words had no secret virtue; for a traveller who knew nothing of our language, observing that the acts accompanying them were but incidents of the daily round, would find nothing more noteworthy in them than in the activities of the anthill, none of which but is plain to read. Thus I, too, gazing down at the bustling streets, the edifices, the industry and commerce of my city, even the care given the sick, saw nothing but a race of animals somewhat bolder, a little more inventive and observant than the common run of animals. Nevertheless it was brought home to me no less positively that in watching them going about their everyday tasks I had learnt not even the first thing of the inner life of men.

For there was something more, something the routine of the ant hill could not account for, something which would have conveyed nothing to me, had I not known the meaning of the words; and this was when I saw them sitting in a circle in the marketplace, listening to a story-teller in whose power it lay, if he were touched with genius, to spring to his feet after he had said his say and, followed by them, set the city ablaze.

Thus have I seen a peaceful crowd lashed to frenzy by a prophet's eloquence, and, streaming forth in his train, melt in the fiery crucible of battle. Compelling indeed must have been the message borne on that flood of words, for the crowd so suddenly to shatter the routine of the anthill and, ablaze with fervor, fling itself on death!

For those few who came back were changed men. And I perceived that we may well believe in magic processes without seeking in the hocus-pocus of sorcerers the secret of their efficacy; since there are certain groupings of words which, acting on my ears, can snatch me away from my home, my work, my habits, and make me welcome death.

Therefore I listened closely to these harangues, marking the difference between the one which created nothing and that which took effect; so that I might learn what it was that was transmitted. For clearly a mere statement carries no weight; else every man would be a great poet. And anyone could become a leader of men by saying, "Follow me to the attack, into the fiery din of battle!" But if you speak thus, only laughter greets you. And not otherwise is it with those who preach virtue.

But by dint of listening and marking that some few succeeded in changing men's hearts, and after praying God for enlightenment, I was enabled to discern in the whirlwind of words those rare currents that transmit the precious seed.

❧ 84

THUS WAS IT that I made a step towards the understanding of happiness, and came to grips with the problem happiness propounds. I saw it as a fruit of the choice of a ceremonial that creates a happy soul; and not as a sterile gift of bright futilities. For it is impossible to confer happiness on men, as something they can store up and possess. Thus my father had nothing he could have given those Berber refugees which would have made them happy; whereas in the bleakest desert and under conditions of the cruellest privation I have seen men whose faces shone with joy.

But think not that for a moment I believe your happiness will be born of privations, loneliness, or the desert. For these can equally well drive you to despair. But I would have you mark the example I have given, which, drawing a clear distinction between the happiness of men and the comforts furnished them, shows that their happiness depends wholly on the nature of the ceremonial in which they participate.

And though experience has shown me that a greater proportion of happy men is to be found in deserts, monasteries, and conditions of self-sacrifice, than amongst the sedentaries of the rich oases or in isles that men call "happy," I have not drawn therefrom the conclusion—which would be inept—that the quality of men's food is antithetic to the quality of their happiness. My conclusion is simply that wherever the good things of the world are most abundant men have more chances of deceiving themselves as to the nature of their joys, for these seem to emanate from those good things, though in reality they derive solely from the meaning those things acquire in a certain empire or domain or dwelling-place. Thus in prosperous conditions they may be apter to deceive themselves and hanker after riches that are but idle toys.

Whereas, being without possessions, those of the desert and the

235

monastery can make no mistake as to whence their joys derive; and thus it is easier for them to keep unscathed the source of their fervor.

But here, once again, the issue is like that of the enemy who makes or breaks you. For if, perceiving the true source whence it springs, you can preserve your fervor in the happy isle or the rich oasis, the man born within you of this fervor will be still greater; even as you may hope to obtain richer sounds from an instrument with many strings than from one with but a single string. And even as the excellence of the wood and the stonework, the meat and drink, could but ennoble yet more my father's palace, where every footstep had a meaning.

And likewise is it with the new-made ornaments which serve no purpose when stored in a shop, and acquire a meaning only when unpacked from their boxes and given their places in a dwelling, beautifying it.

❧ 85

IF YOU SUMMON your police officers before you and bid them build up a world for you, that world, however desirable it be, will never come into being; for it lies not with the police officer, nor is he qualified, to sponsor the faith that is yours. His function is not to weigh men in the balance but to enforce enactments, duly codified, as to the punishment of theft, the payment of taxes, or compliance with such or such a regulation. Whereas the rites and customs of your community are an aspect of its being, molding you into the man you are and not another, and causing you to savor the evening meal amongst your kinsfolk and not another; for they are lines of the field of force that animates you. Meanwhile, in the background so to speak, the policeman is stolidly there, like a wall or a steel framework. Ruthless is he as a law of nature and there is no parleying with him; even as it is a law of nature that you cannot enjoy sunlight in the nighttime, and must wait for a ship if you wish to cross the sea, and if there be no door on the left you are bound to go out by the right. Thus, quite simply, is it with the police officer.

But if you make him go beyond his brief and bid him weigh men in the balance (which no one in the world can do), and track down Evil by the light of his own judgment—and not merely watch men's acts, which acts are his proper concern—then, since nothing is simple and since men's impulses are vague and fluctuant as drifting sand, those alone will have freedom and come to power who are not held back by a profound disgust with the travesty of life you offer them. What the spokesmen of this way of living have in mind is an order somehow antecedent to the fervor of a tree, which their logicians claim to build up with their arguments, and not that of a growing tree born from a seed. Yet order is an effect of life and not its cause; a token of a city's strength, and not its source. Life and fervor and tendencies towards a certain end create order; but never does order create life or fervor or such tendencies.

Thus in a city ordered by logicians those alone will grow great who, because their souls are base, accept the handful of cheap ideas figuring in the policeman's handbook, and barter their souls for a miscellany of rules. For even though your conception of man is lofty and your aims are noble, be sure these will sound base and stupid when formulated by the policeman. For his function is not to point to any higher way of living, but only to forbid certain acts, without knowing why.

The bestowal of total freedom within an *absolute* field of force and the creation of *absolute* constraints (which are invisible policemen)—such is the justice of my empire.

Therefore I summoned my police officers before me and said: "You are to judge men's acts alone, which acts are duly classified in your Regulations. And on these terms I tolerate your injustice; though indeed it may be lamentable that, tied by your rules, you cannot cross a wall, which, may be, at other times serves thieves as a protection, even though a woman who has been set upon is crying for help behind it. Yet a wall is a wall, and the law is the law.

"But I forbid you to sit in judgment on man. For in the silence of my love I have learned that if we would understand a man, it is best not to listen to his words. And also because it is impossible for me to weigh Good and Evil in the balance, and in seeking to burn up Evil like a crop of weeds I run the risk of casting what is good upon the bonfire. Then how should you of all men, you whom I bid to be blind as a blind wall, profess to be capable of this?"

For I have discovered that in burning a criminal I burn a part of him which has beauty and reveals itself only in the flames of his last end. Yet I am bound to accept this sacrifice in the interests of the structure of the whole. For by his death I stiffen springs which must not be permitted to relax.

❧ 86

ON A CERTAIN NIGHT I went forth to visit my prisons. And I perceived that (as was bound to be) my policemen had singled out and cast into durance those alone who had proved their permanence by never truckling and by refusing to forswear the truth that was in them.

Whereas, left in freedom were precisely those who played false and forswore. And here I would have you recall my words: Whatever be the policeman's concept of civilization, and whatever may be yours, if once the policeman has been given the power of judging men for himself, that man alone can hold his own against him, who is ignoble. For every truth, no matter what it be, if it is a man's truth and not that of an obtuse logician, seems foolish, indeed criminal, in the policeman's eyes. For he wants you to be cut to a single pattern, to be the man of a single book, a single rule of life. Thus the policeman's way of building the ship is to begin by trying to suppress the sea.

❧ 87

I AM WEARY of words that flout each other, in vain contention; nor does it seem to me preposterous if I find in the quality of my constraints the quality of my freedom.

And in the quality of the courage of the soldier on the battlefield, the quality of his love.

And in the quality of his privations, that of his luxury.

And in the quality of his acceptance of death, that of his joy in life.

And in the quality of his hierarchy, that of his equality (which I would, rather, name comradeship).

And in the quality of his disdain for worldly goods, that of his employment of these same goods.

And in the quality of his total submission to the empire, that of his personal dignity.

For pray tell me, you who make so much of him, what is the quality of a man left to himself. Too well have I seen how it was with my lonely leper.

And tell me, you who make so much of it, what is the quality of that "free and wealthy" commonalty you cry up. Too well have I seen how it was with my Berbers.

MY FATHER said: "They think to enrich themselves by enlarging their vocabulary. And no doubt I might easily add a new word to mine; for instance, one that meant to me 'October sun,' as contrasted with the sun at other times. But I cannot see what I would gain by coining this new word. Quite otherwise, it seems to me that by doing so I would lose the expression of that interdependence linking up in my mind October, October's fruit and its cool winds, with that word 'sun,' which, having spent its force, no longer speeds the ripening. Few indeed are the words which enable me to conjure up forthwith a whole network of interdependences; words like, for example, 'jealousy.' For this word enables me, without having to set forth at length the network of interdependences it connotes, to convey the analogy I have in mind when I say: 'Thirst is jealousy of water.' For though I have seen men die of thirst, and realized that they were tortured by it, their suffering was not caused by a disease more loathsome in itself than the plague which stupefies you and draws from you but feeble groans. Water makes you scream with longing for it and when in fancy you see others drinking, you feel betrayed, no less than that, by every drop of water which flows elsewhere. Even as you feel betrayed when a certain woman bestows her smiles on your enemy. And your suffering derives not from a disease, but from the faith that is in you, from love and visions more compelling than any physical distress. For your life goes to the rhythm of an empire built not of things but of the meaning of things.

"But my invention for 'October sun' will avail me little, being too personal and private. On the other hand, I increase your powers if I train you in exercises which enable you, while always using the same range of words, to weave divers nets with them, apt to snare any kind of prey. As when you knot a cord, you may dispose your knots in such a way that it can serve for catching foxes, or else for setting your sails so that the wind is trapped in them. And the inflexions of my verbs, the interlockings of my clauses, the cadence of my periods, the placing of my complements, the echoes and recalls—these are figures of the dance that I would have you dance, and, when you have completed it, you will have conveyed to others what you set out to transmit, and grasped in your book what you set out to grasp."

Again my father said: "All awareness begins with the acquiring of a style.

"And," he would add, "awareness does not consist in absorbing a farrago of ideas, that will presently fall asleep. Little use have I for the scraps of knowledge you amass; for they can serve you only as objects or implements for the various tasks I may require of you: building a bridge, or mining gold, or informing me, when I need to know this, of the distance between two capitals. But such miscellanies do not make the man. Nor does the expanding of your vocabulary bring a heightening of your awareness. The only purpose served by enlarging your vocabulary is that it enables you to proceed further in describing the allusive network of a word—for instance, 'jealousy'; but it is the quality of your style and that alone which will sponsor the quality of your endeavors. Else these concoctions of your intellect leave me uninterested; I prefer to hear you say 'October sun' which speaks to my eyes and heart, and moves me more than any newfangled word of yours. First, your stones are stones; then component parts of pillars; then, once these are aligned, cathedrals. But I propose to you these ever vaster combinations only by virtue of the genius of my architect, who devised them for the ever vaster build-up of his style—in other words, the expansion of its lines of force within the stones. And in the phrase, too, you are building something up; and it is, above all, this building up that counts.

"Take that unlettered savage," my father said. "Increase his vocabulary and he will but tire your ears with an endless spate of words. You may pour into his brain the sum total of your knowledge, and it will only make him the more flashily pretentious. And there will be no stopping him. He will intoxicate himself with hollow verbiage. And you in your blindness will ask yourself: 'How can it be that my culture has thus debased this guileless savage and made of him, not the wise man I looked for, but a chattering ape? Now, too late, I perceive how great and pure and noble he was in his ignorance!'

"For there was one gift, and one alone, you should have made him; the gift that more and more you are forgetting and neglecting. And that is the practice of a style. For then, instead of playing with the things he learned from you, as with colored balls tossed in the air, and taking pleasure in their clatter, and being fascinated by his skill in juggling—instead of this you would have seen him using perhaps fewer implements but applying himself to those activities of the mind which lead men up towards the heights. And then, likewise, you would have seen him growing pensive and quiet like the child to whom you have given a box of bricks and who, after getting all the noise he can from them, listens in eager silence when you show him the wonderful forms that he can build with them. Then retiring to a corner of the room, he wrinkles his brows and ponders; and this is perhaps the first step of his progress towards man's estate.

"Begin, therefore, by teaching your ignoramus grammar and the usage of words and their complements. Teach him *how* to act before imparting to him that on which to act. And as for those who make noise overmuch and, as the phrase goes, bubble with ideas, and weary you with their ebullience—wait but a while and you will see them, too, discovering silence.

"And silence alone betokens quality."

❧ 89

IT IS AS THOUGH the nailsmiths and sawyers were to come to me and because a ship is made of planks held together by nails, claim for themselves the right of superintending the building of the ship and its handling at sea. Herein we have an example of that all too common error which consists in a false approach.

For it is not the ship that is born of the forging of nails and sawing of planks; but it is the smithy and the sawpit that are born of the seaward trend and the growth of the ship. The ship comes into being by way of them and draws its sustenance from them in the same manner as the cedar tree draws its sustenance from the rocky soil.

It is for the sawyer and the nailsmith to keep their eyes fixed on their planks and nails respectively, and know all that is to be known of these. Thus in their language love of the ship must become love for the nails and planks employed for it. But I will not come and ask them for advice about the ship.

Thus is it with those to whom I have assigned the collecting of taxes. I will not ask them their opinion as to the trends which should be given to the culture of my empire. Let them but obey me dutifully.

For if I devise a swifter sailing ship and alter the shape of the planks and the length of the nails you will find my craftsmen murmuring, simmering with revolt. To their thinking I am ruining the very essence of the ship, which is dependent, they aver, primarily on their planks and nails.

Whereas in fact it was dependent on my desires.

And similarly you will hear those others raging furiously together if I make some change in the finances of the empire, and therewith in the harvesting of the taxes; for, to their mind, I shall be ruining the empire, which depends, they will tell you, on their time-old procedure.

Let all such hold their peace.

None the less I shall treat them with respect. Once they have been visited by the craftsman's god, I shall not go to the nailmaker's smithy or the sawyer's pit and tender my advice. I have no wish to pry into their craft. The builder of cathedrals fires the sculptors' ardor, from the highest to the lowest, by inspiring them with his ideal; but he meddles not with the sculptor's work, to the point of advising him how to render a certain smile. For that would be mere utopian impertinence, the building of a topsy-turvy world. To busy myself about the nails would be like "inventing" a world not yet in being; which is absurd. Or imposing discipline on that with which discipline has no concern. Herein we see the professor's concept of "order" rearing its witless head. In its due time will strike the hour for giving thought to the planks and nails. If I concern myself with these before their turn, I am but wasting my energies on a world that will never come into being. For the best shape for nails and planks will emerge only in the wear and tear of contact with the realities of life; which realities will make themselves apparent to my nailsmiths and sawyers only.

And the more potent is my constraint—which is that seaward trend I instill in my craftsmen—the less my tyranny will manifest itself. For in the growth of the tree there is no tyranny. Tyranny manifests itself only if you try to force the juices of the soil into the construction of the tree; but not when the living tree itself draws up the juices of the soil.

Thus ever have I sought to make you understand that to build the future is, primarily and exclusively, *to think the present*. Even as the creating of the ship is exclusively the inculcating of a trend towards the sea.

For there is not, nor ever will be, a logical language whereby you can move forward from the raw materials to that which, dominating these, is all that matters to you; just as it is impossible to explain the empire by an enumeration of its trees, mountains, rivers and inhabitants; or to explain the look of melancholy on a marble face by analysing the various lines and masses of the nose, ears and chin; or the thought-laden calm of your cathedral, by beginning from the stones; or the domain, by beginning from the elements of the domain; or—simpler yet—the tree, beginning from the juices of the soil. You are lured into tyranny when, set on accomplishing some impossible task, you chafe against your setbacks, or others' remonstrances, and take to cruelty.

It is because there is no logic in the course of nature that language and logic must ever be at odds. You cannot build up a tree if you have but the juices of the earth at your command; it will grow only if you sow a seed.

The only course of action which has a meaning—though it cannot be expressed by words, being of the nature of an act of pure creation or the repercussion on your mind of such an act—is a course of action leading you from God, the fountainhead, to those objects of the visible world which have been given by Him a meaning, a color and an inner life. Thus, for you, the empire endows its trees and rivers, mountains, herds and dwelling places with a secret power; as the sculptor's fervor endows with secret power his clay or marble, or the cathedral endows its stones with their significance, making them into sanctuaries of silence; and as the tree drawing up into itself the juices of the soil, stablishes them in light.

I find there are two kinds of men who speak to me of a "new empire" that should be founded. Of the one type is the logician who builds with the bricks of intellect. But such activity I call utopian, and nothing will be born of it, for it is nothing in itself. Thus is it when a professor of sculpture shapes a face. For though a creator may be intelligent, creation is not a matter of intelligence. Moreover, such pedagogues ineluctably develop into tyrants.

Then there is that other type of man who is actuated by a passionate faith to which he cannot give a name. Such an one may well be, like a shepherd or a carpenter, lacking in intelligence, for creation calls not for intelligence. Indeed you may see him fingering his clay without any clear idea of what he is about to make of it. He is dissatisfied; shaking his head, he gives a thumb-stroke on the left, then another lower down. But gradually the face that is taking form comes to satisfy something which has no name yet weighs within him like an unborn child. And more and more the face comes to resemble something that is not a face. (Indeed I know not what that "to resemble" signifies, as I use it here.) And, lo and behold, that face of clay shaped into a semblance that no words can define is charged with the power of transmitting to you that selfsame nameless thing which inspired the sculptor. And you are braced together as he was by his creative act.

For this man's creation came not of the intellect but of the spirit. Therefore I tell you it is not intellect but the spirit of man that rules the world.

90

EVEN THOUGH in saying this I well may shock you, I would have you know that the conditions of the "fraternity" you seek derive not from equality; for equality is consummated within God alone, whereas brotherhood is a recompense. Thus is it with the tree which plainly is an hierarchy, yet you cannot say that one part lords it over another. Thus with the temple, which also is an hierarchy; while resting on its foundation, it is held together at its keystone—yet how could you say that one of these claims precedence over the other? What is a general without an army? Or an army without a general? Equality means equality within the empire, and fraternity is given men as a reward. For fraternity does not mean that you can address your neighbor over-familiarly or rudely, as the fancy takes you. Thus it is I say that your fraternity is a "reward"; for it derives from your acceptance of an hierarchy and from the temple that you build each for each.

I have observed households where the father was revered, and the elder son protected the younger, and the younger relied on the elder. Thus a happy glow illumined their evenings together, their feast days and their homecomings. But if they are mere unlinked fragments, if none depends on the other, if they do but rub shoulders and jostle each other like marbles—where is their fraternity? Then if one of them dies, another promptly takes his place, for he was not indispensable. But if I am to love you, I must know where you stand and who you are.

When I rescue you from the waves of the sea, I love you the better for this, being now responsible for your life. Or if I have watched over you and healed you when you were sick; or if it so happens that you were a trusty old servitor, helpful as a lamp; or even the herdsman of my flocks. Then I shall go and drink your goat's milk in your house. I shall receive from you, and you will give; you shall receive from me, and I will give. But I have no truck with him who fiercely declares himself my equal and will neither depend on me in respect of anything or have me depend on him. Him alone I love whose death would wring my heart.

❧ 91

THAT NIGHT, in the silence of my love, I set forth to climb the mountain so that once again, distance having hushed the sounds of the city and stilled its movements, I might gaze down and meditate on it. But half way up the mountainside, compassion made me halt; for I had heard sounds of lamentation welling up from the darkling plain, and I desired to understand them.

They rose from the cattle in the byres, from the creatures of the

247

fields, and the creatures of the sky, and the small creatures on the water's edge. In life's caravan they alone were making their presence heard, since the vegetable kingdom has no speech, and man, though speech is his, living as he does half in the world of thought, has learnt the practice of silence. Thus when a cancer gnaws a man you see him biting his lips, imposing silence on his pain and, rising above the turmoil of all flesh that suffers, transmuted into a spiritual tree that puts forth roots and branches in a kingdom which is not the realm of things but that of the meaning of things. This is why unvoiced suffering harrows you more than suffering that cries aloud. For silent suffering fills the room. And fills the city. There is no escaping it, however far you flee. Thus if your beloved is suffering in a far land, lo, her anguish haunts your mind wherever you may be.

That plaint I heard was the very voice of life; for life was perpetuating itself in the cattle sheds and fields and on the water's edge. Cows great with young were lowing in the sheds. And voices of love rising from the fens ateem with frogs. I heard, too, voices of carnage, for a grouse caught by a fox was shrilling, and bleating piteously a goat that was being sacrificed for your regalement. Now and again some great beast of the forest stilled the whole countryside with one brief roar, carving out a peremptory domain of silence wherein all life crouched, sweating with fear. For these wild beasts are guided to their prey by the acrid smell of terror, tainting the nightwind. And no sooner had he roared than all his victims shone for him, peopling the gloom with twinkling lights.

But after a while the creatures of the field and sky and swamp thawed from their fear-bound stillness, and the sounds of childbirth, love and carnage welled up anew.

"Surely," I mused, "these sounds I hear are but the sounds of portage, for life is being carried forward from generation to generation, and this endless march through Time is like the progress of a heavy-laden cart whose axles creak."

Thus it was given me to understand something of men's anguish, for they too, migrant as it were from within their time-bound selves, are borne forward from generation to generation. And day and night, inexorably, in cities and in fields are taking place these scissions, as it were, of a living flesh that ever rends and then repairs itself. And I, too, felt, like the throbbing of a wound, this process of a slow, perpetual rebirth going on within myself.

"Nevertheless," I mused, "these men live not by things, but by the meaning of things, and thus clearly is it needful that they should transmit the passwords to each other, generation by generation.

"That is why I see them, no sooner a child is born, making haste to inure him in the usage of their language, as in the usage of a secret code; for truly it is the key to their treasure. So as to be able to transport into him this harvest of golden wonders they have reaped, they spare no toil in opening up within him ways of portage. For hard to put into words, weighty yet subtle, are the harvests it behoves us to transmit from one generation to another.

"True, yonder village has a glamor all its own; and true, that old house in it has something that quickens our emotion. But if the new generation lives in houses about which it knows nothing save their utility, what will it find to do in such a desert of a world? For even as your children must first be taught the art of music, if they are to take pleasure in playing a stringed instrument; even so, if you would have them, when they come to man's estate, capable of the emotions worthiest of man, you must teach them to discern, behind the diversity of things, the true lineaments of your house, your domain, your empire.

"Else that new generation will but pitch camp therein, like a horde of savages in a town they have captured. And what joy would such barbarians get of your treasures? Lacking the key of your language, they would know not how to turn them to account.

"For those who have migrated into the land of death, that village once was like a harp, in which every wall and tree, every house and fountain was a string, having its own voice. Each tree had a history all its own, each house had customs all its own, and each well had its own secrets. Thus you could so devise your walk that it was like music, each of your steps striking the note that you de-

249

sired. But the barbarian encamped in it knows not how to make your village sing. It irks him and, fretted it may be by an order forbidding him to enter any of the houses, he throws down your walls and scatters your possessions to the winds. This he does to revenge himself on the instrument which he knows not how to play, and presently he sets the village on fire—which at least rewards him with a little light! But soon he loses interest, and yawns. For you must know what you are burning, if you are to find beauty in its light. Thus with the candle you burn before your god. But to the barbarian the flames of your house will say nothing, for they are not a sacrificial fire."

Thus was I haunted by the picture of a generation ensconced like an intruder in the other's shell. And I saw how incumbent was the tradition of my empire, requiring every man to hand down or to take over his inheritance, as the case might be. For I want dwellers in my land, not campers who come from anywhere and nowhere. This is why I prescribe as being essential those long ceremonies whereby I sew up the rents in my people, so that nothing of their heritage be lost.

True it is that the tree takes no thought for its seeds. When the wind lays hold of them and bears them away, all is well. Likewise the insect takes no thought for its eggs; the sun will see to their hatching. For all that trees and insects own is comprised in their flesh and is transmitted by it. But as for you, who are men, what will you become if nobody, taking you by the hand, has pointed you to the golden treasure of a honey that pertains not to things but to the meaning of things? Doubtless the letters on the page are plain to see; but I must be a hard taskmaster if I am to give you the keys of the poem.

Hence it is that I would have our burials performed with due solemnity. For it is not a matter of committing a dead body to the earth, but of gathering up the heritage which the dead man held in trust, without losing a jot of it; even as one does for the precious contents of an urn that has been broken. Hard is it to preserve all; the dead are long to gather up, and you must mourn them for many a long year, meditating on their lives and observing their anniversaries. Time and again must you cast a backward glance to make sure you have not forgotten anything.

Thus, too, with weddings, which are preparations for the throes of childbearing. For the house you make your home becomes as it were a storeroom, a barn or a treasure-chamber, and who could enumerate all that it contains? Your art of loving, of relishing the poem, of molding silver, your laughter and your tears, your musings and your deeds. And all these must be kept preciously together so that, when the time comes, you may pass them on intact. I wish your love to be like a well-freighted ship, equipped to cross the gulf between the generations; and not a mere concubinage for the sharing out by and by of useless goods you have amassed.

Thus, too, with the rites of birth; for there you have one of those rents of which I spoke and which it behoves you to repair.

These are the reasons why I ordain ceremonies when you wed, when you are delivered of a child, and when you die; when you depart and when you return; when you begin to build and when you begin to dwell; when you garner the crops and when you start the gathering of the grapes; when war begins, or peace.

This, too, is why I bid you bring up your children to be like you. It is not the function of some petty officer to hand down to them their inheritance; for this is something not comprised in his manual of Regulations. And if others than you impart to your son your little stock of knowledge and your little outfit of ideas, he will lose, by being cut off from you, all that is not capable of being put into words or included in the sergeant's manual.

You shall build your children in your image, lest in later days they come to drag their lives out joylessly in a land which will seem to them but an empty camping place, and whose treasure they will allow to rot away uncared-for, because they have not been given its keys.

THERE AROSE a sandstorm which swept towards us the wreckage of a distant oasis, and suddenly the whole camp was teeming with birds. In every tent were some of them, sharing our lives; for they were in no wise timid, and perched readily on our shoulders. Nevertheless, because food was lacking, they died by thousands daily, growing dry and brittle as dead twigs. Then, since they fouled the air, I had them swept up and many great baskets were filled with the small dead bodies. And all this recrement of life was flung into the sea.

Then for the first time we learned what thirst is and daily we watched, at the hour when the heat was fiercest, a mirage building itself up in the glassy air. A town, laid out geometrically in clean-cut lines, was mirrored in the pale smoothness of a lake. One man, losing his wits, uttered a great cry, and fell to running towards that phantom city. And I saw that this man's cry had jangled the others' minds, as the cry of a single wild duck, leader of the migration, thrids the covey. Thus all were itching to follow that madman's lead, to fling forth into the mirage and nothingness. But then a timely bullet laid him low. And, now there was but a corpse prone on the sands, my men took heart of grace.

But presently I saw one of them weeping.

"What is it?" I asked, thinking he was mourning his dead comrade.

But he had just discovered at his feet one of the brittle husks that had once been a bird, and he wept for a sky stripped of its birds.

"When the sky loses its down," he said, "man's flesh is in peril."

We hauled up from the bowels of the well the man I had sent down; he fainted in our arms, but not before telling us the well was dry. For the fresh water underground is ruled by tides, and over some years the tidal course sets towards the north. And then are battles round the wellheads and the northern wells run red again. But this well was pinioning us like a nail in a bird's wing.

And all of us were thinking of those great baskets filled with those brittle husks that had been birds.

Nevertheless we made the El Bahr well at the next day's dusk.

When night had fallen I summoned the guides before me.

"You have misled us as to the condition of these wells. El Bahr is dry. What am I to do with you?"

Gloriously the stars spangled a dome of darkness at once cruel and superb. Thus we had diamonds, if nothing else, served for our repast.

"What am I now to do with you?" I again asked the guides.

But vain is man's justice. Had we not all been changed to brittle twigs?

The sun emerged, sliced by the sand mist into the form of a triangle. Like a chisel whetted for our flesh. Struck on the head by it, men dropped like stones, and on others madness fell. But there were no more mirages to lure them with their cities of shimmering light. Now was neither mirage nor clean-cut horizon, nor any stable form. For the sand bathed us in the red seething glow of a brick oven.

Raising my head, I saw beyond the swirling sand clouds the whitehot brand that kept the air ablaze. "That is God's branding iron," I thought, "and we are His cattle ready for the branding."

"What ails you?" I asked a man who staggered.

"I am struck blind."

I had the bellies of two out of every three camels ripped open and we drank the water of their entrails. We loaded the remaining beasts with all the empty waterskins and, the fate of the caravan being in my keeping, I despatched some men to the El Ksur well, regarding which we had a little hope.

"If El Ksur is dry," I told them, "you may as well die there as here."

But they came back after two eventless days, which cost me the third of my men.

"The El Ksur well," they reported, "is a window opening on life."

So we drank what water remained and set forth to El Ksur, to drink again and replenish our waterskins.

The sandstorm abating, we reached El Ksur in the night. Round the well were some stunted thorn trees. But instead of the leafless skeletons of trees we thought to see, what first met our eyes seemed like a row of black balloon anchors mounted on thin sticks. At first we were perplexed by these curious apparitions, but when we drew closer, the trees, with one accord, seemed to explode in a burst of raucous rage. A huge flock of crows had perched on them and now, when they rose all together in a wild flurry of wings, it was as if the flesh of some black monster had suddenly split asunder, leaving the bare bones. So densely packed together were they that, though a full moon rode in the cloudless sky, we were plunged in darkness. For, instead of making off, the crows kept circling overhead, weaving a black canopy, like a cloud of coal dust, close above us.

We killed three thousand of them, for we were short of food.

How strange was the banquet that ensued! Quickly the men built sand ovens, then filled them with dry dung which blazed up like straw. And soon the air reeked of crow fat. Meanwhile the men on duty at the well paid out and drew in without ceasing a hundred and twenty-yard rope, navel string of the lives of all of us. Others were carrying the full waterskins round the camp, tilting them over thirst-cracked lips, like husbandmen watering the trees of an orange grove in a time of drouth.

Then, slowly walking, I went round the camp, watching my men's return to life. But, after a while, I withdrew from them and, in solitude, uplifted my voice to God.

"In this one day, O Lord, have I seen the flesh of men dried up, then restored to life. My army had grown brittle, like the bark of a dead tree; and now once more it is aflow with life, ready for action, and our limbs refreshed will take us where we list. Nevertheless, one burning hour of sunlight more, and we were wiped off the face of the earth, we and the very traces of our steps!

"I hear men laughing, singing. Freighted with memories is the army I am leading through the desert. It is the key of many a far-off life; for hopes and fears, despairs and joys are in its keeping and it is not self-sufficing, but linked by a thousand human bonds. Nevertheless, one burning hour of sunlight more, and we were wiped off the face of the earth, we and the very traces of our steps!

"I am leading them towards the oasis we are to conquer. They will be as seed sown in a barbarian soil. And bring our customs to tribes that know them not. Hardly will these men who are eating and drinking their full, living tonight a life but little higher than the life of animals—hardly will they have thrust forward into the fertile plains than all therein will change; not only the customs and language, but the form of the ramparts and the temples' style. For these men of mine are charged with a driving force which will take effect for centuries to come. Nevertheless, one burning hour of sunlight more, and we were wiped off the face of the earth, we and the very traces of our steps!

"They know it not. They thirsted and now their bellies are appeased. And that is all they need to know. But the water of this El Ksur well has rescued poems, cities and great hanging gardens —for it was my will to build these—from nonentity. The water of the El Ksur well has changed the world's course. Nevertheless, one burning hour of sunlight more, and we were wiped off the face of the earth, we and the very traces of our steps!

"Those who first came back from it said to us, 'The El Ksur well is a window opening on life.' Thy angels were all ready to gather up my army in their huge baskets and pour it into Thy eternity like the bark of a dead tree. But by this needle's eye we escaped them. Changed hereafter is this Thy world for me. For henceforth, if I but gaze at a common barley field glowing golden in the sun, poised between the dark earth and the light and bearing that by which men live, I shall see in it a vehicle or secret path, though I know not whereof it is the portage and the pathway. I have seen cities, temples, ramparts and great hanging gardens arising from that El Ksur well.

"My men are drinking, glutting their bellies. Their only pleasures are the pleasures of the belly. They were massed around the needle's eye. And at the bottom of that narrow orifice is but a sound of splashes, whenever a pail frets the dark water far below. But when that water is poured on the dry seed—which of itself knows nothing save its pleasure in the contact of the water—it awakens a secret power, which is the motive power of cities, temples, ramparts and great hanging gardens.

"But I can make no sense of all these things unless Thou art their keystone, their common measure and the meaning that pervades them. That barley field, my army, the El Ksur well—all these seem but unrelated things dispersed at random, unless behind the chaos of appearances I discern Thy presence and glimpse, rising up out of them towards the stars, the turrets and battlements of a city coming into being."

❧ 93

PRESENTLY WE CAME in sight of the city. But all that could be seen of it was a line of exceptionally high ramparts which seemed to turn their backs disdainfully on the desert. For they were bare of decorations, bays and battlements, and built, to all appearance, not to be gazed on from without.

Usually, when you approach and look at a city, it returns your gaze, peering through its loopholes, and arrays its towers against you. Then either it opens to you its gates, or shuts them. Sometimes, as if desiring to be loved and graciously smiling, a city welcomes you with a face bedecked with ornaments. Always, indeed, when we captured cities, so clearly had they been built to pleasure those who visited them, that they seemed to be giving themselves to us. Massive gateways and royal avenues—whether you come as a vagrant or a conqueror, you are assured of a right royal welcome.

But there was something uncanny about this city, and my men were uneasy. Looming ever higher as we drew near, the ramparts seemed purposefully to turn their backs on us, sheer as a cliff wall; as though nothing existed, nothing could exist, outside the city.

Thus we spent the whole first day marching slowly round it, seeking for a fissure, some fault in the sheer cliff, or at least some walled-in exit. But there was none. Often we came within easy gunshot, but never a volley broke the stillness, even though some of my men, unnerved by the long suspense, fired salvos, by way of challenge to the foe. But this walled city was like the cayman in his carapace, that disdains, however much you provoke him, to come out of his dream.

From a distant hilltop whence, though it did not overlook the ramparts, one could rake the city with a level gaze, we could see patches of greenery, close-set like cress. Whereas outside the ramparts not a blade of grass grew on the desert. Nothing there was but an endless expanse of sand and sun-scarred rocks; so industriously had the wellsprings of the oasis been diverted to the service of those within the city. The ramparts circumscribed all verdure, as a helmet confines the hair. Like hungry dogs we prowled around the city where, but a few steps' distance from us, was a paradise of serried greenery, an ebullience of trees and birds and flowers, strictly girdled by the ramparts' belt, as by the basalt rim of a crater.

When my men had made sure that there was no rift whatever in the smoothness of the wall, they were seized with fear. For clear it was that never within living memory had a caravan sallied forth from this city or been welcomed into it. No traveller had brought to its denizens the taint of foreign customs; no merchant, the usage of utensils daily employed in other lands. No woman taken in some

257

far foray had infused her alien blood in theirs. Thus my men felt as if they were fingering the hide of some strange, nameless monster having nothing in common with the peoples of the earth. For even the loneliest island has at some time been deflowered by a shipwreck, and always you find something that will make known to you your human kinship and compel a human smile. But, though very plain to see, this monster showed no face.

Others of my men there were who were gripped by a peculiar passion for this city, a love which had no name. For whether it be a woman or a city, you are drawn to her alone who is permanent, well founded, neither mongrel in her flesh nor ill-spoken in her converse and religion; one who comes not of a hotchpotch of nations (like the muddy lake into which a glacier dissolves) in which all is intermingled out of recognition. Ah, how fair was she, that well-beloved, so straitly nurtured in her gardens and her perfumes and her customs!

Thus they and I alike, once the desert crossed, had come up against the impenetrable. For one who stands up against you lays open to you the way of his heart—as that of his flesh is open to your sword—and you may hope to vanquish him, or love him, or die at his hands. But what can be done against one who pays no heed to you? And at the very moment when such thoughts were preying on me, we perceived that ringing that blind, deaf wall, lay a tract of whiter sand; whiter because of the dry bones heaped on it, betokening the fate of expeditions that, like ours, had come from lands afar. And it brought to mind the ribbon of foam into which the ocean swell, coming from far away, dissolves when the long waves meet a granite cliff.

When night came and from the threshold of my tent I gazed at that inviolable mass looming up in our midst, I fell to musing, and presently I perceived that it was far rather we than the city to be taken that were besieged. If you embed a hard hermetic seed in fertile soil, it is not the soil that lays siege to the seed, for all that it encircles it. For once the sheath is broken, the tree upspringing from it will establish its reign over the prostrate soil. Thus if perchance behind those walls there existed some instrument of music unknown to us, from which men called forth melodies of piercing shrillness or of sadness such as never yet had we heard, experience told me that, once we had forced our way into that mysterious fastness and its hoard had been dispersed amongst my men, I soon would find them sitting around the camp fires and seeking to woo from these alien instruments melodies with a new savor for their hearts. And their hearts would be changed thereby.

Victors or vanquished, I asked myself, how can we tell one from the other? Thus is it when you see a man alone, unfriended, silent in a bustling crowd. It pens him in, buffets and constricts him. And if that man be like an empty land, it overruns him. But if he be a man dwelt in, built up within himself—as was that dancing-girl whom once I bade dance before me—and if he speak, then, once he has spoken, he has struck root amongst that crowd, knotted his springes, made good his power, and now, if he starts walking forward, you will see that whole unruly crowd falling into line behind him and multiplying his power.

Thus, methought, if somewhere in the land there dwells but one wise man who, shielded by his silence and rapt in his meditations, has *become,* he is enough, unaided, to outweigh all your weapons, for he is like a seed sown in fertile ground. Did you wish to behead him, you would be hard put to it to distinguish him amongst the others. He reveals himself only by his quiet power and in so far as his work is done. For thus it is with every life that counterbalances the world. Only against the madman who dins your ears with his projects for a new world can you contend effectively; but not against him who *thinks* and builds up the Here and Now, for the Here and Now is none other than as he renders it. Thus is it with all creation: the creator is not visible within it. If from the mountain-top whither I lead you, and from no other place, you can see all your problems solved, how could you defend yourselves against me?

Thus was it with that barbarian who, having torn a hole in the ramparts of a great city, burst into the presence of the queen. And now the queen had no power left, all her men-at-arms being dead.

When you make a mistake in a game you are playing simply because you enjoy this game, I can see you blushing for shame, and
you do your best to put it right. Yet there is none to sit in judgment on you, save that personality which the game has evoked
within you, and which protests. Likewise you take care not to
make false steps in a dance, so that neither your fellow dancer nor
any other may be justified in blaming you. Thus I, so as to take
you prisoner, will not make show of my power, but will give you
a liking for my dance. Then you will come wherever I wish you
to come.

Thus, when that barbarian king broke through the door, swinging his axe like a swashbuckler, all bloated with his power and
filled with a huge desire to strike amaze—for he was a braggart,
puffed up with his own esteem—, the queen turned towards him,
smiling sadly, as though for some secret disillusion or an indulgence a little overtaxed. For nothing thrilled her save the perfection
of silence, and she disdained to hear all that rough sound and fury;
even as you heed not the squalid work of sewermen, though you
condone it as being needful.

Training an animal is teaching it to act in the direction that
serves its purpose best. Wishing to leave the house, you make your
way, without thinking, to the door. When your dog wishes to be
rewarded with a bone he will perform certain acts that you expect
of him, for he has gradually learned that these are the shortest
way to getting his desire—though seemingly they have nothing to
do with the bone. This is founded on brute instinct, not on any
reasoning. Thus, too, the dancer guides his partner according to
certain rules of which they are themselves unaware and which are
a secret language, like that secret understanding between you and
your horse; and you would be hard put to it to tell me what exactly are the movements by which you make your horse obey you.

Now, the weakness of that barbarian king being that he wished
above all to strike the queen with wonder, his instinct soon told
him that there was but one way to this, since all others made her

yet more aloof, more wearily indulgent, more disillusioned—and he, too, began to use the arts of silence. Thus, vanquished though she was, she was beginning to mold him to her wishes, preferring his silent gestures of rough courtesy to the clatter of his weapons.

And so it seemed to me that, by massing round this gigantic lodestone which, wilfully blind though it might be, drew our eyes towards it, we made it play a dangerous part; for our intentness endowed it with the far-flung influence of a monastery.

Therefore, having called my generals before me, I said: "I will take this city by astonishment. We must contrive that those within are led to question us about something."

Though they made nothing of this, my generals, trained by experience, murmured their assent.

Also I had in mind an answer given by my father to some who were insisting that in great matters men yield only to great strength.

"True enough," my father said to them. "Yet you do not advance the argument; for you will tell me that a strength is great when it makes the strong give way—which is a mere tautology. Now consider the case of a proud, avaricious and stoutly built merchant who is carrying with him, on a journey, a fortune in diamonds sewn into his belt. And picture now a little hunchback, poor and puny and cautious, who is not known to our big merchant, speaks another tongue, and yet aspires to get possession of these stones. See you where his strength lies?"

"Nay," they said, "we do not."

"Well, then you shall see," my father smiled. "The day being hot, that puny little man accosts the giant and invites him to share his tea. And clearly you run no risk in drinking tea with a shrimp of a man, when you have your diamonds sewn into your belt."

"Certainly not," they said.

"Nevertheless, when the two men parted, the little man went off with the stones, and the merchant was left gnashing his teeth with rage, being shackled, down to his fists, by the dance that the little man had led him."

"What dance?" they asked.

"The dance of three small dice carved from a bone," my father answered, and, after a while, added: "It may be that the game is stronger than the object of the game. Thus suppose you are a general with ten thousand men under your command. It is the men who have the weapons, and they make common cause with each other. Nevertheless, when you bid some of them hale their comrades to the cells, they obey. For you do not live by things, but by the meaning of things. When the meaning of those diamonds was that of being a stake in the dice game, they flowed away into our small man's pockets."

None the less my generals demurred.

"But how can you make play with them, the men behind those walls, if they refuse to listen to you?"

"There once again, my friends, your love of words has led you into error. Though they can sometimes refuse to listen, how dare you aver that men can refuse to *hear?*"

"Yet, when I seek to win a man over to my side, he may shut his ears to the lure of my promises, if his heart be stout enough."

"That may well be so—since you are showing *yourself* to him. But if there is a certain music that can move him, and if you play this music to him, then it is not you but the music he will hear. Likewise if he is poring over a problem that torments him and you show him the solution, he is bound to take it from you. Whatever his hatred and his scorn of you, how should he make-believe to himself and go on seeking the solution? If you point out to a chess player the move which he has been racking his brain to find, and which alone will save him, you master him, for even while seeming to pay no heed, he obeys you. For when a man gives what you are seeking for, you are bound to take it over. A woman is hunting for a ring she has mislaid or the answer to a riddle. I find the ring and hold it out; or I whisper in her ear the answer. True, she may loathe me so much that she will have none of either. Nevertheless, I have mastered her, for I have sent her back to her chair; she would need to be quite crazy, to go on seeking. . . .

"The men in that city must surely be wanting, seeking, guarding, cultivating, *something*. Else around what would they have built those ramparts? If you fence in a half-dry well with walls and I make for you a lake outside, your walls will fall of their own accord, as having no longer any sense. If you build them round a secret and my soldiers beleaguering your wall shout out your secret for all to hear, then too your ramparts will fall of their own accord, having become purposeless. If you build them round a diamond, and I scatter diamonds like pebbles outside them, then, too, will fall your ramparts, as shielding but your poverty. And if you build them round the perfection of a dance and I dance the selfsame dance better than you, you yourself will make haste to throw down those walls, so as to learn my way of dancing. . . .

"Thus all I would have of the men in that city is that they should hear me, to begin with. And anon they will listen. True, if I but have my trumpets blare at them, they will bide in peace on their ramparts, hearing not that foolish clangor. For you hear only that which is for you. And greatens you. Or, when you are in a quandary, resolves it.

"Thus will I act on them, for all they feign to heed me not. For greatest of all truths is this—that you exist not alone. You cannot stay unchanging in a world that, all around, is changing. I can act on you without touching you for, whether you wish it or not, it is your very meaning that I change, and this you cannot bear. You were custodian of a secret: when it ceases to be a secret, your meaning has changed. If a man is dancing and declaiming in solitude, I have but to surround him privily with a ring of ironical spectators, then whisk away the curtain—and, lo, his dance stops short!

"Or, if he goes on dancing, it means that he is mad.

"Whether you wish it or not, your meaning is made of others' meanings; and your taste of others' tastes. Each act of yours is a move in a game and a step in a dance. When I change the game or the dance, I change your act into another. For you live not by things, but by the meaning of things.

"Thus I will punish the men of that city for their aloofness, for they rely overmuch on their ramparts.

"Whereas the only rampart that can never fail you is the might of the structure that molds you and which you serve. For the cedar's rampart is the might immanent in the seed which will enable the tree to build itself up against storm and drouth and the parsimony of a rocky soil. Then, if you will, you may point to the toughness of the bark as its defense; yet the bark, to begin with, issued from the seed. Roots, bark and leafage are a seed that has fulfilled itself. But a barley seed has but little strength and the barley plant proffers a weak rampart to the onslaughts of the weather.

"One who is well stablished and enduring is equipped to fulfill himself in a field of force according to his lines of force which, at the outset, are invisible. Of such a man I say he is a trusty rampart, for storms will not wear him down, but build him up. They are his servitors. And no matter if he seems naked to them.

"The cayman's carapace guards nothing, if the beast is dead."

Thus gazing at that embattled, well-girt city, my enemy, I mused on its weakness—or its strength. Was I or was the city leader of the dance? Rash it is to let fall a single tare seed in a barley field, for ever the nature of the tare masters that of the barley; and little matter numbers or appearances. Numbers are implicit in your seed, but you must let time roll by before you can assess them.

🌿 94

AT NIGHTFALL I climbed the highest slope of the surrounding countryside, so as to watch the sleeping city and the lights going out one by one in the black patches of my camp spread out around it. I was seeking to reach the heart of the matter, for I knew that my army was power on the march, even as the city was power confined, as in a powder magazine; and that beyond this scene of an army massed round a magnetic pole another scene (whereof as yet

I knew nothing) was taking form and striking root, binding together the same materials in a different way. And I sought to decipher on the black page of the darkness the signs of that mysterious gestation, not in order to foresee it, but to direct its course. For all save the sentries were asleep, and their weapons at rest.

And I seemed to hear a voice which said: "Lo, now you are a ship on the River of Time. Over you has passed the morning light, the blaze of noon, the glow of sunset, bringing some advance to things, like the slow hours of brooding in the nest. Now, after the sun's brisk impulsion, has come the tranquil stress of night. Night flowing smoothly, with a drift of dreams; for those things which come to pass unheeded, like the healing of a wound, or the flow of sap within the tree—only these have continuance. Night made over to the servants, for the master is abed; night, which is a reprieve and a remission of sins, for their effect is put off to the coming day." (Thus I by night, when I am victor, put off my triumph to the morrow.)

Night of vineyards awaiting the grape-gathering; of respited harvests. Night of enemies hemmed in, whom I shall not take captive until the dawn. Night of the game that is over, and the player fallen asleep. Sleepbound, too, is the merchant, but he has given orders to the night watchman pacing to and fro outside his door. Sleeping, too, the general, but he has given orders to the sentries. Sleeping, too, the ship's captain, but he has given orders to the steersman, and the steersman is bringing back Orion, awander in the rigging, to the place where he should be. Night of orders duly given, creation in abeyance.

But night propitious to the evildoer. When marauders steal the fruit, barns are set ablaze, traitors seize citadels. Night of wild cries thridding the silence. Night when the reef entraps the ship. Night of signs and wonders. Night when God bestirs Himself—the thief! —for with tomorrow's dawn she whom you love will be no more.

Night when you hear a sound of creaking backbones. For ever have I heard this sound by night—the stirring of that unseen angel

whose presence I feel diffused amongst my people and whom it
behoves me, one day, to set free.

Night of embosomed seeds.

Night of God's patience.

✣ 95

"I," SAID MY FATHER, "am responsible for the deeds of all men in
my empire."

"Yet," one who heard him said, "some of them play the coward,
and some the traitor. How can you be to blame for this?"

"If a man plays the coward, it is I. And if a man betrays, it is
I playing traitor to myself."

"How could you play traitor to yourself?"

"I," answered my father, "endorse certain patterns of events, in
terms of which they serve me. And for each pattern I am responsible, since I enforce it. And it becomes the truth. Thus it is my
enemy's truth that I am serving."

"But why? Are you, perchance, a coward?"

"I call that man a coward," said my father, "who, having given
up moving, lays himself naked and supine. Who wails, 'The river
is carrying me away;' for, were he not a coward, he would set to
and swim." And, to sum up, my father added: "Him I call a coward and a traitor who lays the blame on others, or on his enemy's
power."

But none could understand his meaning.

"Nevertheless, surely there are happenings for which we are not
responsible?"

"No," my father answered.

Taking one of the guests by the arm, he drew him to the window.

"What does that cloud remind you off?"

The man gazed at it for some moments before answering.

"A sleeping lion."

"Now," said my father, "we will let the others look at it."

And having divided the company into two groups, he led one to the window. They all saw the sleeping lion which the first man pointed out to them, tracing its outline with his finger.

Then my father drew them aside, and brought another man to the window.

"What does that cloud remind you of?"

The man gazed at it for some moments before answering.

"A smiling face."

"Now let those others look at it."

And all those of the second group saw the smiling face which the second man pointed out to them, tracing its outline with his finger.

Then my father led the company of guests away from the windows.

"Try to come to an agreement as to what that cloud resembles."

Furiously they raged together, but to no avail; that smiling face was too plain to see for some, the sleeping lion for the others.

"Thus events," my father said, "have no form save that which the creative mind chooses to impose on them. Thus all forms are equally valid when you compare them."

"As for the cloud," someone observed, "we understand that; but not as regards life. For when the dawn of battle rises, if your army be contemptible as compared with the foe's resources, it lies not in your power to influence the issue of the day."

"True enough," my father said. "But even as the cloud extends in space, so events extend in time. If I wish to impose my pattern on them, I must have time. I can change nothing of what is bound to come to pass before the nightfall of today, nevertheless tomorrow's tree will arise from the seed I sow. And that seed exists today. Creating is not discovering a sleight of today that would have spelt your victory, had not ill hap concealed it from you. Such an evasion of the issue would lead to nothing, being like a drug that masks the symptoms of a disease, leaving its cause intact. To create is to render victory or cure as inevitable as a tree's growth."

But still they did not understand.

"The logic of events . . ." one of them began.

Whereat my father grew wrathful, and he gave free rein to his scorn.

"You fools!" he said. "You gelded cattle! Historians, logicians, pundits—you are but vermin battening on corpses, and never will you grasp anything of life."

Then, when his gust of anger had passed, he turned to the prime minister.

"The king, our neighbor, is set on war. But we are not prepared. Creation means not the molding for me of armies not yet in being, within the space of a day. Nay, it means the molding for me of a king, our neighbor, who has need of our love."

"But, Sire, it is not within our power to mold him. . . ."

"A woman sang to us," my father answered, "the other evening, and I shall call her song to mind, if you continue to weary me with your discourse. She sang of a poor, faithful lover who dared not voice his love. I saw even my general-in-chief weeping—a rich man, puffed up with pride and, what is more, a wencher! Yes, the magic of her song had transformed him in a few minutes' space into that humble, guileless lover, whose bashfulness and sorrows he made his."

"I," the statesman answered sourly, "am not a *prima donna!*"

❧ 96

You GIVE BIRTH to that on which you fix your mind. For, by defining a thing, you cause it to be born, and then it seeks to nourish, perpetuate and augment itself. To make that which is extrinsic to itself become itself. Thus is it when you belaud a man's wealth. Forthwith he esteems himself in virtue of his affluence and, though hitherto perhaps he paid little heed to this, from now on he bends his mind to the increasing of his wealth. For this has come to mean for him his whole significance.

Desire not to change a man into something other than he is. For it is certain that good reasons, against which you can do nothing, constrain him to be thus and not otherwise. But you can impart a change to that which he is already; for a man has many parts, he is virtually everything, and you are free to select in him that part which pleases you. And to limn its outline, so that it is evident to all, and to the man himself. Then, once he perceives it, he will accept it (having readily enough accepted it the day before), even though he has no special ardor to second him therein. And likewise once, by dint of having fixed his attention on it, it has been integrated within him, and indeed become a second nature, it will live the life of all beings which seek to perpetuate and augment themselves.

For you will always see a man giving the slave-master a certain toll of work, but refusing to exceed this. Such is life, for assuredly he might, if he were so inclined, give more work or less. But, supposing you wish that one part should absorb the other—that, for example, the work should absorb the leisure—you will say to him who works: "You, who accept this toil, exacting though it be, because in it alone you find your human dignity and a field for your creative gifts—surely you do well; for it behoves you to create where creation is possible to you. And to grieve that the slave-master is not a different man were but vain regret. He *is,* even as *is* the age into which you were born. Or as *is* the mountain in your land."

Thus you have neither asked him to work more, nor fomented his inner conflicts. Rather, you have implanted in him a truth reconciling the two parts of himself, and the man will now have life more abundantly and go forward willingly with the work assigned him.

Or you may prefer that the part of him which calls for leisure should absorb the part which urges him to work; and then you will say: "You are one who, despite the lash and the pressure of your daily needs, give to the work assigned you but the very minimum, failing which you would starve. Courage indeed is needed thus to act. And how right are you—for if you wish the slave-master to flinch, your sole resource is to begin by thinking you have bested him! Whatever you concede not in your heart is so much rescued from his clutch. And logic governs not creations."

You have neither bidden the man work less, nor fomented his inner conflicts. Rather, you have implanted in him a truth reconciling the impulses that were at strife within him. And now he will have life more abundantly, and go forward towards rebellion.

Therefore I have no enemies. I fix my gaze on the friend within the enemy, and he becomes a friend.

I gather in all the fragments. It is not for me to change them, but I bind them together by a changed language. And then the selfsame being takes a different course.

Therefore I accept all the raw materials you bring me, and I call them true. But I well may call regrettable the picture they compose. Then, if *my* picture comprehends and reconciles them, and takes the form I wish for it, surely you will be the better for it.

Therefore I say that you do well to set up your walls around wellsprings. But I reveal to you that there are other wellsprings outside your walls. And then, being the man you are, you pull down your walls and fall to rebuilding them. But now you rebuild them on my terms and I become the seed within your rampart.

❦ 97

I BLAME YOUR VANITY but not your pride; for, if you dance better than another, why depreciate yourself by bowing down to one who dances badly? There is a form of pride which is love of the well-danced dance.

But love of the dance does not mean love of you, the dancer. Your significance flows from your work of art; it is not the work of art that draws its prestige from you. And never will you perfect yourself, save in death. Only a vain woman is satisfied with herself. She has nothing to get from you but your applause. But we despise such cravings, we the eternal seekers, aspiring Godwards; for nothing in ourselves can ever satisfy us.

The vain woman has called a halt within herself, for she believes that her true visage can be achieved before the hour of death. Hence she is no longer capable of receiving or giving, but like one who is dead.

True humility impels you, not to demean yourself, but to open your heart. It is the key to giving and receiving. And I admit no distinction between these terms, which are but two names for the selfsame rule of life. Humility is not submission to man, but to God. Even as the stone is submissive not to the other stones but to the temple. When you serve, it is creation you are serving. The mother is humble towards the child; the gardener towards the rose.

I, the king, will submit without demur to the teaching of a farm hand, for he knows far more about husbandry than does a king. And while he is grateful for instructing me, I shall thank him therefor without feeling I am lowering myself. For it is fitting that the lore of husbandry should proceed from the farm hand to the king. But, disdaining vanity, I shall not ask him to admire me. For judgement proceeds from the king, its fountainhead, towards the laborer.

GOING UP to the mountain-top which overlooks the city, I made this prayer to God.

"These men, O Lord, are seeking to learn from me their life's meaning; awaiting from me their truth. But, O Lord, that truth has not yet been given form. Bestow on me the light of understanding. For however much I knead the dough so that the leaven may take root in it, nothing as yet is bound together, and qualms of conscience haunt my sleepless nights. Yet also I know how slow it is, the ripening of fruit. For all creation must first be steeped in Time, and long is the process of becoming.

"They bring me their desires and aspirations, and their needs, and heap them on my workyard, like so much raw material for me to assemble, for the building of the temple or the ship.

"For I have perceived that subordinating means receiving and setting in place; as when I subordinate a stone to the temple and it no longer lies at random in the workyard. Nor is there any nail which I put not to the service of the ship.

"I shall not heed the voices of the greatest number, for they see not the ship, which lies beyond their range of vision. Were the nailmakers in the majority they would insist on subordinating the sawyers to their own craft, and never would the ship be built.

"I will not create the peace of the antheap by multiplying executioners and prisons, though thus peace would certainly ensue; for, created by the antheap, man would live for it alone. But little wish have I to perpetuate a race of men which does not transmit its legacy from generation to generation. True, the making of the cruse comes first, but what gives it value is the liquor it contains.

"Nor shall I compromise. For compromise means being contented with a tepid brew in which iced and scalding drinks are feebly reconciled. But I wish to preserve for men their fullest savor. For all they seek after is desirable; all their truths are valid. And it is for me to create the vision, the pattern that embraces them all. For the common measure of the sawyers' truth and the nailmakers' truth is—the ship.

"Surely an hour will come, O Lord, when Thou takest pity on my anguish, whereof I have drunk to the last bitter dreg. For ever I aspire towards that shining peace which comes of conflicts resolved; but not towards the peace, half love, half hatred, of the partisan.

"When, O Lord, I wax indignant, it is because I have not yet understood. When I cast men in prison or have them slain, it is because I know not how to shelter them. For he who makes for himself a fragile truth (such as preferring freedom to strict discipline, or discipline to freedom), since he fails to master the vagaries of a language whose words rebuff each other—such a man boils with rage when someone ventures to contradict him. If you shout loudly, it is because, your own language being inadequate, you want to drown others' voices. But wherewith, O Lord, should I wax indignant, if I have had access to Thy mountain-top and seen work well done despite the makeshift words that sponsored it. Him who comes to me will I welcome; to him who sets himself up against me will I speak gently, comprehending where his error lies, so that he may return. Yet nothing in this gentleness will spell concession, flattery, or a desire to curry favor; I shall but be turning to account what I read so clearly behind the outward man—the fervor of his desire. And thus I shall make him mine; for I shall have taken him, too, into myself. Anger does not blind us; it comes of our being blind. You wax indignant with a man who shows his rancor. But it opens his garment, so that you see the cancer gnawing him—and presently you forgive. Why be wroth with a despair so piteous?

"The peace which I have in mind is won through suffering. I accept the ordeal of my sleepless nights, since ever I am drawing nearer to Thee who hast revealed Thyself: towards an end of questionings and silence. I am a slowly growing tree and by Thy grace I shall resorb into myself the juices of the earth.

"Well, O Lord, I know that the spirit rules the intellect. For the intellect studies the material parts, but the spirit alone perceives the ship. Thus, once I have envisaged the ship, they will lend me their intellects for the carving and adorning, strengthening and bodying forth of the visage I have created.

"Why should they naysay me? I propose nothing to oppress them; far otherwise, I set them free, each to fulfill his love."

❦ 99

I WISH YOU to be well stablished and perduring. Thus I would have you faithful, and the beginning of faithfulness is being true to oneself. You can get nothing of unfaith, for long in the tying are the knots that will hold your life together, quicken your energy, and endow you with significance and light. Thus is it with the stones of the temple. I do not begin anew each day and scatter them at random, groping my way towards better temples. If you sell your domain so as to buy another that is better in appearance, you lose something of yourself that never will you regain. How comes it, you wonder, that in this new house your days are so tedious? Surely it is more comfortable, nearer what you were always hankering after in that old house which always gave you so much trouble? Your well used to tire your arms and you dreamt of a fountain. But now you miss the tinkling of your little pulley, and the sheen of living water drawn up from the womb of the earth.

Think not that I would hinder you from climbing the mountain-side and rising higher; or have you cease renewing yourself and moving forward hour by hour. But the fountain wherewith you beautify your home, when it is a work of your own hands, is quite other than the comfort you take over in another's shell. For successive gains (as when new treasures are added to a shrine), gains that bespeak the growth of a tree developing according to its nature, are other than a change of house for mere convenience' sake, not love's.

I cannot feel sure of you when you cut loose, for in so doing you run the risk of losing your most precious possession—which is not things in themselves but the meaning of these things. . . . Thus ever have I seen that emigrants were sad.

Herein I would have you keep your mind alert; for we are apt to be the dupes of words. He who has found his meaning in travel, is constantly moving from place to place, and I will not say of such an one that he impoverishes himself. Nevertheless, another loves his house, and in his home is his continuance. Were he to change it daily, never would he have joy of it. When I speak of the "sedentary," I have not him in mind who loves his home above all else. I speak of one who has ceased to love it, or even to see it. For your home, too, is a never-ending victory—as is well known to your wife who remakes it with the dawn of each new day. . . .

Thus now I can explain to you the meaning of unfaith. For you are a nucleus of relations and nothing else; you exist by your links, and your links exist through you. The temple exists by each of its stones. If you take one away, it falls. You belong to a temple, a domain, an empire. And these exist through you. It is not for you to sit in judgment on that to which you belong, as an outsider, not bound up with it, might do. When you judge, it is yourself you judge. This is your burden; but it is also your highest good.

Therefore I despise the man who when his son has sinned speaks evil of his son. His son is part of himself. It is his duty to reprimand his son, to condemn him—punishing himself withal if he loves his son—and drum his truths into the wrongdoer's ears; but not to go from house to house complaining of him. For, in thus loosening the ties between himself and his son, he ceases to be a father, and the peace of mind he gets from this is but a diminution of himself, and like the peace of death. Poor indeed they always seemed to me, those who had ceased knowing whereto they belonged. You see them, day in, day out, seeking for a religion—anything to give meaning to their lives—and pleading like beggars for admittance. But all they get for their pains is the mere wraith of a welcome. For there is no true welcome save at the level of the roots; you need to be well planted, laden with rights and obligations, and responsible. But you do not take on the duties of a man in life, as you would take up a load of bricks in a workyard at the bidding of the slave-master. And so, if you play false to your true self, lo, your hands are empty!

That father I esteem who, when his son does wrong, takes the dishonor on himself, mourns over it and does penitence. For his son is part of him. But, being thus tied up with his son and perforce guided by him, he will likewise guide his son. For I know no road going one way only. If you decline to hold yourself responsible for your defeats, you have no right to glory in your victories.

If you love the woman of your house, your wife, and if she sins, you will not join with the crowd in judging her. She is yours and you will begin by judging yourself, for you are responsible for her. Has your country fallen short? I bid you condemn yourself; for you belong to it.

Doubtless, men from other lands will come to you and air their views, and you will blush for your country. And to purge yourself of shame, you will dissociate yourself from its lapses. Yet surely there must be some with whom you make common cause. With those who spat on your house? "Alas, they were only too right!" you will tell me. Perhaps. Nevertheless I would have you be of your house, and keep aloof from those who spit. It is not for *you* to spit; better were it to go back to your own people and cry in their ears: "O shame, why am I so unsightly when your shadow falls on me?" For if they take effect on you, by bringing shame on your head, and you accept this shame as yours, then you, too, can influence them and embellish them. And in so doing it is yourself whom you embellish.

Your refusal to spit is not a covering up of guilt. It is a sharing of the guilt so as to purge it.

You will hear those who repudiate their kinsmen, and, worse still, hound the foreigner on against them, protest: "Surely they are rotten to the core! We do not belong to them." But those who speak thus belong nowhere. Perhaps they will tell you they are making common cause with mankind, or God, or righteousness, or whatnot. But these words, unless they signify knots that bind together, ring hollow. God comes down to the home and makes Himself house, and, for the humble man who lights his taper, God is in the duty of the lighting of the taper; and for him who is at one with men, mankind is not a mere word in his vocabulary; mankind means those for whom he is responsible. Too easy is it to slink out of the race, and prefer God to the lighting of the taper. But mankind I know not; I know *men*. Not freedom, but free men. Not happiness, but happy men. Not beauty, but beautiful things. Not God, but the pure flame of tapers. Those who bend their minds on definitions otherwise than as wellsprings of significance, prove but the void of their hearts, and their own inanity. And they will neither live nor die, for men do not live or die by words.

But the man who sits in judgement, cutting the ties between himself and others, judges for himself alone, and you come up against his vanity as against a wall. What counts for him is the figure he shows the world, and not his love. Not himself as a link, but as an object to be gazed at. Which proves his futility.

Thus when you are ashamed of those of your own household, your domain, your empire, and you tell me you proclaim this on the house-tops with the object of purifying them, since you belong to them, this is a vain pretence. In the eyes of others you have ceased belonging to them, and you are redeeming merely your own good name. For rightly enough it will be said to you: "If they are like you, why are they, too, not here to spit as you are spitting?" You are plunging them deeper in the slough of shame, and battening on their disgrace.

True, a man may be disgusted by the vices, the foulness, the ignominy of his household, his domain, his empire, and forsake them so as to retrieve his honor. And thus he becomes an emblem of the honor of his kind; an envoy of what honor still survives amongst them, and an intimation that others also may be struggling up towards the light. But hazardous is this function, and it calls for yet more valor than does the facing of death. There will always be someone to call him to order. "But you yourself come of this scum!" And if he looks into himself he will answer, "Yes—but I have cut loose from it!"

Your one hope of remaining loyal lies in sacrificing the vanity of the figure of yourself you have set up, and saying, "I think like them, and I am indistinguishable from them." And you will be scorned.

But little will scorn matter to you, for you form part of their community, and you will act on it. You will impart to it your own direction, and as for your honor, it will be bestowed by theirs. Indeed there is nothing else for you to hope for.

If you are justly ashamed, show yourself not. And nurse your shame in silence. And salutary is this gnawing pain which will constrain you to set your house in order. For it depends on you. But be not like him who, because his limbs are ailing, cuts them off. That man is a madman. You may go forth to death so that your people may be respected in your person; but you may not repudiate them, for thus you would be repudiating yourself.

But good and evil is your tree. Not all its fruits may please you, yet some are well-liking. Too easy were it to flatter yourself for the latter and disown the others. Too easy to choose out certain branches and reject the others. Be proud of those which are good; and if the evil branches outnumber the good, keep silent. It is for you to withdraw into the tree trunk and ask yourself: "What shall I do to cure this trunk?"

He who gladly forsakes his country disowns his people and is disowned by them. Thus is it ineluctably. You have accepted other judges, and it is right that you throw in your lot with them. But it is not your land—and you will die of it.

It is your own nature that works the harm; your mistake lies in discriminating. There is nothing you are qualified to reject—yet here you feel out of place. But the blame lies with yourself.

I disown him who disowns his wife, his town, or his country. Perchance you are dissatisfied with them? Nevertheless, you are part of them; indeed that part of them which strives towards their betterment. And you should draw the rest in its wake. Not judge them from outside.

For two judgments must be rendered. The judgment you pass on yourself, acting as judge. And the judgment passed on you.

For there is here no question of building an antheap. You disclaim a home—and you disclaim all homes. If you disown a wife, you disown love. You may leave this woman but you will not find love.

❧ 100

MY BELOVED PEOPLE, you have lost your honey, which is not distilled from things but from the meaning of things, and though I see you eager as ever for life, you can no longer find the way of life. Once I knew a gardener who, when at the point of death, bethought him of his garden lying fallow. "Who will prune my trees? Who will sow my seeds?" Then he prayed for a few days' grace for the building up of his garden; for he had all his flower seeds ready sorted in his storeroom, and in his workshed all his tools for opening up the soil, and, hanging at his belt, his pruning knife—but now all these were for him but so many scattered objects and their significance had passed away like a forgotten rite. Thus is it for you with the things you have stored up; with your seeds and thatch, your desires and feuds and pities, and your old crones nearing death, and the worn lips of your wells, and your mosaics, and your singing water, all the which you have not yet learned to unite by the miracle of that knot celestial which binds things together (and alone can quench the thirst of heart and mind) into a village and its fountain.

✣ *101*

SCORNING BIG-BELLIED OPULENCE, I tolerate it only as a condition of what is higher than itself; as with the noisome activities of my sewermen, which are a condition of the cleansing of the town. Having learned that no contraries exist and that perfection is tantamount to death. Thus I tolerate bad sculptors as a condition of good sculptors, bad taste as a condition of good taste, the disciplining of the man within as a condition of man's freedom, and big-bellied opulence as the condition of an excellence which neither comes from it nor serves it, but comes from and serves those alone whom it nourishes. For if, by paying men to make their sculpture, wealth acts as a granary which the good poet can draw on for the grain he needs to feed him—which grain has indeed been pilfered from the husbandman's toil, since all he has got in exchange for it is a poem for which he cares not a jot, or a work of sculpture on which, likely as not, he will never set eye—and it is clear that, were there no such pilferers, the sculptors would not survive, little do I care if this granary bears a fat man's name. It is but a means, a portage, and a vehicle.

If perchance you blame the granary for thus becoming and being a receptacle of the poem, the work of sculpture, nay, even of the very palace, because it cheats the people's eyes or ears of these good things, I reply that, far otherwise, the vanity of the fat rich man will lead him to display his treasures to all and sundry (which plainly holds good also as regards the palace), since a civilization depends not on the using of things made with hands, but on the fervor of creation—as it is with those empires whereof I have spoken to you, where the art of the dance flourishes, though the fat-bellied rich man cannot store up in his showcases the dances that they dance, any more than the townsfolk can store them in their museums, since the dance is something that admits no hoarding.

And if you tell me that nine times in ten, the big-bellied man is a vulgar boor, patronizing those poets who babble of silver moonlight, and sculptors of the "lifelike," I answer that little does this matter, since if I would have the flower of the tree, I needs must accept the whole tree as it is, and, for the same reason, tolerate ten thousand bad sculptors if I wish one good sculptor to emerge. So I counterbalance the ten thousand receptacles of bad taste with the one gifted with enlightenment.

Thus, though the sea is a condition of the ship's being, some ships are swallowed up by it. And likewise there may be big-bellied men who are other than vehicles, portage, means to an end (and thus conditions), and devour the people for the pleasuring of their big bellies. So we must see to it that the sea does not devour the ship, or discipline devour freedom, or the bad sculptor the good, or the big-bellied man the empire.

You may ask me here to turn my logic to account and describe a system which will avert this peril. There is no such system. You do not bid me tell you how to direct the stones so that they gather together in a cathedral; for the cathedral is not within their competence, but within that of the architect who has sown the seed, and, like a tree, it draws its sustenance from the stones. It behoves me to *be* and with my poem generate an inclination towards God; then it will draw into itself the fervor of my people, the grain stored in the granary, even the doings of the big-bellied man, for His greater glory.

Do not think that I am interested in preserving the granary because it has a noble name, any more than I preserve the stench of the sewermen for its own sake. But the sewerman, too, is a vehicle, a pathway and a portage. Do not think that I am interested in the rancors the raw materials have for whatever differs from them. My whole people is but a vehicle, a portage, and a pathway. Disdaining alike the music and the flattery of the great, the hatred and the plaudits of the crowd, and serving God alone, beyond and through them, I am lonelier on my mountainside than the wild boar of the caves, and firmly rooted as the tree whose life's work is to transmute the rocky soil into a cluster of flowers whose seeds it scatters on the wind—making the blind dust live in flying motes of light. For in my ineluctable remoteness, I stand aloof from all their futile controversies, being neither for one group against the others, nor for inferiors against superiors, but overruling classes, factions, parties, I fight for the tree itself against its component parts, and for the components for the tree's sake—and who shall hold this up against me?

❦ 102

Now THERE BEFELL this quandary: that I could lead my people to the light of truth only by deeds, and not by words. For life is something that needs building up like a temple, if it is to take form and a meaning. What could you make of days that, like stones set in a row, were all alike? But when old age overtakes you, I wish to hear you say: "I have duly hallowed my elders' anniversaries, brought up my sons to manhood, and seen them wedded—and, as for those whom God took untimely to Himself (for some He garnered in before their prime), I have buried them with due regard."

For it is with you as with that wondrous thing, the grain of wheat which exalts the earth into a radiant hymn, an offering to the sun. And thereafter you exalt the sheen of harvest into the light in the eyes of your beloved when she smiles towards you, then shapes for you the words of the prayer that rises to her lips. Thus already when I sow the seed, a sound of the evening prayer is echoing in my ears; for I am one who goes his way slowly, scattering the good seed under the stars, nor can I fulfill myself if I keep my eyes too near the ground, like a shortsighted man. From the seed will arise the blade, and from the blade the ear of wheat to be transmuted into the flesh of man, and from the man will arise the temple to God's glory. Thus I can say of the wheat that it has the power of bringing the stones together, and a seed borne on the wind suffices to transmute the earth into a temple.

❧ 103

HATEFUL TO ME is the "intelligence" which is but that of accountants, who are perpetually striking their futile balances of things that serve for a moment and are gone. Thus, walking on the ramparts, you see (if you are such an one) one stone, then two stones, then three. But some there are who have the sense of time; they do not linger over this stone or that; do not regret this stone or that, nor hope to get their due from this particular stone or that. Simply they take a walk along the ramparts round the town.

NOTHING HAVE YOU to hope for if yours is the misfortune of being blind to that light which emanates not from things but from the meaning of things. Thus when I see you standing listless on your threshold and ask: "What are you doing there?" you cannot tell me, and you bemoan your lot.

"Life has nothing more to give me. My wife is sleeping, my wheat ripening, my ass idling in the stall. I am waiting, marking time futilely, my days are empty of concern."

A child without a game to play, you cannot discern what lies behind appearances. And, steeped in lost time, you are plagued by the distress of not-becoming. Then I sit down beside you and instruct you. . . .

For others tell you: "A man must have an aim." Joyful is swimming when it brings you nearer a shore slowly emerging from the sea. And joyful the creak of the pulley, bringing you the water for which you thirst. Thus with the golden wheat, the shore delectable of your black tillage; thus with the smile of the child that is the landfall of wedded love; and thus with the gold-inwrought mantle patiently made ready for the festival. What do you become within yourself if you turn the handle merely so as to hear the pulley, or sew the mantle merely for the mantle's sake, or practise the act of love for its own brief delight? All these things are soon exhausted, for they have nothing to give you.

I have spoken of the convict prison where I confine those who have lost their quality of men. The strokes of their pickaxes are but so many hollow thuds upon the rock, following mechanically. And nothing is changed in their substance. They are like swimmers moving in a circle, going nowhere. And there is no creation, for they are not a pathway or a portage towards some distant gleam. But though you toil under the selfsame sun, along the same hard road, and, like theirs, your sweat flows thickly, nevertheless, if but once a year it befalls you to win a diamond from the rocks, yours is the inner light that comes from God. And each stroke of your pickax is fraught with the meaning of the diamond, which is of a different nature. Thus you enjoy the quietude of the cedar tree, and the meaning of life—which is a gradual ascent towards the glories of the Kingdom—fulfills your heart.

You sew for the festival, you break the rocks to win the diamond, you plough the fields for the crop to grow thereon. And as for those whose happiness you envy, what more than you have they, save a knowledge of that divine knot which binds all things together?

You will not find peace if you transform nothing according to the light that is yours; if you do not make of yourself a vehicle, a pathway and a portage. For thus alone does the blood circulate within the empire. But in your folly you wish to be revered and honored for yourself, and you seek to get something from the world that is for yourself alone. But you will get nothing, for you *are* nothing. And you scatter your gifts and talents pell-mell in the cesspit.

You were awaiting a visitant from outside; as it were an archangel in your own image. And what more would you have gotten of his coming than of a visit from your neighbor? But having discerned that, though when you see them on their way they look alike, these three men are not the same—this one walking towards his sick child, a second towards his beloved, and a third towards an empty house—I make myself that something beyond things-as-they-are which is a destination or a meeting; and then all is changed. I am the harvest beyond the tillage, the man beyond the child, the fountain beyond the desert's rim, the diamond beyond the toil and sweat.

I constrain you to build a house within yourself: once it is built, there comes the visitant who sets your heart aflame.

It was revealed to me that the acceptance of the risk of death and the acceptance of death are very different. Many a young man I have known who proudly defied death—generally because there were women to applaud him. You come back from the wars, and gladdening is the hymn their eyes sing to you. Therefore you welcome the ordeal of cold steel and call your manhood into play, for that alone exists which you proffer and risk losing. This is something which the dice-player who risks his all on a throw of the dice knows well, for at that instant nothing of his fortune is directly serving him; it is but a stake pledged on the dice, dramatically dwindled to some tiny cubes held in the hollow of his hand. But when you cast these golden emblems on the rough-hewn table they become a vast expanse: plains, pastures and harvests of your domain.

Thus a young warrior returns, haloed by victory, his shoulders bowed with the weight of the weapons he has conquered, and decked, it may be, with the red flower of blood. And so he shines in glory—for a while only, perhaps; yet for a while. For you cannot *live* on your victory.

Thus the acceptance of the risk of death is the acceptance of life; and love of danger is love of life. Even as your victory was the risk of defeat bested by your creative valor; and never have you seen a man who reigns at no risk to himself over tame animals, boasting of being a conqueror.

I would have you form part of a tree, and subordinated to the tree. I would have your pride lodged in the tree, and likewise your life, so that it may possess a meaning.

The acceptance of risk is a gift you make yourself. For you enjoy breathing freely and bedazzling young women with your splendor. Also you feel a need for telling of these risks, which are goods that can be traded. Thus my petty officers are boasters all; but they do honor only to themselves.

One thing it is to lose your all on a throw of the dice, because you wish to hold and contain it in its entirety in the hollow of your hand, to feel it there, solid and substantial, intensely present in that fateful moment, with its garnered wheat and straw, its cattle grazing in the fields, its villages above which rise the wisps of smoke that betoken human life; and another thing it is willingly to strip yourself of these same granaries, cattle and villages, so as to go to live elsewhere. One thing it is to whet your fortune to a point and make it sting like fire in an all-decisive moment; and another to renounce it like a man doffing his garments one by one, and disdainfully letting his sandals fall on the sand, so as to wed, naked, the sea.

To wed, you must die.

You must die to yourself and thus survive like those old women who wear their eyes out sewing the ritual garments with which they clothe their God. Thus they transform themselves into a divine vestment. And by a miracle wrought with their fingers a haulm of flax becomes a prayer.

For you are but a bridge, a passage, and your life's reality lies in that which you transform. The tree transforms earth into branches; the bee, the flower into honey; and your tillage, the black earth into a blaze of wheat.

Thus my chief concern is that your God shall be more real to you than the bread you grip between your teeth. Then you will achieve the ecstasy that leads to the great sacrifice of self, which is wedlock in love. . . .

But you have ruined and wasted all, by losing touch with the significance of the feast day and thinking to enrich yourself by dispersing on daily needs the stores you have amassed. For you misunderstand the meaning of time. Your historians, logicians and pundits have misled you: gazing only at the surface of material things, and reading nothing behind them, they urged you to enjoy them to the utmost. Thus you would not hear of fasting, which is a pre-condition of the banquet on the day of festival, and would not suffer the loss of that moiety of the wheat which, burnt in the festal rite, creates the light of the wheat. And, blinded as you are by your base arithmetic, you no longer understand that one crowded moment may be worth a lifetime.

❧ 106

FOR YOUR EQUALITY is your undoing. You say: "Let us share this pearl amongst all. Any one of the divers might have found it."

But then the magic of the sea is lost; no longer is it a source of joy, and rife with promises to him whose stars are kind. And each man's dive is no more a ceremonial prelude to a miracle, and an adventure marvellous as a fairy tale, by reason of that black pearl another won from the depths a year ago.

Even so I would have you save, nay, stint yourself, all the year round for the sake of that one great yearly festival, whose significance lies not in its rejoicings, for these are fleeting (the festival being like a hatching-out, a victory or a royal visit); but whose purport is the sweetening of your whole year with a savor of happy expectation or of remembered joy—for only that road is beautiful which leads towards the sea. Thus the nest is prepared in expectation of the hatching-out, which is different in essence from the nest. Thus, too, you strive manfully in battle in expectation of a victory that is different in essence from the clash of arms, and you spend a twelvemonth making your house worthy of the prince's visit. Wherefore I dissuade you from levelling men out at the behest of an impracticable "justice"; for never will you make an old man equal to a youth, and your equality will always be a cumbrous makeshift. Sharing out the pearl will leave none the richer; therefore I bid you decline the paltry share that might be yours, so that the finder of the pearl may bring it home entire and with plenary delight, and when his wife questions him he will hold up his fist, saying, "Guess!" For he wants to whet her curiosity, rejoicing in advance for the happiness he has but to open his fingers to bestow.

Indeed all are the richer for his treasure-trove. For it proves that the divers' gropings on the seabed are not drudgery. Thus, too, the love songs sung by my minstrels teach you the delights of love, and the beauty they extol sheds lustre on all women. For if there is one woman in the world for whose winning a man will gladly lay down his life, she is a proof that love can be worth dying for, and, through her, all women are beautified, englamored; for may not any woman hide in her bosom, like the sea, her bright particular treasure, a peerless pearl? And then each time you draw near a woman your heart will beat faster, like the hearts of the divers in the Coral Gulf, when they wed the sea.

You are "unjust" to ordinary days when you bend your thoughts on the feast day, yet the mere prescience of high festival sweetens those common days, and you are the richer for its prospect. Injustice is done you if you do not share in your neighbor's pearl, but the pearl he lit on will beacon your gropings underseas, even as the fountain in the heart of a far-distant oasis spreads enchantment on the desert.

That justice of which you prate bids one day be like another, one man like another. True, if your wife is shrill-tongued you can put her away and take another whose voice is gentle. But my wish is to perpetuate love, since it exists only when irrevocable is the choice; for we must be limited in order to *become*. The pleasure of the ambush, of pursuit and capture, is different from that of love. For then your significance is that of the hunter; the woman's that of the prey you are pursuing. And so, once captured, she has served her end and means nothing to you. What does the poem when once it has been written, matter to the poet? His function is to go beyond it in a new creation. But once I have closed the door on the couple in your house, you needs must go beyond her. Your significance now is that of the husband; and the woman's her wifehood. I charge the words with their utmost weight of meaning, and when you say "my wife," there is an echo in the depths of your heart. Yet you will discover other joys; and other sufferings assuredly. But these are the condition of your joys. You are willing to die for her, since she is yours as you are hers. But you do not die for a captured prey. Your fidelity is that of a believer, not that of a wearied hunter—whose fidelity is different and sheds, not light, but boredom.

True, there are divers who never find a pearl. And men there are who never find aught but sorrow in the bed that they have chosen. But the ill hap of the unsuccessful divers is a condition of the sea's bright lure. Which holds good for all, including those who never find the pearl. And the sorrows of the husband are a condition of love's magic which holds good for all, including those whose love is ill-starred. For yearnings and regrets and grief for love's eclipse are better than the torpor of the well-fed beast to whom love means nothing. Even as when, parched with thirst in the desert, you are struggling through the briars, you prefer regret to forgetting of the wellsprings.

Herein lies an enigma which it has been given me to understand. Even as you stablish that with which you concern yourself, for or against which you fight (this is why you fight badly if it is mere hatred of your enemy's god that sends you into battle, whereas when you bravely run the risk of death it is the love of your own god spurring you on)—even so you are enlightened, nourished and ennobled by that very thing whose absence you deplore and for which you sigh and weep, quite as much as by the fruits of victory. Thus a mother within whose heart bereavement, having taken on its full meaning, has beatified itself, lives on the memory of her dead child.

If I ruin for you the true conditions of love, by ensuring that you do not suffer by it, what have you to thank me for? Is a desert without a wellspring any more acceptable to men who have lost the trail and are dying of thirst?

But if the wellspring has been lovingly hymned and tended in your heart, it will yield for you, in that fell hour when you are wedded to the sand and ready to put off your husk of mortality, the waters of that peace ineffable which comes not from things but from the meaning of things, and I shall call a smile to dying lips when I tell you of the sweetness of the melody of the wellsprings.

How, then, could you turn against me? I give you your life's meaning; with a regret I make your sand enchanted; I open to you the gates of love, and with a fragrance build a kingdom in your heart.

✼ 107

To BESTOW CULTURE, my father said, is to bestow thirst; then all the rest comes naturally. But replete bellies call for artificial potions.

Love is a craving for love. Thus is it with culture, whose very essence is a thirst, a craving. But how can thirst be cultivated? You crave for that alone which is a condition of your permanence. The man whom strong drink has stablished craves for strong drink. (Not that he is the better for it; indeed he dies of it.) One who has been molded by your civilization craves for your civilization. The supreme instinct is that of permanence; it rules even the life instinct.

Many men have I seen who preferred death to a life cut off from their village. Thus is it with even gazelles or birds which, in captivity, prefer to die. And you too, if you are reft from your wife and children and your habits—if the light by which you live is put out in the world (and that light shines even from the cloister of a monastery)—then it may well be that you die of this.

Thus, in order to save you from death, it is enough that I build up for you a visionary empire in which your beloved is as it were immanent, a welcoming presence. Then you will be glad to go on living, biding your time in patience. Though very far away, your home befriends you in the desert, and likewise your beloved will befriend you, though very far away and sleeping.

But the worst thing that can befall you is that a knot should give way, letting all it held together fall apart and be dispersed. And when your gods die, you die. For you live by them. And you can live by that alone whereby you can die.

If I awaken in you some compelling emotion, you will pass it down from generation to generation. You will teach your children to glimpse this vision behind the flux of things, even as the domain is perceived behind the scattered objects it comprises—and it alone compels our love.

For certainly you would not die for material objects, which belong not to you (for you are but a pathway and a transit), but to the domain. And you subordinate them to it. But once the domain comes into being you will lay down your life to save it from disruption. You will die for the *meaning* of the book, not for the ink and paper.

For you are a nexus of relations and your personality does not consist in your face and body, your chattels or your smile, but in a structure that is built up through you; and it depends on a vision of the world that at once derives from, and stablishes, you. Thus, though you contribute to the building of its unity, in return you owe yourself to it. Rarely can you speak of this vision; there are no words to convey it to another person.

Thus is it with your beloved. If you tell me her name, these syllables have not the power of conveying to me your love. For that, you would need to show her to me—which falls in the domain of deeds, not words.

But the cedar tree is known to you, and when I say "a cedar" I implant its majesty in your mind. For your eyes have been opened to the cedar tree, which is something more than the trunk, branches, roots and leafage.

It is only by having you sacrifice to love that I can stablish love within you. As for those sedentaries whose provender is fed to them on their litters, what gods are theirs? You may seem to exalt them by puffing them up with gifts, but these will be their death. You can live only by that which you transform and whereby, since you barter yourself for it, you die a little day by day.

A truth of which the old women of my empire, who wear their eyes out plying their needles, are well aware. One day you advise them to save their eyesight. And, lo, their eyes serve them no longer; by your well-meant advice you have ruined their bartering of themselves!

But those whose appetites you set out to glut, for what can they barter themselves? True, you gratify and stablish their thirst for possessions, but owning is not bartering. You can make good their lust for amassing embroidered cloths. But all you make good is the cult of the warehouse. How, indeed, could you expect to stablish a thirst for wearing out one's eyes on needlework? Which thirst alone is a thirst for life in its true meaning.

In the silence of my love I observed the lives of my gardeners and the women spinning my wool; and I saw that while little was given them, much was required of them. Indeed, it was as if the destiny of the world depended on them.

Thus I would hold every sentry responsible for the whole empire. As the gardener is responsible for warding the garden against the caterpillars. It may be that the woman making the golden chasuble infuses but a feeble radiance, but that faint gleam adorns her God, and it is a God more richly adorned, who, in turn, sheds His radiance upon her handiwork.

To say you "uplift" man has no meaning I can see, unless it means to teach him to discern the secret visage behind material things. I perpetuate the gods. Thus is it with the pleasure of a game of chess. I ensure it by maintaining the rules; but you would

293

provide men with slaves whose duty it is to win their games for them!

You think fit to supply men with love letters ready-made, because you have seen men weeping for joy when they received letters from their loves—and then you are surprised because you fail to make them weep!

Giving is not enough. You need first to build up him who receives. For the pleasure of the chess game the player needs first to be built up; and for that of love, the thirst for love. Thus, too, the altar is built, in the beginning, for the god's reception. And I have built the empire in my sentries' hearts by enjoining them night-long to pace the ramparts.

108

I HAVE HEARD men insisting on their claim to gratitude; they have done this or that for others. But, in truth, there are no gifts that can be garnered in and stored away. Your gift is an act of transmission from one to another. Once you cease giving, you have given nothing. You will tell me: "I did a good deed yesterday and its reward is mine to keep." But I answer: "No! True, had you died yesterday, you would have died with the merit of your act still yours; but you did *not* die. Count only upon that which you have become when your last hour strikes. Generous you were yesterday; but now you have conjured up from within yourself the niggard of today. And your last end will be a niggard's."

You are the root of a tree which draws its life from you. You are bound to the tree, and its welfare is your concern. But the root may say, "I have sent up too much sap." Then the tree dies. Can the root preen itself on having a claim to the tree's gratitude?

When the sentry tires of watching the horizon and falls asleep, the city dies. He cannot lay up a stock of rounds already gone, any more than you can lay up somewhere in your body a reserve stock of your heartbeats. Even your granary is not a store laid up; it is but a port of call. And even while you till the earth you are plundering it. For you befool yourselves in all such matters. You fancy you can dispense with the effort of creation by filling museums with already created objects. What you are shutting up in them is your people itself. But as for "objects"—these have no independent existence; you have only the various meanings given to the same thing according to the language of the speaker. Thus "a black pearl" does not mean the same for the diver, the courtesan and the merchant. The diamond has divers values—when you win it from the rocks, when you sell it, give it, lose it, retrieve it, and when it sparkles on a forehead at a festival. The thing-in-itself means nothing; the diamond, as a mere "object," is but a silly pebble. The woman who owns one knows this well; she locks it up in her most secret coffer, for it to sleep there. Only on the king's birthday does she bring it forth—at the prompting of her pride. She was given it on her wedding's eve, and then love prompted the gift. And once, for the man who broke its matrix, it was a miracle.

Flowers serve the pleasure of the eye. But fairest of all flowers are those with which I once bedecked the sea in honor of the dead. And none will ever set eyes on them.

Sometimes you hear a man flaunting his past. "I am he who did this or that." I am quite willing to do honor to such a man— but on condition that he is dead. Never have I heard my friend, that one great geometrician worthy of the name, basing his good name on his triangles. He was a servitor of triangles, a gardener in a garden of signs. One evening I said to him, "You must be proud of your work, you have given so much to men."

For a while he kept silence; then he answered: "There is no question of giving, I despise him who gives or receives. How could I revere the insatiable appetite of the prince who is always expecting gifts? And this holds no less good of those who let

themselves be devoured. The greatness of the prince negatives
their greatness; you cannot have both at once. But if the prince
abases me, I despise him; I am of his household and he owes it to
himself to greaten me. And, if I am great, I greaten my prince.

"What have I given men? I am but a part of them, an embodiment of their share of meditation on triangles. Through me they
ponder on such matters, as through them I eat my daily bread.
And I have drunk the milk of their goats, been shod with leather
from their oxen.

"I give to men, but receive all from men. Wherein lies the
superiority of one man over the other? If I give more, I receive
more. And the nobler is the empire to which I belong. You may
see this even in the case of your vulgarest captains of industry.
Incapable of being sufficient unto themselves, they lavish a fortune
in emeralds on some courtesan. Thus she shines forth, and they
share in her radiance, rejoicing in the reflected splendor that is
theirs. Yet they are paupers—dependents on a courtesan! Another
man has given all to the king. 'Whose man are you?' he is asked
and answers, 'I am the King's man.' And thus his lustre is enhanced."

❧ 109

I HAVE KNOWN a man so much wrapped up in himself as to despise
all others, down to the courtesans. Already have I told of that
pot-bellied, heavy-lidded minister of state who, after betraying me,
forswore and abjured himself, thus playing the traitor to himself
as well. How indeed could he have done otherwise? If you belong
to a household, a domain, a god, an empire, you are ready to
preserve that to which you belong by sacrificing yourself, if needs
be. Thus is it with the miser who belongs to a treasure, and has

made his god of a unique diamond; he will lay down his life defending it. But it is not so with the pot-bellied man; he is his own idol. True, his diamonds belong to him and honor him; but he is not theirs reciprocally. He is a barrier, a blind wall, not a pathway. And if one day you exercise your power and threaten him, what god has he to die for? He is all belly.

A love which parades itself is a vulgar love. He who truly loves communes in silence with his god. The branch has found its root; the lip, its breast; and the heart throbs in silent prayer. Nothing care I what others may think or know. Thus even the miser hides his treasure from all.

Love is silent. But riches call for drums and trumpets. What meed has wealth that is not flaunted? What is an idol without worshippers? Else it is but an effigy of painted wood, relegated with other rubbish to an outhouse.

Thus my pot-bellied, heavy-lidded minister of state was always crying, "*My* domain, *my* herds, *my* palaces, *my* women, *my* golden candelabra!" Somehow he had to make his existence felt. He heaped riches on those who bowed down before him. In like manner the wind, which has no weight or savor, assures itself that it exists by harrying the wheat fields. "I am," it thinks, "because I lay low."

Thus my minister relished adulation, but he relished hatred no less. For the smell of it tickling his nostrils was another proof of his existence. "I am," he thought, "because I make men talk!" And so he rode roughshod over the bellies of the people.

Moreover he was but a windbag, bloated with vulgar verbiage. For so that you may *be,* it is needful that the tree to which you belong should rise sunwards; you are but a pathway, a transit, and a portage. And, to believe in you, I need to see your God. But my minister was but a pit for the storage of raw materials.

Therefore I summoned him before me and said: "By dint of hearing you declaim so often 'I . . . I . . . I,' I have thought fit graciously to respond to the summons of your drums and trumpets and to contemplate you. And all I have seen is a hoard of random merchandize. What purpose do you serve by possessing these things? You are but a shop, a cupboard, and no more useful, no more real, than they. Doubtless you like to hear people saying, 'The cupboard is full,' but what of that?

"If I have you beheaded so as to spare my eyes your ugly leer, will anything be changed in the empire? Your coffers will remain where they are. What did you bestow on your wealth, of which your passing would deprive it?"

The pot-bellied man did not understand my question; but he fell to breathing heavily, for he was uneasy.

I continued: "Think not that I am actuated by some vague ideal of 'justice.' The treasure stored in your cellars is admirable, and it is not this that shocks me. True, you have plundered the empire. But the seed, too, plunders the earth to build the tree. Only . . . show me the tree that you have built!

"It troubles me not that the sculptor's woollen garment and his loaf of bread are levied on the shepherd's and the husbandman's sweat, so that he may be clad and eat his daily bread. For their sweat has been transmuted into the statue, even if they know it not. The poet, too, plunders the granary since he consumes the wheat without contributing to the harvest. But he provides a poem. I, too, use the blood of the sons of the empire for building victory. But thus I stablish the empire, whose sons they are. Sculpture, tree, poem, empire—show me which you serve. For you are but a vehicle, a pathway, a portage.

"Though for a thousand years you go on jangling my ears with your 'I . . . I . . . I,' how can this tell me what services you render? What have your estates and jewels and gold ingots become by way of you? Think not that I set myself against the glacier on behalf of the swamps, or reproach the seed for its gluttony and pillage. It is but a leaven that forgets itself, and indeed itself is pillaged by the tree that it sends forth. You, my friend, have pillaged—but who else profits by your plunder?"

✦

Nevertheless I would not have the high justice that I served mistaken for a mean and paltry justice. Favored by base practices, I told myself, a treasure has been got together which, divided up, would yield nothing. It greatens its owner; but its owner should greaten it likewise. I could divide, distribute and change it into bread for my people were I so minded, but they would be little the better for the extra day's food it would provide for them, numerous as they are. Once the tree has fulfilled itself, if it be tall and straight, I prefer to change it into a ship's mast; not to share it out in logs burning an hour or two. For my people would be little the better for an extra hour's fire. But all will be the nobler for the launching of a tall ship.

Around this treasure I fain would build a golden myth, gladdening the hearts of all. I would restore to men their happy faith in miracles; and it is well that the pearl-fishers, who have poverty for bedfellow—for hard is the harvesting of the fruit of undersea—should believe in a supreme pearl of great price. Richer they are for a pearl found by a single man, once in a while, which changes his whole life, than they would be for the paltry addition to their daily fare that would come of an equitable sharing out of all the pearls of the sea. For only that which is unique, unfindable, illumines the seabed for all alike with the glamor of a dream.

❧ 110

You come to me with a long sad tale of the sufferings of little children—and then you catch me yawning. Your tale has taken me nowhere. "Ten children were drowned," you say, "in that shipwreck." But such arithmetic means nothing to me; and if twice as many had been drowned, I would not shed twice as many tears. Moreover, since the beginning of the empire, children have died by hundreds of thousands; yet can you deny that you enjoy life and are happy?

I shall be moved to tears if you can take me to an individual child, by a path leading to him alone, and (even as a single flower brings home to us all flowers), by way of him, I shall feel for all children, and weep not only for the children, but for suffering mankind.

I remember your telling me of a lonely little boy whom you once saw in a village; how he was lame and darkly freckled, and how the villagers loathed him, for he had no kinsmen there, but had drifted into the village one evening from heaven knew where, and lived on charity.

"You are a blot on the face of our village," they shouted after him. "A canker on our stem."

When you first saw him you asked compassionately: "Haven't you a father, Freckles?"

He made no answer.

Or again, since the only friends he had were animals and trees: "Why don't you play with the other boys of your age?"

He merely shrugged his shoulders. For the other boys threw stones at him because he limped and hailed from some far-away village, certainly wicked as are all "foreign parts."

When he wanted to join in their games the biggest boys would scowl at him: "You walk like a crab. It's no wonder your own village spewed you out! How dare you come and spoil the look of ours, where we all walk properly, with your ugly, slouching gait?"

You saw him turn, without a word, and limp away.

Another day you asked him: "Haven't you a mother, Freckles?"

But he made no answer. Only he flashed a look at you, and his cheeks reddened. Yet, in judging him as sad, embittered, you misread his quiet gentleness. For thus he was—such an one, and no other.

An evening came when the villagers took counsel and resolved to drive him out of the village with sticks and stones.

"Let that spawn of crippledom go and make its nest elsewhere."
After protecting him from their attack you asked: "Haven't
you a brother?"

Then his face lit up, he looked you straight in the eyes.

"Yes! I've a brother."

Flushing with pride, he told you about his elder brother: his
very own brother, and not another's.

Captain somewhere in the empire, he had a horse of such and
such a color and not another. And (so he told you) on a certain
memorable occasion, his brother had taken him riding behind
him on the crupper of his horse. On that particular day and not
on another. Surely one day his brother would come here and take
him riding—him the limper, him the cripple—under the eyes of
the whole village! "But," the boy said, "this time I'll ask him to
let me ride in front of him, instead of on the crupper. Then it's
I who will look ahead, and say, 'Turn right! Turn left! Quicker!'
I'm sure my brother won't refuse this—why should he? He loves
to see me happy. And then there'll be the two of us."

He is something more than the pariah of the village, half crip-
pled, darkly mottled. He can fall back on something other than
himself and his ugliness, on his soldier brother. And he had had
his day of glory unforgettable, when he went riding on a warhorse.

Then one morning you came back to that village and saw the
boy sitting on a low wall, his legs dangling. And the other boys
were throwing stones and jeering at him: "Why don't you run,
squinty-legs?"

But he looked at you and smiled. You and he had a secret
shared, an understanding; you knew better than those foolish
boys who saw in him only Freckles, the cripple, the outcast; you
knew he had a soldier brother who rode a warhorse. You shared
his dream.

One day will come his brother and wash him clean of the spittle
of his tormentors; his glory will be a bulwark against their stones.
And he, the weakling, will be refreshed, renewed, by the shrill wind

of the speed of a galloping horse. His ugliness will be redeemed by his brother's beauty. He will be purged of his humiliation, for his brother is all-glorious within, a sun in whose effulgence he can bask. And, having recognized him riding past, those other boys will ask him, from now on, to join in every game. "Come and play with us, Freckles. If we'd known you had a brother . . ." And in him they will glimpse a reflection of his brother's glory. Then he will ask his brother to take them, too, one after the other, for a ride on his charger, so that they, too, may be refreshed by the wind of speed. How could he nurse a grudge against these youngsters for their ignorance? Rather, he will make friends with them and say, "Each time my brother comes, I'll invite you to gather round him, and he will tell you of the battles he has fought. . . ."

But you had come to bid him cast out of his thoughts that paradise, with its sun and promise of redemption. You had come to strip him of the armor enabling him to brave the stones. You had come to thrust him back into his mire. You had come to say, "My little man, try to reshape your dream, for your hopes of riding on a warhorse are but moonshine." And how bring yourself to tell him that his brother had been dismissed from the army; that he was shamefully returning to his village, limping along and looking so abject that stones were cast at him on the way?

And then if you round off your tale by telling me, "I myself drew up his dead body from the pond in which he had drowned himself; for, now his sun had set, he could live no longer"—then indeed will I weep for the wretchedness of man's estate.

And this will be by reason of the picture you have conjured up of a certain boy with a freckled face and not another, a certain warhorse and not another, a certain ride the boy had on one memorable day and not another, an indignity he suffered on the outskirts of a certain village and not another, a certain pond which you have described to me, with its ducks and humble washing fluttering on its banks. Thus you will rouse my compassion, a compassion so vast that by way of men it will lead me towards God; for you will have pointed me the one true way, by telling me the story of this one small boy and not another.

III

WERE I TO PRESENT you with a fortune ready-made (as happens with an unexpected legacy), in what respect would I increase you? Were I to make you a gift of the black pearl at the bottom of the sea, dispensing with the ceremonial of divings, wherein would I augment you? You are augmented only by that which you transform; for you are a seed sown in the ground. No gift advances you. Therefore I wish to reassure you, when you are in despair over your "lost opportunities." There are no lost opportunities. A certain man carves ivory, transmuting it into the image of a goddess or a queen whose beauty stirs our hearts. Another man carves pure gold and perhaps what he makes of it is charged with less emotion. Neither to one nor to the other has the ivory or gold been given; each is but a pathway, an intermediary. You have a temple to build, the raw materials are at your disposal, and there is no lack of stones. Thus the cedar tree does not lack earth. But the earth may well lack cedar trees and remain a stony waste land. Of what do you complain? No opportunity has been lost, for your function is to be a seed. If no gold be available, carve ivory; if no ivory, carve wood; if you have no wood, pick up a stone.

That pot-bellied, heavy-lidded minister of state whom I cast out from my people never found in all his domain, his cartloads of gold and the diamonds heaped in his coffers, a single opportunity to turn to account. Whereas he who, when out walking, stumbles on a pebble has stumbled on a marvellous opportunity.

When a man complains that the world has failed him, it means that he has failed to do his duty by the world. When a man complains that love has not given him his heart's desire, it means that he is mistaken as to love—which is not a gift to be had for the asking.

Opportunity of loving does not fail you. You can become a soldier in the service of a queen. For you to have your heart's desire it is not necessary that the queen should know you. Thus, watching my astronomer, I could see he was in love with the stars; he could transform a ribbon of light into a law of the mind. He was a vehicle, a pathway, a conveyor—a bee extracting its honey from a glittering flower; and I saw him die happy by reason of some signs and figures for which he had bartered his whole life. Thus was it also with my gardener, who had brought a new rose into being. The stars may lack their astronomer, and the flowers a gardener. But you will never lack stars, nor gardens, nor round pebbles on the lips of the sea. So never lament to me that you are poor. . . .

Thus I understand the bearing of my sentinels when they come off duty and are at their evening meal. They bandy jokes, they stuff their bellies, they slap each other's shoulders. And heartily they curse the hours of sentry-go, the long night watches. Now that their spell of duty is ended, they rejoice. That duty was their enemy. True enough. But besides being an enemy, it was also the condition of their lives. Thus with war and love. I have told you how the warrior adds his lustre to the lover; and how the lover, facing the perils of war, magnifies the valor of the fighter. Thus the man who dies in the desert is more than a mere fighting-machine, broken now and derelict. He says, "Look after my beloved, my house, my children, I entreat you." And then you hymn his sacrifice.

Thus I watched attentively those Berber refugees who never bandied jests, never thumped each other's shoulders. And think not that here it is a question of mere contrast, as it is with the sense of relief that follows the extraction of a rotten tooth. For

poor and paltry things are contrasts. True, you can breathe new
life into water (which means nothing to you if you merely quench
successively your small, recurrent thirsts) by forcing yourself to
drink but once a day. Then your pleasure is enhanced. But it
is still only a pleasure of the belly, and of little interest. Thus were
it with my sentries' meal when they come off duty, if it were
only a respite from their task. You could find nothing in it but
a new lease of appetite whetted by their work. Thus all too easy
would it be for me to breathe new life into my Berbers merely
by bidding them eat on feast days only.

But I have built up my sentries in their hours of vigil, and
therefore these men at their meal are men indeed, and their
repast is very different from the fodder fed to livestock to increase their girth. It is a communion of sentries in the breaking of
the evening's bread. True, none of them is conscious of this.
Yet even as the wheat that has gone into the bread will, through
their intermedium, be transmuted into vigilance and the safeguarding of the city, so their vigilance and safeguarding of the
city adds, through their intermedium, a religious significance to
the bread they break together. And thus it is not the same bread
that is eaten.

If you would learn their secret (whereof they themselves are
unaware), you need only watch them when they visit the brothel
quarter and pay court to the women. You hear one of them saying: "There I was on the ramparts, and I heard three bullets
whizzing past my ear. I stood my ground, I wasn't afraid." And
you, in your blindness, mistake what is love's diffidence for a
drunkard's bragging. For when the soldier tells about this experience on his sentry beat, it is far less to glorify himself than
to satisfy a feeling he is at a loss to voice. Even to himself he
cannot confess his love for the city; he is willing to die for a
god whose name he cannot tell! Already he had made himself
over to this god, but he will not have you know it. And he im-
poses a like ignorance on himself. For to seem to be the dupe of
big, pretentious words would lower him. And because he knows

not how to express himself, he instinctively refuses to expose his fragile god to your irony. Thus you may see my men playing the braggart and the swashbuckler—and delighting in your false impression—so as to relish somewhere deep down inside them, surreptitiously, the rare savor of a gift gladly made to love.

If the woman says to them, " 'Tis a cruel shame that so many of you will die in battle," you will hear them noisily assenting. But they assent with oaths and grunts. Yet she has wakened in them the secret joy of being known for what they are—men who will die for their love's sake.

If you talk to them of love, they will laugh in your face. You are taking them for numskulls who let themselves be duped to their death by pretty phrases! And they play the braggart, to hide their love from prying eyes. Nor are they wrong; for sometimes you wish them dupes. You enlist their love of the city for the defending of your granaries. Little care they for your precious granaries! Scorning you as they do, they choose to make you think it is out of vanity that they accept death's challenge. But you, you the replete, have no notion of what love of the city truly means. With their love they will save the city, without asking your advice; and then, since your granaries are lodged within the city, they will fling to you contemptuously, as one flings a bone to a dog, those precious granaries of yours that they have saved.

✕ 112

I PITY YOU in your disputes and reconciliations, for they take place on a plane other than that of love. For love is, above all, a communion in silence, and to love is to contemplate. There comes an hour when my sentry weds the city. And comes an hour when you meet your beloved—and its import lies not in one gesture or another, in one expression or another of her face, in one word or another that she utters, but in *her*.

There comes an hour when her name alone suffices as a prayer; no further words are needed. And comes an hour when you ask for nothing, neither her lips nor her smile, neither her gentle arms' embrace nor the fragrance of her presence. It suffices that she *is*.

But women there are who bid you justify yourself and who sit in judgment on your acts. They confuse love with possession. What good were it to answer? What joy will you have in meeting such an one? Your desire was to be received in silence; not for the merit of this gesture or another, this quality or another, this word or another—but because, with all your unworthiness, you are what you are.

✿ 113

IT BEFELL ME to repent of having failed to use in due measure the gifts bestowed on me (which were but signposts or stepping-stones) and, because I coveted them for their own sake, of having found in them but a barren wilderness. For, mistaking a certain parsimony of the heart or the flesh for a sense of measure, I sought not to employ them to their full. It pleases me to set a whole forest ablaze, so as to warm myself for an hour, for thus I invest fire with a more regal splendor. And when, riding my charger, I hear bullets whistling past me, it seems to me of little interest to economize my days. I have the value of what I am in each passing moment, and a fruit that has missed a single stage of its ripening never attains fruition.

Wherefore ridiculous he seemed to me, that ink-slinger who, when the city was besieged, refused to show himself on the ramparts, because of his scorn (as he said) for physical courage. As though a state, not a transition, were involved; an end, not a condition of the survival of the city, were at stake.

Likewise I scorn mere eating for eating's sake; my life is not to be assessed by the quarters of lamb I have digested. But I made those quarters of lamb serve the white impact of my sword-stroke, and my sword subserve the permanence of the empire.

Furthermore, though in the heat of battle I do not stint my blows so as to spare my sinews or because fear has made me craven, it would displease me were the historians of the empire to portray me as a mere wielder of the sword; for it is not in my sword that I reside. And though I mistrust the squeamish who eat their meat as if it were medicine, closing their noses to its savor, I would not have my chroniclers describe me as a huge meat eater, for 'tis not in my belly I reside. I am a tree well knit to its roots, and despise nothing of the roughage they absorb; for I build my branches with it. . . .

One day it became clear to me that I had been mistaken as to women. And there came the night of my repentance when I discovered that I knew not how to handle them. I was like the robber chieftain, ignorant of the appointed rites, who, when he joins you in a game of chess, moves his men wildly and unprofitably, then in a gust of petulance sweeps them off the board.

That night I rose from her bed with anger in my heart, for I had learned that I was no more than a stalled beast. And, O Lord, Thou knowest I am no body-servant of women.

One thing it is manfully to climb the mountain, and another, after having been carried to the summit in a litter, to sweep your gaze across the varied scene, in quest of some perfection. For hardly have you spanned the horizon of the blue plains than you are weary of this beauty and tell your bearers to carry you elsewhere.

I sought in woman that gift which she alone can give. Thus I wished a certain woman whom I had chosen to rouse echoes in my heart, like bell notes, charged with fond regrets. But who would wish to hear the same bell note night and day? Very soon he would relegate the bell to a loft, as something that had served its time. Another I enjoyed for the subtle cadence of her voice when she said, "You, my lord . . ."; but soon one tires of an oft-heard cadence and dreams of another song.

Were I to give you ten thousand women whom, one after the other, you quickly drained of that personal quality which made each delectable, even these would not avail fully to satisfy your heart's desire, for you yourself are variable as the seasons, the days, the winds that blow.

Nevertheless, since I have always held that none can achieve full knowledge of another's soul and that, in the secret places of his heart, each has an inner world of inviolable plains, vales of silence, great mountains, secret gardens, and that I could discourse to you of any man whatsoever a whole life long without ever being unduly prolix—such being my belief, it passed my understanding why what each woman brought to me from her store was so meagre, barely enough for a single evening meal.

But now, O Lord, I see my error. I failed to regard them as arable land to which year-long I must betake myself before the daybreak, my boots caked thick with mud, with my plough, my horse, my harrow, my bag of grain, my lore of husbandry, my prescience of storms and showers, and above all my faithfulness, so as to receive from them that which is for me. Instead of this, I reduced them to the level of those puppet-like creatures whom the notables of some humble village, which you visit in the course of a survey of the empire, thrust forward to falter some set phrase of greeting or to pay homage to you with a basket of choice fruits. True, you greet them affably, for charming is the ripple of their smiles, graceful their gesture proffering the fruit, and childishly simple is the small set speech; nevertheless you have drained them of their honey in a moment and used up their gifts, once you have patted the blushing cheeks and savored the sweet confusion of their gaze. Yet these young girls, too, are arable lands with vast

309

horizons, in which perhaps, did you but know the way of access, you might lose—and find—yourself for ever.

I sought to harvest from hive to hive the honey ready-made, instead of seeking to enter those vast spaces which at first give nothing but demand of you a long wayfaring, step by toilsome step; for you must walk a great while in silence beside the lord of the domain if you would make of them your homeland.

I who have had for a friend the one true geometrician, a man who could instruct me night and day and to whom I brought my quandaries, not to have them solved, but studied by him from his own angle; for being himself and not another, he did not hear this or that note of music as I did, nor see the sun as you see it, nor get the same taste as you do from the selfsame food, but, of the materials submitted to him, composed a fruit with a quality peculiarly its own and not another (neither measurable nor definable, but pregnant with a certain quality and not another, and pointing in a certain direction and not another)—I, who found in him the significance of Space and had recourse to him as one has recourse to a sea wind or solitude, what would I have gained from him if I had made appeal not to the man himself, but to what he could supply—not to the tree, but to the fruits—and aspired to satisfy my mind and heart with some dry formulas of geometry?

For him alone who tills his field and plants the olive tree and sows the good seed, for such an one alone strikes the hour of transfiguration, which he could never enjoy did he buy his bread from the baker. For him sounds the hour of the festival of harvest, and the festival of the garnering, when slowly he swings to the creaking granary door upon its hoarded sunlight. For the mound of seed grain stored behind that door, above which lingers a glow of yellow dust, has the power, when its hour comes, of flooding your black fields with rippling gold. . . .

I have taken the wrong road, I told myself. I made blind haste to go among women, like a traveller on a journey whose end he knows not. I have struggled through a wilderness unpathed, without horizons, seeking for the oasis that is not the oasis of love, but lies beyond it. I sought for a treasure hidden there, as for an object to be discovered amongst other objects. But I was going nowhere. Hurried as an oarsman's was their breathing when I bent above them, and I measured their perfection in their eyes. Familiar to me was the grace of their young limbs, the soft curve of an elbow like the handle of a ewer wherefrom one fain would drink. My anguish pointed the way, and for my thirst there was a remedy; but I had taken the wrong road. Thy truth, O Lord, was plain to see, yet I perceived it not.

For I was like one of those madmen whom we see prowling at night amongst the ruins of an old castle, carrying a spade, a pickaxe, and a crowbar. We watch him dismantling walls, upending stones, thumping great flags to find if they ring hollow. For, possessed by a black fervor, he desperately hunts for a legendary treasure that has slumbered for centuries in its hiding place, like a pearl in its shell—an elixir for the old, a warrant of wealth for the moneygrubber, a gage of love for the lover, of pride for the proud, of glory for the vainglorious. And yet it is but dust and ashes, vanity of vanities. For there is no fruit that comes not of a tree, no joy save the joy you make yourself. Vain is it to seek amongst stones a stone more exalting than another; and for all his rummaging in the ruins, the treasure-hunter will get of them no glory, wealth or love.

I, too, even I, like that madman plying his pick by night, have got nothing of my sensual pleasures but the morose and futile satisfaction of a miser's greed. Seeking, I found but myself. And I am weary of myself; the echo of my own pleasure rings hollow in my ears.

Wherefore I would build up a ceremonial of love so that its joys may be a portal opening on a world beyond them. For nothing of what I seek and for which I thirst (and for which, indeed, all men thirst) is on the level of the raw material at our command. And it is but wasted effort when a man seeks amongst the stones for something not of their essence, when he might put them to a worthy use in the building of his temple; since his true joy lies not in the extracting of one stone from amongst others, but in the ceremonial order of the stones, once the cathedral has been built. And thus it is with the woman on whom my choice has fallen; I can make nothing coherent of her if I fail to perceive what lies beyond her, her significance.

True, O Lord, when I watch a young wife sleeping in her sweet nakedness, pleasant it is for me to feast my eyes on her beauty, the frail grace of her limbs, the soft warmth of her breasts—and why should I not have my joy of her? But I have understood Thy truth. It is for me to ensure that she who now is sleeping and whom presently I will awaken, merely by letting my shadow fall on her, shall not be like a blind wall against which I knock my head, but a portal opening on another world; and that I do not disintegrate her, seeking for an impossible treasure amongst the fragments, but bind her together in oneness, a tight-drawn knot, in the silence of my love.

And how could I be disappointed of my hope? True, the woman who is given a jewel is ever disappointed; for there is an emerald fairer than the opal you have given her, a diamond fairer than the emerald, and the King's diamond, loveliest of all. But I care nothing for a thing cherished for itself, if it fail to adumbrate the meaning of perfection. For I live not by things but by the meaning of things.

Yet this ill-carved ring, this faded rose embroidered on a strip of linen, this ewer of common pewter which serves for our tea before the hour of love—all these things are irreplaceable since they minister to a rite. Only of the god himself I ask perfection, but the clumsiest wooden object, once it has served to grace his worship, shares in his perfection.

Thus with the sleeping wife. Did I appraise her for herself alone, soon would I grow weary and quest elsewhere. For it may well be that she is shrewish; or, even though she be perfection's self to look on, that she sounds not that sweet bell note on which my heart is set, that she says badly, "You, my lord . . . ," whereas these words would chime like music on another's lips.

But sleep untroubled for your imperfection, imperfect wife. I do not knock my head against a blind wall, for, though you be not a fulfillment, a reward, a jewel venerated for itself—of which I soon would weary—you are a vehicle, a pathway, and a portage. And I shall not grow weary of becoming.

✻ 114

THUS BECAME CLEAR to me the meaning of the festival, which marks the moment of your passing from one phase to another; when observance of the ceremonial has conditioned your rebirth. Herein is it as with the ship (of which I have already spoken). As a result of having been for a long while a house in the building, in the phase of planks and nails, it becomes, once rigged, a creature wedded to the sea. And you preside at its wedlock. This is a moment of high festival. But you do not settle down for life in the rejoicings which attend the launching of the ship.

Also have I spoken to you of the birth of your child; likewise an occasion for rejoicing. But you do not continue day after day, years long, rubbing your hands for joy that a child has been born to you. For your next festival you await a change of state, such as that which ensues when the fruit of your tree, bringing forth a new tree, carries your dynasty a stage farther. I have spoken, too, of the reaping of the wheat. Then comes the festival of harvest home. Then, anew, seedtime. Then the festival of spring, when the fields shimmer like a lake flooded with green tree-shadows. Then once more you bide your time, and comes again the festival of reaping, and again the harvest home. And so on, from festival to festival; for there can be no storing up of past rejoicing. And no festival

313

I know save that which you attain by coming from somewhere, and from which you go on. You have travelled many a mile. The door opens. This is the moment of the festival. But the room you enter is no more an abiding place than was the one preceding it. Nevertheless I would have you rejoice whenever you cross the threshold which leads somewhere; and keep your joy for the moment when you break through your chrysalis. For commonly you glow with but an uncertain light; and that clear radiance which is the sentinel's visits you at rare moments. I reserve it, so far as may be, for great occasions of victory when drums beat, bugles blow. Indeed it is needful that something should recuperate itself within you; something that, like desire, calls for recurrent periods of sleep.

Thus I walk slowly, one slow step on a golden flagstone, another slow step on a black flagstone, in the depths of my palace. One slow step on a golden flagstone, another slow step on a black flagstone, slowly I perform my task, like the team of workers sinking a well and hauling up the earth and sand to the surface. And timing the tug of the rope to the smooth rhythm of their sinews. I know whither I am going—and no longer is this land *my* land.

From hall to hall I make my way. In each the walls are of a different hue. And different the ornaments hung on them. I make my way round the big silver table on which are candlesticks of many branches. And now and again I stroke a marble pillar as I walk by. It is cold to the touch. Always. Presently I enter the precincts that are dwelt in, and the vague sounds coming to me from them are as echoes of a dream—for no longer is this land *my* land.

Nevertheless those homely sounds ring sweetly in my ears. For pleasing ever is a song that flows unheeding from the heart. Nothing is ever quite asleep. Even your dog, when sleeping, will sometimes give a few short, stifled barks, and stir a little, dreaming of the hunt. Thus is it with my palace, though high noon has plunged it in repose. The thud of a closed door jars the silence. Whence came that sound? you wonder. And tell yourself, "Surely it is the serving-women at their task. They have folded the new-washed linen in their baskets and, two by two, conveyed it down the corridors. And, now it is laid in order on the shelves, they are shutting the doors of the tall cupboards." There, in the recesses of the palace, a task has been performed, a duty well and truly done. Something has just fulfilled itself; and doubtless now will come repose. But what has that to do with me? No longer is this land *my* land.

From hall to hall, stepping now on a black, now on a golden flag, I make my way around the palace kitchens. I hear a familiar clatter of china, then the silvery tinkle of a ewer. Then again the faint thud of a closed door. Then silence. Then a noise of hurried steps. Something has been forgotten, something that needs your instant presence—as when milk is boiling over, or a child utters a sudden cry, or, simpler still, the abrupt cessation of a familiar, murmurous sound. Perhaps something has gone suddenly amiss in the water pump, or the spit, or the flour mill—and you whose steps I hear are hurrying to restart that humble prayer. . . . A moment later the sound of steps has died away; the milk has been saved, the child consoled, and now the pump or spit or mill is droning again its toneless litany. A danger has been averted, a wound healed, a lapse atoned for. Which? I neither know nor care. No longer is this land *my* land.

And then I enter the region of odors. For my palace is like a cellar slowly maturing the fragrance of its wines, the honey of its fruits. And now I shape my course between isles perfumed like those of tropic seas. Here is a store of quinces; if I shut my eyes, I feel their redolence cloying the air afar. Here is a pungency of coffers of sandalwood, and, farther on, rises the simpler smell of newly washed flagstones. Each smell has been carving out its province for many generations, and indeed a blind man could find his way here by his nose. Doubtless my father in his time reigned over these fragrant provinces. But I go my way, paying little heed to them. No longer is this land *my* land.

Following the ritual of such encounters, the slave drew back close against the wall as I went by. But I was moved to kindness and said, "Show me your basket," so that he might feel his importance in the world. Arching his glistening bare arms he grasped the basket on his head and lowered it. Then, his eyes fixed humbly on the ground, he proffered me his homage of dates, figs and tangerines. I sniffed their fragrance, and smiled. Then the man's smile broadened and, transgressing the ritual of these encounters, he looked me straight in the eyes. And slowly, arching his arms, he put the basket back on his head. "What portends this lamp aglow?" I wondered. "What is the secret fire burning in the depths of my palace behind these walls? For surely they spread like forest fires: rebellions or love." And I gazed intently at the slave, as one who peers into the abysmal depths of sea. "How vast," I thought, "is the mystery of man!" and went my way, leaving the enigma unresolved; for no longer was this land *my* land.

I crossed the hall of recreation; I crossed the Council Chamber in which my footfalls echoed and re-echoed. Then slowly I went down the stairway leading to the last vestibule. And no sooner had I begun to cross it than I heard a quickly muffled outcry and a clatter of arms. I smiled indulgently, having guessed that my guards had been asleep, for under the fires of noon my palace was like a drowsy hive, its languorous repose hardly ruffled by the brief unrest of a fretful few whose eyes refused to shut; or of that eternal process of reshapement which is for ever amending and perfecting you, and dismantling something within you. Thus in a flock of goats always there is one who bleats; and always from a sleeping town rises an inexplicable cry; and in the black silence of a mausoleum always there is a night watchman going his round. Thus with slow steps I went my way, lowering my eyes so as not to see my men hastily standing to their posts. For what cared I? No longer was this land *my* land.

Then, having stiffened to attention, they saluted and opened to me the great double doors. Under the fierce impact of the sun I half closed my eyes, and lingered for a moment on the threshold. Yonder, I saw the countryside: rolling hills proffering my vineyards to the sun, my wheatfields laid out in squares. Yonder a smell of sun-scorched chalk was rising from the ploughlands, and therewith rose an earthborn music from bees, crickets and grasshoppers. I was aware of passing from one civilization to another. For I was about to breathe the air of noontide brooding on my empire. . . . And in that moment I was reborn.

❧ 115

THUS IT WAS when I paid a visit to my friend, the one true geometrician in my empire.

I was touched at seeing him so intent on the tea and the little charcoal fire, on the kettle and its gaily singing water, then on the tasting of a trial sip, then on the time of waiting; for slowly tea brings forth its aroma. And it pleased me to see that during these meditative minutes, he was more absorbed in the tea than in a problem of geometry.

"So you, who know so much, do not despise the humbler joys of life?" I said.

For a while he kept silent. Only when he was quite satisfied with the tea did he make answer.

" 'I who know so much'—what has that to do with it? Why should a guitar player despise the ceremonial of tea merely because he knows something about the relations between notes of music? Somewhat I know of the relations between the lines of a triangle. Yet the song of the boiling water and the little ceremonial in honor of my friend, the King, rejoice me—and why not?" After a pause he added: "I wonder now! I doubt if my triangles can enlighten me as to the pleasure given me by the tea. Yet it may well be that this pleasure can throw a little light on my triangles."

"What do you mean by that, my friend?"

"When I experience an emotion, a need comes on me to describe. Thus when I love a woman, I will talk to you of her hair, her eyelashes, her lips, her gestures which are music for the heart. Would I talk of her gestures, lips and hair and eyelashes, were there not the face I have discerned behind these things? I can describe the elements of beauty in her smile; nevertheless the smile came first.

"I would not bid you pore upon a heap of stones, and turn them over and over, in the vain hope of learning from them the secret of meditation. For on the level of the stones there is no question of meditation; for that, the temple must have come into being. But, once it is built, a new emotion sways my heart, and when I go away, I ponder on the relations between the stones.

"Nor do I hope to find the 'explanation' of the orange tree in the salts of the earth that nourish it; for at their level the orange tree has no meaning. But by dint of watching the rising of the tree, I shall explain through it the rising of the salts of the earth.

"I must begin by feeling love; and I must first observe a wholeness. After that I may proceed to study the components and their groupings. But I shall not trouble to investigate these raw materials unless they are dominated by something on which my heart is set. Thus I began by observing the triangle as a whole; then I sought to learn in it the functions of its component lines. You, too, began by loving a concept you had formed of Man, in terms of an inner fervor personal to you. And starting from this you built up your ceremonial, so that your vision of Man might be comprehended in it—like a living creature held in a snare—and it might thus be consecrated in the empire. But what sculptor would be interested in a nose, an eye, or a beard for its own sake only? And what rite of the ceremonial will you enjoin for its own sake only? And what can I hope to deduce from the lines if they do not belong to a triangle?

"So, to begin with, I practise contemplation. After that, if I am able, I analyse and explain. Thus I have never scorned love; indeed the repudiation of love is but pretentious folly. Often have

318

I esteemed a woman who knew nothing about triangles—but she knew far more than I about the art of the smile. Have you watched a woman smile?"

"Indeed I have, my friend."

"Well, the woman I have in mind could, with the muscles of her face, her lips and her eyelashes (which are but raw materials, intrinsically without significance), build up for you, effortlessly, an inimitable masterpiece; and by grace of witnessing that smile one dwelt for a fleeting moment in a world of shining peace and love's eternity. Then, under your eyes, she undid her masterpiece—so swiftly that you had but just the time to make a timid gesture and momentarily lose yourself in a land of dreams where you could cherish such wild fancies as a great fire from which you rescued her and she acclaimed you her savior—so potent was the emotion she inspired. And had I any reason to belittle that woman, because her creation left nothing behind: none of those visible traces which enrich museums? From already built cathedrals I can draw conclusions, but there I saw her, building her cathedral under my very eyes!"

"And what did she teach you as to the relations between lines?"

"Little matter the actual things that are linked together; it is the links that I must begin by apprehending and interpreting. I am old. Thus I have seen those whom I loved die, or sometimes recover. An evening comes when she whom you love, her head drooping on her shoulder, refuses to drink of the bowl of milk, like the babe already on the deathward slope, turning his head from the breast whose milk has grown bitter to his dying lips. She has a weak smile, which is a plea for forgiveness; for your look betrays your grief that she no longer takes the food you proffer. But she needs you no more. Then you go to the window to hide your tears. And yonder lie your fields and pastures. Then you are conscious of your link, like a navel-cord, with the world of things: the barley fields and wheat fields and that orange tree in flower which will assuage your hunger; and the sun, which from time immemorial has been turning as it were the mill-wheel of the water-springs that quench your thirst. A rumbling of cart wheels comes to you from the new aqueduct in building, which will bring water to the city now that the old one is falling into ruin; or perhaps it is a simpler, rustic sound—of a farmer's wagon, or an ass, slung with his panniers, ambling by. Thus you grow aware of the all-pervading sap that causes things to endure. And slowly you walk back to the bed. Gently you wipe the sweat from her glistening cheeks; she is still here beside you, yet you feel her thoughts awander, half way to death. No longer does the countryside sing for her its song of an aqueduct in the building, a farm cart, or a trotting ass. No longer is the fragrance of the orange trees for her; nor your love.

"Then perhaps you recall two warm friends whom once you knew. One of them would go to wake the other in the middle of the night, simply because he felt a sudden need of his jests or his counsel, or, more simply still, of his mere presence. And if one were away, travelling, the other pined for him. Then one day an absurd misunderstanding parted them. And now when they meet they feign not to see each other. And the amazing thing is that neither feels the least regret. Regret for love is love. Yet what they two got from each other, neither will get from any other person in the world. For each man jests, gives counsel, or simply breathes, in his own manner and not in another. Thus, now, they are diminished, mutilated, yet quite incapable of recognizing this. You see them loitering in front of the merchants' windows, each wrapped up in himself. Neither of them will waste any more time in his friend's company, and they eschew any effort that might link them up again with that garner whence they used to draw their nourishment in common. For dead is the part of themselves which once lived thereby, and, now that this part has ceased to be, how could it crave aught?

"But you, as you go your ways, observe with the gardener's eye, and see what is amiss with the tree. Not from the tree's point of view, for from the tree's point of view nothing is amiss; it is perfect! But not so from yours, the point of view of the tree's

god who grafts each branch at the point beseeming it. Your task
is to retie the broken strand, relink the navel-cord. You reconcile
the erstwhile enemies. And, lo, they set forth again fulfilled with
fervor.

"I, too, have reconciled. And I have known that magic hour
when, after the night's alarms, she whom you love asks you for a
bowl of goat's milk and a morsel of soft bread. Then, with an
arm around her shoulders, you gently raise her from the pillow
and, holding the bowl to her pale lips, you watch her drink. You
are a pathway, a vehicle, a portage—for it now seems to you that
you are not so much tending her or even healing her, as relink-
ing her with all those things with which she used to be at one—
those fields and crops, sunlight and the water-springs. Almost it
might be for her that the aqueduct is being built; almost for her
that farm cart clatters down the road. And because she seems
to you this morning like a child, undesirous of deep talk or sage
remarks, but anxious rather for news of the household, her play-
things and her friends, you say 'Listen . . . !' and she recognizes
the steps of the little ass ambling by, and smiles, and looks up,
all eager to be loved by you, her sun. . . .

"Thus have I, your old geometrician, my King and friend, been
schooled by life; for indeed the only relations between things are
those which you create in your mind. You say, 'The same holds
good for this as well'—and, lo, the problem ceases to exist! I
restore to a man the desire for his friend, and, lo, I have reconciled him! I restore to a woman her desire for milk and for love;
I say, 'The same holds good for you,' and, lo, I have healed her of
her sickness! When I point to the relationship between a stone
that falls and the courses of the stars, what else have I done than
say, 'The same holds good for both'? Thus, too, when I show a
relationship existing between lines, I say, 'In the triangle this or
that holds likewise good.' And so, from death to death of questionings and problems, I slowly make my way towards God, in
whom all questions cease."

Leaving my old friend, I walked slowly away. . . . And now my angers of the past were leaving me, for there emanated from the mountain I was climbing that true and perfect peace which mere renunciation, compromise, concession, can never bring. For now, where others see cross-purposes, I see a condition of life. Thus is it with my discipline, which is a condition of the freedom I bestow; and with my rules restricting love, which condition love; and with my beloved enemy, who is a condition of my self—for, without the sea, never could the ship take form.

From reconcilement to reconcilement with my enemies, but likewise from new enemy to new enemy, I, too, make the long ascent leading me to God's peace. For I know there can be no question, for the ship, of humoring the onsets of the sea, nor, for the sea, of dealing gently with the ship—for, in the first case, the ship will sink, and, in the second, it would soon degenerate into a mere ungainly barge. But I know, rather, that it behoves us never to flinch or come to terms, out of a mawkish loving-kindness, in this war without respite which is the condition of peace, but rather, leaving on the way those who fall (since their deaths are a condition of life), to accept the hardships which are a pre-condition of the day of festival and of the night of the chrysalis which is a pre-condition of the wings. For well, O Lord, I know that thus it is Thou moldest me, according to Thy will, into something loftier than myself, and that apart from Thee I shall never know love or peace, for within Thee alone can he who reigned beyond the northern marches of my empire, my well-loved enemy, and I find our reconcilement, because we both shall have been fulfilled; even as in Thee alone will the man whom, much as I respected him, it behoved me to chastise, and I become at one, because we both shall have been fulfilled; for it is in Thy peace alone, O Lord, that love and love's conditions, all conflict stilled, merge at last and are at one.

UNJUST INDEED is the hierarchy which thwarts you and prevents you from becoming. Nevertheless when you take arms against this injustice, you will proceed from destruction to destruction of what has been established, until all is levelled out like the stagnant lake into which the glory of a glacier is melted. You would have men be like each other, confusing the "equality" you seek with sameness. But I would call them equal when all alike they serve the empire. Not when they merely resemble each other.

Thus with a game of chess; there is a winner and a loser. Sometimes it happens that the winner smiles superiorly, so as to humiliate the loser. For such is the way of men. Then you intervene, with your "justice," and forbid victories at chess. "Wherein lies the merit of the winner?" you say. "He happened to be cleverer or knew the game better. Thus his victory is but the outcome of a state. Why should a man preen himself on being nimbler than his neighbor, or hairier or less hairy, or having ruddier cheeks?"

But I have seen a constant loser go on playing chess for years, in the fond hope that one day he may have the thrill of victory. Thus, though she on whom your heart is set is not for you, you are the richer for the fact that she exists. Thus, too, with the pearl at the bottom of the sea.

For make no mistake regarding envy; it is the sign of a line of force. Suppose I found an order of merit. You will see those on whom it is bestowed flaunting, proud as peacocks, the bauble on their chest. Then the others wax jealous of those whom I have decorated. And now you step in with your justice, which is a spirit of compensation, and enact that all men shall wear these baubles on their chests. And, thereafter, who will trouble to bedeck himself with a thing so trivial and meaningless? For it was not the bauble itself, but its significance, that counted.

"Yet only look!" you will bid me. "I have reduced the sum of men's discontents. For I have cured them of hankering after baubles which most of them could never hope to have." Clearly, what you have in mind is envy, and true it is that envy causes pain. And you go on to conclude that the object of envy is an evil thing. Thus you would allow nothing to exist that is outside our reach. The child stretches his arms towards a star, and cries because he cannot have it. Therefore your justice bids you extinguish the star.

Thus with the ownership of precious stones. You have them deposited in museums and "Now," you say, "they are everybody's." No doubt on rainy days you will see the townsfolk filing past the show cases. But that bright array of jewels merely makes them yawn, for no longer is there a ceremonial to endow them with significance. And indeed wherein are they more brilliant than cut glass?

You have purged even the diamond of its essential virtue. Because it could not be for you. You have gelded it of that eminence which came of its being desirable. Thus, too, with women if you forbid the possessing of them; however beautiful they are, they will mean no more to you than wax figures. Never have I seen a man ready to lay down his life for a woman whose likeness, however beautiful, has come down to him on the bas-relief of a sarcophagus. She brings to him the grace or the poignant glamor of an earlier age, but not the bitter craving of desire.

Likewise your diamond which none can possess will not be the same. Its virtue has gone out of it. For hitherto it glorified you, honored you and shed its lustre on you. But now you have made it an exhibit in a show case; and doubtless it does honor to the show case. But, not wishing to be a show case, you do not wish to have the diamond.

And if now you burn one, so as to commemorate with this burnt offering a day of great rejoicing, and thus to multiply its effulgence in your heart and mind, you will be burning—nothing! For it is not you who sacrifice the diamond. Its donor is your show case. And much the show case cares about its fate! No longer can you play with the diamond, which has ceased to mean anything to you. Or were you to immure it in the heart of a pillar of the temple, as a gift to the gods, it would be no gift of yours. The pillar would be but a place of storage, only little more discreet than the show case, which, too, is discreet when the hot summer days make your people flee the city. Then your diamond has no value as a gift, being not a thing that is given, but something put into store, in one place or the other, temple or museum. It has lost its lure; its divine lines of force are gone. And what have you gained thereby?

And suppose I forbid those who are not descendants of the Prophet to wear red? Wherein have I wronged the others? Hitherto no one dressed in red, and red signified nothing whatsoever. But now, lo, everybody dreams of wearing red! I have stablished the prestige of red and thereby you are the richer, though it be not for you to wear it. And the envy which you now feel means that a new line of force has come into being.

To you the empire would seem perfect if a man could lounge his life away, sitting cross-legged in the heart of the city until he died of hunger and thirst. For you would have seen to it that there was nothing to attract him to the right rather than to the left, forwards or backwards. And he would receive no orders, any more than he would give them. No impulse would he feel towards an unpossessable diamond, nor towards a badge of honor pinned on the chest, nor towards a red garment. Were he in the shop of a cloth merchant you would see him yawning away for hours on end, waiting for me to endow with my significances the trend of his desire.

But, now I have forbidden him the wearing of red, you will see him furtively eyeing a near-red violet. Or if he be a man of mettle, restive, free-minded, averse from honors, unruled by conventions, and scorning the meanings of colors (which meanings I have arbitrarily assigned them)—then you will see him ransacking the shop, paddling the contents of drawers, in his quest of the color most opposed to red—a garish green, for example—and turning up his nose at all he sees until he finds the color he has set his heart on. And presently you will see him parading the city in his new clothes of garish green, and preening his disdain for my hierarchy of colors.

But it is to me he owes the zest that lasts him through the day. Else, dressed in red, he would have spent the day yawning in a museum; for it is raining.

"Sometimes," my father used to say, "I am moved to found a festival; but it is not so much a festival I found as a set relation between Man and Time. Then the rebellious spirits pour scorn on it and promptly launch a counter-festival. Yet it is the same relation that they are asserting and perpetuating. I imprison them a little, to give them pleasure—for they wish their ceremonial to be taken seriously. As I do mine."

❊ 117

WHEN THE EMPIRE is decaying, all have contributed to its decay. If the majority tolerate this process of corruption, how may they disclaim responsibility? If a child is drowning in your pond and you do not hasten to its rescue, I call you a murderer.

Thus my efforts will be worse than futile if, befooled by my imagination, I try to remold a Past that has run its course, and fall to beheading the corrupters as being abetters of corruption, the cowards as abetters of cowardice, the traitors as abetters of treason; for, once started on this path, there is no stopping, and I shall wind up by destroying even the better elements of my people, on the ground of their supineness, connivance or stupidity, since they stood tamely by with folded arms. True, I would be claiming to eliminate that part of man which is capable of being infected with disease and of providing a soil apt for the growth of tares. But all men are liable to fall sick, being a soil apt for the growth of divers kinds of seeds. So I should have to exterminate them all! And then at last I should have a perfect world, purged of every vice. But well I know perfection is a virtue of the dead and the dead alone. Bad sculptors and bad taste act as stepping-stones on the pathway of ascent, and I do not serve the cause of truth if I execute every man who makes mistakes, for truth is slowly come by, error by error. Nor would I serve the creative process by executing every man who botches his work, for creation, too, progresses setback by setback. I do not stablish a truth by executing him who practises another truth; for my truth is a growing tree. And I deem the soil which has not yet nourished my tree none the less arable for that. I go my way, and I am the Here and Now. The past of my empire is an heritage that has been handed down to me. I am the gardener walking across his land, and I have no mind to reproach it for nourishing briars and cacti. If I am the seed of the cedar tree, not a jot care I for cacti or briars.

I scorn hatred, not out of laxity, but because, coming from Thee, O Lord, in whom all things are present, the empire for me is, at every moment, a real presence. And at every moment I am beginning anew.

Well I remember how my father used to say: "How foolish is the seed that grumbles because, traversing it, the earth becomes a lettuce instead of a cedar tree! When the truth is, it was but a lettuce seed!"

Also he said: "The cross-eyed man gave the young girl a smile. But she turned away towards those who look you straight in the eyes. And now the cross-eyed man goes round declaring that the straight-eyed men are corrupting the young girls!"

Befooled in their own conceit are those self-righteous pedants who fancy that they owe nothing to the gropings and blunders, injustices and misdeeds which pass their comprehension. How fatuous is the fruit that contemns its parent tree!

THERE CAME to visit me that sour-faced prophet, in whom, night and day, smoldered a holy rage, and who, moreover, was cross-eyed.

"The righteous few," he said to me, "must be cherished."

"That is so," I answered. "No good reason can I see for punishing them!"

"So as to distinguish them from the sinners."

"That, too, is so," I answered. "The most perfect should be held up as an example. To set upon your pedestal you choose the best statue by the best sculptor. You read the best poems to your children. You wish the most beautiful women to be queen. For perfection is a direction you do well to point men to, though it is beyond your power to attain it."

Then, ablaze with zeal, the prophet cried: "And, once you have sorted out the company of the righteous, you must so arrange that it alone is saved, and stamp out, like the vermin that they are, the race of evildoers."

"Ah, now," I said, "you are going too far. For what you want to do is to sever the flower from the tree. To glorify the harvest by suppressing the manure. To safeguard great sculptors by beheading the bad sculptors. But as for me, I know but more or less imperfect men, and I see that the tree rises from the dark squalor of the soil. And, to my mind, the perfection of the empire is based on shameless men."

"So you honor shamelessness!"

"I honor quite as much your foolishness, for it is well that virtue

328

should be held up as a state of perfection wholly desirable and attainable. And that we should form a picture of the virtuous man, though none such exists, firstly because of human frailty, and also because absolute perfection, wherever it is found, spells death. But it is well that the road you follow, your direction, should appear to you an end, for otherwise you would weary of faring towards something that can never be attained. Well do I know it, the ordeal of a journey through the desert, which at first seems hopelessly impracticable. And then I picture a lonely sand dune, far ahead, as being an ideal halting place, grateful as a promised land. But when I reach it, lo, all the magic has gone out of it! Then I tell myself that a certain notch on the horizon is surely the ideal halting place; but here, too, when I reach it, the glamor is departed. Then I select another target, and thus, from target to target, I make my way out of the wilderness.

"Shamelessness is either a sign of innocence and simplicity (as is that of the gazelles), in which case, so but you deign to instruct it, you can change it into guileless purity of heart; or else it takes its joys in outraging others' sense of shame. But therein it bases itself on modesty, lives by it and stablishes it. When drunken soldiers are going by, you see mothers hustling their daughters into the house, and forbidding them to show themselves. Whereas the soldiers of your chaste Utopia, being trained decorously to lower their eyes, would be men whose presence meant no more than their absence, and you would see nothing against the young girls of your country bathing stark-naked in the river. But the sense of shame in my empire is more than a mere absence of shamelessness (for, on those terms, the dead would take the palm for modesty). It is a secret fervor, a guardedness in conduct, self-respect and courage. It ensures the safety of the honey that has been laid up, with a view to love's coming. And if somewhere a drunken soldier is going by, true were it to say that he is stablishing the sense of shame within my land."

"So you approve of your drunken soldiers' shouting their foul words in the streets?"

"Nay, the truth is otherwise; I punish such men, so as to inculcate in them a due sense of shame. But it is no less true that, the better I inculcate this, the stronger is the temptation to commit some outrage. More joy do you have in scaling a lofty peak than in walking up a gentle slope; or in vanquishing an enemy who resists than a poltroon who shows no fight. Only in lands where women veil themselves are you all eagerness to see their faces. And I gauge the tension of the lines of force within the empire by the severity of the punishments that counterpoise men's frowardness. When I dam a mountain torrent, it pleases me to gauge the thickness of the wall. For it is a sign of my power. Whereas a strip of pasteboard would suffice against the trickle from a pond. Why should I want eunuchs for soldiers? Rather would I have men lunge mightily against the wall; thus only will they be great in crime or in the creation which transcends crime."

"So you wish to have your men seething with desires for rape and lechery?"

"No," I answered. "You have utterly failed to understand."

❧ 119

IN THEIR LUSH STUPIDITY my police officers, having stolen a march on me, insisted on a hearing.

"Sire, we have discovered the reason of the empire's decadence. A certain sect is responsible, and we must root it out."

"Is that so?" I asked. "And how do you know that these men are working in concert?"

Then they told me of certain signs they had noticed, showing that these men formed a secret society, and of certain coincidences in the things they did, even naming the place where they held their meetings.

"And how do you make out that they are a danger to the empire?" I asked.

Then they told me of their crimes, the peculations of some, the rapes committed by others, and the ignobility of several, and their repellent appearance.

"Well," I said, "I know a secret society that is still more dangerous, for no one has ever thought of fighting against it."

"What is it, Sire?"

And now they were all agog with eagerness; for the police officer, being born to use his fists, wilts if there be none on whom to ply them.

"The secret society," I answered, "of those men who have a mole on the left temple."

Whereat they gave a loud grunt of approval, having—naturally—failed to take my meaning. For the police officer needs not understand in order to ply his fists, which have no brains in them. All that is asked of the policeman is to lay about him.

One of them, however, who had formerly been a carpenter, coughed once or twice.

"But there are no signs of their being banded together. And they have no meeting place."

"Quite true," I answered. "And just there the danger lies. Nobody notices them. But all I need do is to issue a proclamation denouncing them to the public, and then you will see them singling each other out, banding together, sharing their resources, and in their stand against the righteous indignation of the people, growing conscious that they form a caste."

My police officers nodded approval. "Only too true!"

But the former carpenter coughed again. "I know a man with a mole on his left forehead. He is honest, gentle, open-hearted. What's more, he was thrice wounded, fighting to defend the empire."

"That may well be so," I answered. "Because women as a sex are light-headed, need we assume that there are no intelligent exceptions? Because generals as a class are blusterers, does it follow that you will not sometimes find, exceptionally, a shy one? But waste no time over the exceptions. Once all the men who bear that mark have been traced out, look into their past. You will find they have been concerned in all manner of crimes: from rapes and kidnappings to embezzlement and treason, and public acts of in-decency—not to mention their minor vices such as gluttony. Dare you tell me they are innocent of such things?"

"No, no!" exclaimed the police officers, whose fists now were wide awake, and itching for blows.

"When a tree gives rotten fruit," I said, "do you blame the fruit or the tree for this?"

"Surely the tree," they answered.

"And do some few healthy fruits exonerate the tree?"

"No, no!" again cried in chorus my police officers, who (as in deed is fitting) are devoted to their profession, in which "exonerat-ing" plays no part.

"Therefore it were well to purge the empire of these men who have a mole on the left temple."

But the ex-carpenter coughed again.

"State your objections," I said to him. But, the while, I saw his colleagues casting suspicious glances at the man's left temple.

Indeed one of them went so far as to suggest, scowling darkly at the suspected man: "May not that man whom he says he knows, and speaks so well of, be perchance his brother, or his father, or, anyhow, one of his kindred?"

Whereat the others growled approval.

Then blazed up my anger. "More dangerous still is the 'sect' of those who have a mole on the right temple. And, in our in-nocence, we never gave them a thought! Which means they hide themselves yet more cunningly. Most dangerous of all is the 'sect' of those who have no mole on their faces, for clearly such men disguise themselves, like foul conspirators, so as to do their evil work unnoticed. So, when all is said and done, I can but condemn the whole human race—since there is no denying that it is the source of all manner of crimes: rapes and kidnappings, embezzlement and treason and public acts of indecency. And inasmuch as my police officers, besides being police officers, are men, I will begin my purge with them, since 'purges' of this sort are their function. Therefore I order the policeman who is in each of you to lay hold of the man who is in each of you, and fling him into the most noisome dungeon of my citadel."

But when the carpenter was going out, I called him back. Whereat he made much show of modesty, lowering his eyes.

"As for you, my man," I said, "I dismiss you from my police. The carpenter's truth, which is subtle and rife with contradictions by reason of the wood which resists his handicraft, is no truth for police officers. If the code sets a black mark against those who have a mole on the back of the neck, it is my pleasure that my police officers, at the mere mention of such a man, feel their fists clenching. And it is likewise my pleasure that your sergeant major weighs your merits by your skill in doing an about turn. For had he the right to judge for himself he might condone your awkwardness because you are a great poet. And likewise forgive the man beside you, because he is a paragon of virtue. And likewise with the man next after him, because he is a model of chastity. Thus justice would prevail. But now suppose that, on the battlefield, a swift and subtle feint, hinging on an about turn, is· called for, then you will see my troops blundering into each other, huggermugger, and the enemy profiting by their confusion to wipe them out! And much consolation will it be to the dying that their sergeant major thinks well of them! Therefore I send you back to your boards and planks, lest your love of justice, operating where it is misplaced, lead one day to a useless shedding of blood."

🌿 *120*

CAME TO ME one who questioned me regarding equity and justice. "Equitable acts I know," I told him, "but of equity I know nothing. Thus it is equitable for you to be supplied with food according to the work you perform; to be cared for if you fall sick; to be free if you are pure. But all this proves little. Save that equitable is all that conforms with the Custom of the empire.

"I bid the physician cross the desert, even if he has to crawl the last miles on his hands and knees, to bandage the wound of a man who has been wounded—even if the wounded man be a miscreant. For thus I stablish the respect due to Man. Nevertheless, if my empire is at war with that man's empire, I bid my soldiers cross the selfsame desert and lay bare to the sun the entrails of that selfsame miscreant. For thus I stablish the empire."

"Sire, I do not understand you. . . ."

"It is my pleasure that the makers of nails, who sing the nailsmiths' song, try to steal the tools of the sawyers of planks, if these tools further their nail-making. And likewise it pleases me if the sawyers try to entice away the nailsmiths so that they, too, may work in the sawmill. And I find it good that the architect in charge of the work offend the sawyers by showing favor to the nailsmiths, and the nailsmiths by favoring the sawyers. For it is from this tension of the lines of force that will be born the ship, and I can expect little of half-hearted sawyers who pay respect to nails, or of half-hearted nailsmiths who pay respect to planks."

"Then you approve of enmities?"

"I can stomach enmities—and override them, but it is only love that I approve of. And love is to be achieved only on a plane above the rivalry of planks and nails—in the completed ship."

✦

Thereafter, having withdrawn from men's sight, I prayed to God.

"I accept, O Lord, as partial and provisional truths (though it is not of my present estate to discern the keystone linking them together), the contradictory truths of the soldier who seeks to wound and the physician who seeks to heal. I do not try to reconcile, in a lukewarm potion, drinks that are icecold and others scalding hot. For, whether it be a case of wounding or healing, I would not have it gone about half-heartedly. I punish alike the physician who declines to minister to a sick man, and the soldier who refuses to deal blows. Little care I if certain words may seem to shoot their tongues out at each other! For often it so happens that this trap alone, made of seemingly incongruous elements, can capture my prey in its wholeness—meaning a certain man, of a certain personal quality, and not another.

"Thus, gropingly, I seek to discover Thy divine lines of force and, lacking those proofs which it is not of my present estate to discern, I maintain that the rites of my ceremonial are well chosen, if so be that therein I can breathe freely and fulfill myself. Is it not thus, O Lord, with my sculptor when a certain thumb-stroke on the left gives him—though why he could not say—exactly what he wanted; and it seems to him that in no other manner could his clay have been charged with power?

"I go towards Thee like the tree developing according to the lines of force implicit in its seed. The blind man knows nothing of the nature of fire. But fire has lines of force to which the palms of his hands are sensitive. And he gropes his way painfully through the briars, for painful is all sloughing off of one's old self. By Thy grace, O Lord, I fare towards Thee, ascending that long upward slope, which is the slope of my becoming.

"Thou dost not deign to come down to this world of Thy creation, and I can hope for nothing other to enlighten me than the heat of the fire or the tension of the forces implicit in the seed. Even as the caterpillar knows nothing of wings. Nor have I any hope of being enlightened by some celestial puppet-show of archangels descending in a cloud of glory; indeed such a show could tell me nothing of advantage. For it is as useless to talk of wings to the caterpillar as of the ship to the nailsmith. Let it suffice that by virtue of the shipwright's conception, the ship's lines of force exist. And, owing to the chrysalis, the wings' lines of force. And, owing to the seed, the tree's lines of force. And, as for Thee, O Lord, quite simply, that *Thou art*.

"Icecold sometimes is my loneliness, and in the desert of my dereliction sometimes I pray that a sign may be given me. But in a dream, Thou didst reveal to me the folly of my prayer. And I thus learned that no sign could help me, for wert Thou on my level, Thou wouldst not constrain me to rise above myself. And how small, how unworthy is the man I now am!

"Thus ever I go forward, shaping prayers to which no answer is vouchsafed, and so blind that all I have to guide me is a faint warmth on my wasted hands—nevertheless, praising Thee, O Lord, for that Thou dost not answer; for did I find that which I seek, I would cease *becoming*.

"Wert Thou to take, of Thy good pleasure, the step, that is the visitant archangel's, towards Man, Man would be fulfilled, his task accomplished. No longer would he saw his planks or hammer nails for the ship in the making; no more would he fight the foe or tend the sick. No longer would he sweep his room or cherish his beloved. How, O Lord, could he wander through the world, seeking to honor Thee through his fellow men by acts of charity, did he see Thee face to face? For, once the temple is built, I see the temple only, not the stones.

"O Lord, Thou seest me, that I am old and weak as is a tree before the fury of the winter gales. Weary of my foes, weary of my friends. Troubled in mind by the compulsion to kill and to heal, as it were, in the same breath—for Thou hast given me that craving to master and to reconcile such contradictions, which makes my lot so hardly to be borne. Yet this it is that urges me upon my upward way, through ever fewer questionings, towards Thy silence, in which all questions have an end.

The Wisdom of the Sands

"O Lord, grant of Thy favor that at last we three be made at one, my well-loved enemy, who is sleeping his last sleep beyond the northern confines of my empire, my old friend, the only true geometrician, and I myself who, having, alas, passed the summit, am leaving behind my generation on the downward slope; grant that, for Thy greater glory, we be united, when I am sleeping my last sleep in these desert sands, where I have labored to perform the task Thou gavest me."

✻ 121

THERE CAME to me the logicians, historians and pundits of my empire, and waxed great in argument, each deducing, by dint of a long chain of causes and effects, his favorite system. And all in it was rigorously precise. Vying with each other, they drew their divers pictures of forms of society, civilizations and empires which, according to them, would foster, nourish and enrich the human race.

After they had addressed me at great length, I put them a simple question: "If you wish your disquisitions regarding Man to carry weight, were it not well to start by telling me what is the most important thing *in* Man and *for* Man?"

Then right gleefully they fell to expounding their views on Man, for if you give such persons the least pretext for a harangue, you will find them gripping it by the mane and galloping blindly ahead upon their hobbies, till you might be witnessing a troop of cavalry thundering by to charge the foe, the yellow sand churned up around the horses' hoofs and the air humming with the speed of them. Only they are going nowhere!

When their noise had subsided, and now they were waiting for compliments (for such persons do not indulge in these feats so as to be of service, but to be seen, heard or admired for their fine horsemanship, and, once the caperings and curvettings are over, you see them assuming an air of becoming modesty), I made answer.

"So then, if I have taken your meaning, you claim to foster that which is the most important thing in man and for man. But only this is evident: that your systems make sure his girth is adequate—which is certainly all to the good; yet this is but a means, not an end, since the structure of a man's frame imports neither more nor less than the robustness of a vehicle. Or else they ensure his health, which, too, is a means, not an end, and corresponds to the upkeep of the vehicle; or else his numbers, also a means and not an end, like the quantity of vehicles you have at your disposal. And most certainly I would wish the empire to have a great number of men, and all of them stalwart, healthy and well-fed. But, in stating these obvious requirements, I still have failed to touch on that which is essential—except in so far as the man of the empire is as it were a raw material placed at my disposal. But what shall I make of him, whither lead him, and what must I bestow on him to greaten him? For he is but a vehicle, a pathway, a portage."

Thus they discoursed of men, like market gardeners discoursing of a lettuce. But the generations of lettuces which have followed each other in my kitchen garden have left nothing behind them worthy of remembrance.

Thus they could not answer me; for, being near-sighted, glueing their long noses to the paper, they took stock only of its quality and the lettering, and not of the meaning of the poem.

So I continued: "I, who deal with realities, refuse to dabble in the mush of dreams. And the siren islands men go forth to seek mean nothing to me unless they are solid and abiding. I am not, like the money-makers, bemused by airy phantoms of the imagination; and it comes naturally to me, who respect the lessons of experience, to set the art of the dance above the arts of peculation, moneygrubbing and double-dealing, since it provides more pleasure and its significance is clearer. For, after amassing your riches, you are bound to put them to some use, and (since all men are charmed by the dancer's art) you will doubtless buy some dancing-girl; but, knowing nothing of the dance, you will choose her stupidly and gain nothing by the purchase. Likewise, I who observe and comprehend (for, in the silence of my love, I listen not to the words) have discerned that nothing counts for a man so much as the homely smell of beeswax on a certain evening of his life, or the golden glint of a bee in the grey of dawn, or a black pearl unpossessed at the bottom of the sea. And I have seen even the rich man exchange a fortune laboriously built up—by double-dealing, peculation, moneygrubbing, grinding the faces of the poor, and long sleepless nights spent on stock-takings and ponderings over the next move—I have seen such a man exchanging his fortune for a stone no bigger than a nut, that looks for all the world like a morsel of cut glass; yet, in that it bore the name of diamond and was a fruit of the ceremonial of delving in the womb of earth, had for him the value of that remembered smell of beeswax or the gold flash of the bee, and was worthy of being preserved from robbers, even at the cost of a man's life."

Thus it was revealed to me that the one gift of great price is that of the pathway giving access to the festival. And that, if I would assess your civilization, I must begin by having you tell me about your festivals and what is their savor for the heart; and likewise—since these festivals bespeak moments of transition, of thresholds crossed, of a breaking-forth from the chrysalis when a great change has come—I would have you tell me whence you have come and whither you are advancing. Then alone will I know what man you are, and if it is worth while taking pains to ensure that all goes well with your health, your girth, and your numbers.

And since, if you are to choose a certain path, it is needful that you should feel a craving to advance in that direction and no other, and that it will ensure your ascent, guiding your steps and quickening your talents (even as it is with the inclination towards the sea, which I need but foster in you to ensure the getting of ships)—I would have you enlighten me as to the nature of the cravings you implant in those around you. For man is so built that, essentially, love is a thirst for love, culture a thirst for culture and the joy of the ceremonial quest of the black pearl, a thirst for the black pearl lying at the bottom of the sea.

❧ 122

THERE ARE THOSE who, ever in a flutter, would have you think them fired with high enthusiasm night and day. They lie.

Lies, too, the sentinel who dins your ears night and day with the tale of his devotion to the city. He is more devoted to his evening meal.

Lies, too, the lover who tells you that night and day he is haunted by visions of her he loves. A mere flea will divert his mind from her; for a flea bites. Or even mere boredom, and he yawns.

Lies, too, the traveller to far lands, who professes that night and day he is enraptured by the new sights that greet him. For when the ship plunges steeply into the waves' trough, he sees no sights, but only vomits.

Lies, too, the saint who tells you that he spends his nights and days contemplating God. For sometimes, like the sea, God withdraws Himself from him. And then he is drier than a tropic beach when the tide is low.

He also lies who weeps his dead night and day. Why thus weep night and day, when you loved not each other all the time, but had your hours of bickerings, or weariness, or pleasures nowise concerning love? True, the dead are more present to us than the living, for, now all cross-purposes are over, we can see the dead man or woman steadily and whole. None the less you are unfaithful even to your dead.

All these persons lie, because, in the blindness of their hearts, they perceive not their hours of apathy. And when you suffer a bereavement, you even come to doubt yourself, for hearing them protest their fervor, you believe in their constancy, and thus you, too, blushing for your moments of apathy, change your voice and demeanor when others look at you.

I know but one mood that can be permanent, a mood of listless indifference. Which comes from the infirmity of your mind, when you fail to see the vision and the meaning informing the multifarious stuff of life. Thus is it when a man looks at chessmen arranged on a chessboard, without grasping that here a problem is involved. But if so be that now and again, as a reward for your fidelity in the chrysalis, you are vouchsafed that fleeting moment of illumination which comes to the sentinel, the poet, the believer, the lover, or the traveller, grieve not that you cannot contemplate this beatific vision at every hour. For some visions blaze so brightly that they wear out the eyes of him who contemplates them overlong. And thus not every day can be a day of festival.

Hence you err when you blame men for going about their everyday tasks—as did that cross-eyed prophet in whose breast smoldered night and day a holy rage. Well I know that a ceremonial is all too apt to degenerate into a dull routine. And that the practice of virtue is all too apt to degenerate into concessions to the policeman's code. And that the loftiest principles of justice can be twisted into a cloak for evil practices. But what matter? I know, too, that it befalls man to sleep. Must I then lament his nightly apathy? Of the tree, too, I know that it is not a flower, but a condition of the flower.

I HAVE SOUGHT to stablish within you love for your brethren. And, in so doing, I stablished sorrow for separation from your brethren. I sought to stablish in you love for your spouse. And I stablished sorrow for separation from your spouse. I sought to stablish in you love for your friend. And, lo, I stablished in you sorrow for separation from your friend; even as he who builds fountains, builds their absence.

But, having perceived that deprivation afflicts you more than any other ill that man is heir to, I resolved to heal you, and teach you what presence signifies. For to him who is dying of thirst the absent fountain, for all its absence, is nevertheless sweeter than were a world in which there were no fountains. And though you be exiled from your house for ever, you weep when you learn it is burnt down.

I know presences lavish as great trees, which spread their branches widely for the giving of shade. For I am he who dwells, and I will show you your dwelling place.

Remember how sweet is love's savor when you kiss your wife, now that daybreak has restored their color to the vegetables whose shaky pyramids you build up on your ass's back, for it is the hour of setting forth to sell them in the market. Then your wife smiles to you, as she stands on the threshold, ready, like you, for the day's task; for soon she will sweep the house, polish the utensils, and set to cooking a certain tidbit whose surprise she is concocting for you. And watching the simmering pot, she thinks: "If only he doesn't get back too soon! All my pleasure will be spoilt if he catches me making it." Thus though seemingly you are going far away, and she even hopes your return may be delayed, nothing has parted her from you. And with you it is the same; for your journey serves the house whose wear and tear you remedy

and whose gaiety you nourish. Also you have in mind to buy with
your profits a certain deep-piled carpet and, for your wife, a
certain silver bracelet. Therefore you go towards the city, singing,
and though to all seeming you are leaving it behind, dwell in
love's radiance. You are building your home with each tap of
your little stick as you guide the ass and straighten the baskets
now and then, rubbing your eyes, for the day is very young. Indeed you are more at one with your wife just now than in those
hours of leisure when, standing in your doorway, you gaze at the
horizon, with no thought of turning round to look at anything of
your little kingdom. For perchance you are dreaming of a wedding
far away at which you would have wished to be present, or of
some irksome duty, or of a friend you have lost sight of.

But soon, with the swelling light, you are more awake, and when
your ass, to show his mettle, breaks into a little trot, you listen
to the clattering hoofs that make the pebbles ring and, musing
on the morning that lies ahead, you smile to yourself. For already
you have made up your mind about the shop where you will
bargain for that silver bracelet. You know well the shrewd old
huckster, and he will show delight at your coming, for you are
(he will tell you) his dearest friend. He will ask for news of your
wife, that pearl among women; especially of her health, for
surely frail is one so exquisite. Thus he will say a world of
kindly things about her, in a tone so convincing that even a
boorish passer-by, hearing his praises, will judge her worthy of
a bracelet of pure gold. But you heave a sigh. Such is life—alas,
no king are you, but only a market gardener! And the huckster, too,
will sigh. And when you are done with your joint sighings in
honor of the golden bracelet, he will confess to you, as a great
secret, that really he prefers silver bracelets. The great thing in a
bracelet, he explains, is for it to be heavy; and gold ones are light.
The one he is about to show you will be the first link of the
chain binding you together; and pleasant it is, in love, to feel the
weight of the chain. When she raises her arm, with a pretty
movement, to straighten her veil, the bracelet should weigh heavy,

for thus it gives a message to the heart. Then, after going to the back of his shop and returning with the heaviest of his bangles, the man invites you to feel its weight, resting it on the palm of your hand and shutting your eyes, the better to gauge the pleasure of owning it. And, having done so, you nod approval. But sigh again. For such is life—alas, you are no leader of a great caravan; your sole possession is your ass! You point to the small animal waiting outside, and draw attention to its lack of strength. "So paltry is my wealth, that this morning he even trotted on the way, bearing upon his back my little all!" Then the huckster, too, heaves another sigh. And when you both have had your fill of sighs in honor of this heavy bracelet you can never own, he confesses to you that, after all, the lighter bracelets are better, as being more daintily carved. Then at last he shows you the one on which your heart was set. For, many days ago, after taking counsel with your wisdom, like a chancellor of the exchequer balancing his budget, you came to a decision. A part of your monthly profits was to be set aside for the purchase of a deep-piled carpet, another for a new garden rake, another for the daily food, another for a bracelet.

So now begins the veritable dance; for the huckster is versed in the ways of men. Once he guesses that the hook is holding firmly, he pays out no more line. You, however, telling him the bracelet is far too costly, take your leave. Then he calls you back. He is your friend; he will make a sacrifice to the beauty of your young wife; it would pain him too much to think that this exquisite bracelet were gracing the arm of some ill-favored wench. You come back, but with seeming reluctance, at a snail's pace. You make a faint grimace. You test the weight of the bracelet in your hand. Surely, being so light, it can't be worth so much! Also, the silver is rather tarnished. In fact you cannot make up your mind between a mere trinket and a length of really fine material you have seen in the next-door shop. But, on the other hand, you must not overdo your show of disdain, or he will lose hope of selling you anything, and watch you go away, without recalling you. And then you would blush for the feeble pretext you must trump up for coming back to him.

True, one who knew nothing of men would think he watched the dance of avarice—whereas it is the dance of love he sees—and hearing you talk of your ass and your vegetables, or sagely appraising gold and silver or quantity and quality, and thus deferring your return by long discourse and transactions, would glean the impression that you are far indeed from your home—whereas in reality you are dwelling there, despite appearances, at this very moment. For there is no absence either from the home or from your love, when your every step forms part of the ceremonial dance of love or of the home. Far from parting you, your absence binds you together; far from isolating you from her, it unites you. And can you tell me where you would set the landmark beyond which absence means a sundering? If the ceremonial be firmly knit together, and if you keep your eyes intently on the god within whom you twain are one, and if that god burns with an ardent flame—who can separate you from your friend or your own house? Sometimes have I been told by the son of a man who has died: "My father died without completing the left wing of his house. I am building it. Without completing the planting of his trees. I am planting them. My father, on his deathbed, vested in me the duty of carrying on his work. I am carrying it on. And that of remaining loyal to his King. I am loyal." In such houses never did I feel that the father was no more.

Thus is it with you and your friend. Provided you seek elsewhere than within yourself, and elsewhere than within him, the underlying truth you share in common, and provided that there exists for both alike, beyond the diversity of the visible world, a knot divine binding things together—then neither Time nor Space can sunder you; for the gods within whom your unity is stablished laugh at walls and seas.

There was an old gardener who liked to speak to me about his friend. Before life separated them, for many, many years the two had lived like brothers, drinking the evening tea together, observing the same feast days, each repairing to the other when he needed counsel or wished to confide his troubles to a friendly ear. Yet true it was that they spoke rarely to each other; far oftener one would see them, after the day's work was done, walking together and, without uttering a word, gazing at the flowers and gardens, trees and sky. But when one of them bent down, and shaking his head, touched a plant, the other, too, would bend and, seeing the traces of caterpillars on the leaves, would likewise shake his head. And both showed equal delight when they came on flowers in full and perfect bloom.

It befell on a certain day that a great merchant hired one of them and bade him accompany, for some few weeks, his caravan. But forays of predatory nomads, wars between great empires, storms and shipwrecks, deaths and disasters, divers mischances and the need to earn his living tossed the man to and fro, like a cask buffeted by the waves, until from garden to garden, he was carried away to a far country, on the very margent of the world.

Years went by and, after half a lifetime's silence, my gardener received a letter from his friend. God alone knows how many years that letter had been awandering; what ships and caravans, horsemen and diligences had sped it on its devious ways, with the tenacity of the myriad waves of the sea, before it reached his garden. So that morning he was beaming with delight and, wishing others to share in it, he begged me read the letter, as one begs a friend to read a poem. And watched my face, so as to see the emotion it quickened in me. True, there were but a few words, for the two gardeners were, as befitted them, handier with the spade than with the pen. Indeed all I read was: *This morning I pruned my rose trees.* Then, meditating on those essential things which, methought, cannot be expressed in words, I slowly nodded my head, as they, too, would have done.

But now a change befell my gardener: his peace of mind was gone. You might have heard him sedulously enquiring as to distances, sea routes, couriers, caravans and the wars in progress on the desert's face. Then three years later, as chance would have it, I had occasion to despatch envoys to the edge of the world. So I sent for my gardener. "Now you can write to your friend." Whereat my rose trees suffered a little, and in the vegetable garden, too, the caterpillars held high festival. For now he took to spending whole days in his room, jotting down phrases, crossing them out, starting again, sticking out his tongue the while, like a schoolboy poring over his lesson-book. He knew he had something most important to say, and somehow he must transport himself, lock, stock and barrel, as it were, to his absent friend. For he had to build a bridge over the sundering gulf and, communing with the friend who was his other self, across Space and Time, make known to him his love. Thus a day came when, blushing, he came to me and showed his answer, hoping to glimpse on my face a reflection of the joy that would light up that of its recipient, and to test on me the power of his message. And when I read it, I saw these words, written in a careful yet unskilled hand—earnest as a prayer coming from the heart, yet how simple and how humble!—*This morning I, too, pruned my rose trees. . . .* And could he indeed have imparted to his friend news more important than this, standing as it did for that for which, supremely, he was bartering his life, like those old women who wear their eyes out over their needlework in the making of some altarcloth for their God? And, having read, I fell silent, musing on that essential thing which I was beginning to perceive more clearly; for it was Thou, O Lord, whom they were honoring, fusing their lives together within Thee, above and beyond their rose trees, though they knew it not.

And now, O Lord, having striven my utmost to instruct my people, for myself I pray. For the task I received at Thy hands was too great to permit me to attach myself to any one in particular of those whom else I might have loved. Thus I had no choice but to wean myself from those all-too-human intimacies which alone afford the heart its pleasures; for ever pleasant is it

347

to return to one fixed, cherished place and not to another, and sweet are the sounds of familiar voices and the childish confidences sobbed into your ears by her who thinks she is weeping for her lost jewel, when (though as yet of this she has no inkling) it is for death, which brings a parting from all jewels, that she is weeping. But Thou hast condemned me to silence so that, beyond the rumor of words that weave the wind, I may overhear their true significance; for it behoves me to bend my mind upon men's anguish, whereof I fain would heal them.

It was Thy will that I should be frugal of the time that else might have been squandered on idle chatter or outcry over a lost jewel (and no end can there be to such repinings since what is here at stake is more than a jewel, it is death), and likewise on friendship or love. For in Thee alone is the true knot of friendship, and of love, made fast, and it is Thy will that I should attain these only by way of Thy silence.

Nothing look I to receive, since I know it would ill beseem Thy dignity or Thy solicitude to visit me on my level, nor is anything to be expected of the puppet-play of archangels descending in a cloud of glory. For I who bestow not my care on a chosen few, but no less on the workman than on the shepherd, have much to give and nothing to receive. And it so happens that a friendly smile from me can thrill my sentry with delight—for I am his King and the empire unified in me is built up with his and his comrades' blood, and thus the empire recompenses their blood, through me, with my smile. What, O Lord, have I to get from the sentry's answering smile? From none of these do I crave love for myself, and little care I if they are indifferent or hate me; so only they respect me as the pathway leading up to Thee. For Thee alone I ask their love—for Thee, from whom they proceed as I proceed—and, gathering together in a sheaf their acts of worship, I make these over to Thee; even as I assign to the empire, not to myself, my sentry's genuflexion; for mine is the function of the seed that, drawing forth the juices of the soil, converts them into leafage proffered to the sun.

Wherefore it is that sometimes—since for me no king is there to recompense me, like the sentry, with his smile and I must go my lonely way until the time comes when Thou deignest to receive me and unite me with those I love—therefore it is that now and again a great weariness of being alone descends on me, and a craving to mingle with my fellow men; for, seemingly, I am not yet pure enough.

Thus, esteeming the old gardener who sent that letter to his friend a happy man, I am sometimes seized with a desire to form, like him, a bond of amity with the gardeners of my empire under the aegis of their god. And then, at the first peep of day, I go down the steps of my palace and slowly walk towards my gardens, and it is ever to the rose garden that I wend my way in the grey light. I take stock of my roses, lingering to bend attentively over a young, flower-laden branch—I, who when noon has come, will make decision of a man's pardon or his death, of war or peace. Then straightening up with an effort, for I am growing old, I enter into communion with all gardeners, living and dead, through the only channel that conveys such messages, the way of words that well up silently from the heart: *This morning I, too, have pruned my rose trees.* Little matters if the message pursues its silent way for many years, or in the end reaches this man or that. So as to enter into communion with my gardeners I have taken the simplest course; I have done homage to their god, which is a rose tree glimmering in the dusk of dawn.

Thus, O Lord, is it concerning my beloved enemy, whom I shall meet only beyond my earthbound self. And for whom it is likewise, since he resembles me. Thus I dispense justice according to my lights; and he dispenses justice according to his lights. Often these seem contradictory and, when they clash, engender wars between us. Yet, though following different paths, we follow, groping our respective ways, the lines of force of the same inward fervor. And in Thee, O Lord, our paths converge and end as one.

Thus, having fulfilled my task, I have embellished the soul of my people. And he too, his task fulfilled, has embellished his people's soul. And I who think of him and he who thinks of me, even though we meet not on a common ground of words, when we have dispensed judgment or ordained a ceremonial, can each of us say, I on his behalf and he on mine: *This morning I have pruned my rose trees.*

For Thou, O Lord, art the common measure of us twain. Thou art the knot supreme, binding all things together.